Buchan Claik

BOOKS BY PETER BUCHAN

Mount Pleasant	Buchan Observer	1961
Fit Like Skipper?	Aberdeen Journals	1984
Fisher Blue	Peter Buchan	1988
Buchan Claik (with David Toulmin)	Gordon Wright Publishing	1989
Collected Poems and Short Stories	Gordon Wright Publishing	1992

BOOKS BY DAVID TOULMIN

Hard Shining Corn	Impulse Publications	1972
Straw into Gold	Impulse Publications	1973
Blown Seed	Paul Harris Publishing	1976
Harvest Home	Paul Harris Publishing	1978
Travels without a Donkey	Gourdas House Publishers	1980
A Chiel Among Them	Gourdas House Publishers	1982
The Tillycorthy Story	Aberdeen University Press	1986
The Clyack Sheaf	Aberdeen University Press	1986
Buchan Claik (with Peter Buchan)	Gordon Wright Publishing	1989
Collected Short Stories	Gordon Wright Publishing	1992

BUCHAN
CLAIK

The Saat an the Glaar o't

**A Compendium of Words and Phrases
from the North-East of Scotland**

Peter Buchan
and
David Toulmin

GORDON WRIGHT PUBLISHING
25 MAYFIELD ROAD, EDINBURGH EH9 2NQ
SCOTLAND

British Library Cataloguing in Publication Data
A catalogue record for this book is
available from the British Library.

ISBN 0-903065-94-0

Photo on the cover: Gordon Wright.
Cover design: John Haxby.

Typeset by Gordon Wright Publishing Ltd., Edinburgh.
Printed by The Cromwell Press, Trowbridge, Wilts.

Contents

Biographical Notes

Peter Buchan was born in Peterhead in 1917, the son of a fisherman. Educated at Peterhead Academy, he was off to sea on a fishing boat as soon as he left school at the age of sixteen and he spent most of his life amongst boats.

In 1940 he married Agnes Cowe, a Peterhead quine, and the couple had two daughters.

After the war he started writing poems. A collection, *Mount Pleasant*, appeared in 1961 and reprinted six times. He then started to write short stories to portray the 'middle ground' in fisher life which had formerly been portrayed at the two extremes of either drunkenness or religious fanaticism and he found a large readership for his work at home and abroad. He broadcast regularly on radio and was interviewed several times on television. He was Vice-President of the Buchan Heritage Society from 1988-1990, then Patron until his death. He also edited five editions of the Society's magazine, *Heirskip*, from 1987-91.

Peter died on 12 December 1991 and is buried in Peterhead.

His *Collected Poems and Short Stories* were published in 1992.

David Toulmin is the pen-name of John Reid, who was born at Rathen in Buchan, Aberdeenshire, in 1913. His father was a farm worker, and at the age of fourteen, John left school to work on the farms as a 'fee'd loon'.

In 1934 he married Margaret Jane Willox and the couple had three sons.

An interest in writing which began in his schooldays developed into an absorbing hobby and in 1947 his first article was published in a local newspaper. Since then, he has had nine books published; a number of his short stories have been broadcast on the radio and he has made several appearances on television.

In 1986 he was awarded an Honorary Degree as Master of Letters (M. Litt.) by Aberdeen University for his services to Scottish literature.

In December 1992 he was incapacitated by a stroke which ended his writing career and on 13 May 1998 he died at his home in Aberdeen.

His *Collected Short Stories* were published in 1992.

* * *

Following the publication of the first edition of this book in 1989 the two authors continued to collect words and phrases as they came to mind adding a further forty pages to this second edition.

Each entry is followed by either a (T) or a (B) to identify the author concerned.

It has been impossible to standardise the spelling of Scots words, as each author had his own pronunciations and spelt words accordingly. We have resisted the temptation to explain too many words in the text and trust you will find most words explained as individual entries.

Gordon Wright.

David Toulmin's Introduction

It was being said a hundred years ago that the Doric language was dying, and since that time, many of the older words have become obsolete and survive only in the pages of the *Scottish National Dictionary.*

In the North-East of Scotland, the language was very much alive in the first half of the present century when many of the words were in general use, particularly in the farming and fishing areas, where a great number of them were associated with the land, animals and farm implements; the sea, fish and boats.

The Buchan speech is largely based on an agricultural structure which influenced town and village society and many of the words disappeared with the advent of mechanisation and the consequent depopulation of the land, recently accelerated by the Government's 'Set Aside' non-cultivation policy for British farming. The current influx of farmers from England and beyond has also contributed to the deteriorating useage of the 'Mither tongue'.

Despite the effect of the fashionable desire of the academic pundits and the genteel upper classes to become 'Englified' in the eighteenth century after the Union of Parliaments, and the influence of an English education system in the nineteenth century, the dialect speech of Buchan, and indeed of Scotland, is under greater threat today than it was a hundred years ago.

The twentieth century has given us the gramophone, radio, television, tape recorders, video and the compact disc; effective transport throughout the world, and most of all, the cosmopolitan effect of the oil industry, all of which have had a detrimental effect on Buchan speech and social habits.

In the last twenty years, many new, small, Scottish publishing houses have become established and a generous part of their output has been work in the Doric, and television, radio and the theatre have also made a significant contribution.

Doric 'spik' is sometimes the comic relief in the drama of our lives, in print and on the concert platforms, though I must admit that some of the performers excel in their burlesque imitation of what was natural, instinctive behaviour within my own life span.

So let us hope that this book is not a tombstone for our dialect, but at the very least, a record of how the language was spoken, and if it helps to inspire and promote a reviving interest in the Buchan tongue, that will be an added bonus.

During the exacting and lengthy period of research required to compile my contribution to this book I was grateful for the assistance of Mr John Morrison of Ellon, Mrs F McDonald of Insch, and to several friends and relatives who prefer anonymity. To all of them I extend my sincere thanks. Finally, I must give special thanks to my wife, Margaret Jane, for her patience, encouragement and invaluable assistance in collecting so many samples of the language she grew up with and still uses.

David Toulmin 1989.

Peter Buchan's Introduction

When I was invited to share in the writing of this book, I agreed rather reluctantly, thinking that there simply couldn't be enough material to fill more than a few pages. In that I was completely mistaken, as I soon discovered.

On one thing I was adamant ... I would not attempt to resurrect words and phrases which are long since dead and gone. That, I was sure, would serve no useful purpose. There are already plenty books on that subject. Nor would I consult anyone, relying rather on the stock of Doric speech which I use or hear every day. I must admit that, by making such a decision, I have probably narrowed the field to a great extent, for I am NOT an authority on anything. Still, if I have been successful, I have nobody to thank; if I have failed, I have nobody to blame. One way or the other, I have enjoyed myself; yea, weel awyte, I have amazed myself.

Naturally, I have tended to stick to the fisher side. Could you expect anything else? That was the purpose of the exercise. I have on occasion strayed inland, but even then, the great expected overlap of fisher and country has failed to materialise. Fit think ye o that, noo?

The spelling of the Buchan tongue may present a slight problem. This book was never meant to be a dictionary, with precise definitions and impeccable spelling. But the problem (if any) is far from being insurmountable, especially if you take the book for what it is meant to be ... a light-hearted look at a tongue which is far from being dead. This prompts me to say that we are not at a wake ... yet!

It gives me great pleasure to know that my speech requires occasional translation to those who might be deeply offended, were I to classify them as ignorant. It is my humble opinion that a race is a race so long as it retains its language; without that, it sinks into the mire of mediocrity. And who wants to be mediocre?

Oh, jingers, I've jist mined on anither word!

Peter Buchan 1989.

Pan Loff

There are among us those who fain
Wid treat wi scorn an great disdain
And, gien the slightest chance, wid hain
The Doric phrase.
To hear them spik, ye'd think that they
Were born five hunner miles away,
Instead o 'tween Burnhaven Bay
And Ugie's braes.

They think it impolite to say,
When freen meets freen, 'Fit like the day?'
Oh no, that's not the proper way!
It's 'How d'ye do?'
At phrases sic as oors they scoff;
They toss their heids an spik 'Pan loff'.
They dinna hoast. Oh no, they cough!
Their bleed is blue.

But drap a haimmer on their feet,
Or stick a needle in their seat,
Ye'll get the Doric pure an sweet,
Aye! Rich an rare!
If they were richt, they'd need nae shock
To gar them spik like Buchan folk;
They widna be the lauchin-stock
That noo they are.

Peter Buchan 1949.

AA: All; everything; completely. 'The sea's aa watter, but it's nae aa fish!' 'It's dung for aa, min, dung for aa! Ye canna beat it!' (Organic slogan.) 'Is't aa oo?' 'Aye, aa ae oo.' 'Is it completely made of wool?' 'Yes, all one kind of wool.' (B)

AA COME: All there; sane. (B)

AABODY: Everybody. 'Aabody kens fit I should dee wi my problems. Aabody but me, ye ken.' 'Is aabody fine?' Is everybody well? (B)

AAL: Old. In Buchan, the 'au' sound doesn't exist. (B) **AALEST:** Eldest. 'Erchie wis the aalest in the faimly.' (T)

AAL EEL: Old Yule. The old date of Christmas was 6 January. (B)

AAL-FARRANT: Old-fashioned; obsolete. 'Tooshie's ower aal-farrant an jist refuses tae modernise the placie, but time an money, or the want o't wull catch up on im yet, aye fegs!' (T)

AATHING: Everything. 'Aathing his an end but a mealie pudden his twaa.' Which is more factual than moralistic. (T)

AAWYE: Everywhere. 'I hope ye're nae lookin for the perfect job, my loon. There's dubs aawye, ye ken.' (B)

ABEEN: Above. 'Sic a mess o nettles at yon fairmtoon, especially roon aboot the fairm hoose itsel; it's that bad that afore I could get near the front door I hid tae hud ma haans abeen ma heid or I wid a been stung tae death. (T)

ABLACH: A dwarf. (B)

ACHT: Eight. 'Ye'll get saiven or acht o these for a powen!' (B)

ACKER: Scraps thrown overboard to attract fish. Any poor unfortunate passenger being sick over the side may be said to be 'Giein them acker the day.' (B)

ACQUANT: 'To be acquant with' means to have knowledge of something, i.e. 'Yon skipper's richt weel acquant wi the Wast side', in that he knows every hole an bore from Cape Wrath to the Mull of Galloway. The word also deals with personal relationships. You can be 'Weel acquant', 'fine acquant', 'richt acquant', or 'nae acquant avaa' with someone. It's all a matter of degree. An MP, on the verge of a nervous breakdown was advised to take a few days' holiday in a quiet Buchan village. On his second day there, he discovered that he had left his shaving gear at home and was advised to seek the aid of the blacksmith, since there was no barber in the place. The smith agreed to do the job and sat his guest down on the studdie (anvil) before draping him with a leather apron. Then he produced, from a rickety wooden press, a bowlie of shaving soap and a cut-throat razor. The startled politician was soon to discover that the smith was no ordinary barber, for he kept spitting on the soap to work up a nice lather with the brush. 'My dear fellow!' says he, 'Why on earth do you spit on the soap?' 'Oh,' says the smith, 'That's cos we're nae richt acquant! If we wis richt acquant, I wid spit on yer face!' (B)

AE: One. 'Tae fisher folk, ae sheep's jist the same as anither.' 'I jist got the ae fish for the hale day.' 'Aa in thegither, like the wifie's ae coo.' (B) 'Tak ae day at a time.' (T)

AFFA: Awful. **AFFA DOON:** Awful down; depressed; fed up. 'That holiday in Banff. It rained aa wik. We were affa doon.' **AFFA FINE:** Marvellous; first class. (T)

AFFAIR: Consequence. 'Keep the change, lassie, for aa the affair.' It is of little consequence. (B)

AFFRONTIT: Mortally embarrassed. (T)

AFORE: Before. 'I get up afore the wife tae mak the tay.' (B)

AGLEY: Astray; off course. 'The best laid schemes o mice an men gang aft agley.' (Burns.) (B)

AGYAAN: Going on. What's going on or what's on offer. 'Ye'll jist hae tae tak fit's agyaan.' (T)

AHIN: Behind. 'Ye're like the coo's tail, lassie, aye ahin.' (T)

AIFTERHIN: Afterwards; after the event. 'I nivver thocht onything aboot it at the time, bit aifterhin, fin I hid time tae think aboot it, I changed ma mind!' (T)

AIK: Oak. 'Aikey Brae.' Oakey Brae. 'Aikenshill.' Hill of the Oaks. (T)

AIRISH: Chilly. 'It's gey airish in the mornin afore the sun rises.' (B)

AIRT: Direction; district. 'Fit airt div you come fae onywye?' (T)

AISE or AISS: Fine ash dust. 'Watch that ye dinna faa ower the aiss bucket as ye ging oot.' (B)

AISHAN: Pronounced like nation without the 'n'. The same breed or branch of a family. The Duncans and the Reids are the same aishan as the Robertsons in the clan system. (T)

AIVEN: Even; evenly. 'Space the letters oot aiven, they'll look a lot better.'

12

AIVEN OOT: Honest; straightforward. 'He's fairly aiven oot, yon lad. Ye fairly ken fit's in him.' (B)

AIWAAN: A.1. For as long as I can remember, the fisher folk have used the term 'Aiwaan' for all types of aerated waters. This was from the days when the choice was limited to lemonade, ginger beer and cream soda. (B)

AIXE: An axe. (B)

AKE: Alex or Alec. (B)

ALEEN: Alone. 'Keep yer haans tae yersel an leave me aleen.' Keep your hands to yourself and leave me alone. 'Aa ma leen.' All on my own. 'He's nae his leen.' He is not alone. (T)

ALISS!: Ouch! An exclamation of pain. 'Aliss min, that wis sair!' (T)

ANENT: Across from; in line with; beside; regarding; in opposition to. 'Ye ken far the lavvy is, divin't ye? Jist anent the lobby press.' (T)

ANETH: Under; beneath. 'Aabody aneth the ae reef.' Everybody under the one roof. (B)

ANEUCH: Enough. (B)

ANITHER: Another. **ANITHER KIND:** Greatly improved. 'Fit like's the wife noo, Sandy?' 'Anither kind the day, man; anither kind. We're affa pleased.' (B)

ANNWALL: Annual. (T)

ANTRIN: Occasional. 'Pocket money, did ye say? Man, fin I wis a loon, I wis pleased to see an antrin maik (halfpenny).' (B)

APOTHICK: 'The hale apothick.' The whole sorry mess. (B)

ARLES: When a herring curer was recruiting women and girls to work for him, he would give every recruit her arles, a small sum of money for her verbal promise. There was never any written agreement, but the arles were morally binding. (B) Farm workers got arles from the farmers at the feeing markets, a shilling or a half-crown. (T)

ASWARN: I'll warrant; I reckon. 'Aswarn there's three hunner folk here the nicht.' (B)

ATE OR AIT: Eat. 'Ate up stem-mull man, an ate up that ither stem-mull man an aa!' This was the invitation of an over-anxious farmer's wife serving as table-maid on a threshing day with the hired portable plant. She and her kitchiedeem had a lot of extra work feeding all the lads engaged for the job, which might last for more than one day, depending on the size of the farm. Yet she was determined to earn a good reputation with the two stem-mull (steam-mill) men who were in charge of the operation, and as they moved about the parish they would give her credit for looking after them. Most farms were renowned or otherwise by the quality of the cuisine offered to the enlarged staff on threshing days, and the farmers' wives were keen to compete for a fair share of the praise. Others didn't care and were sometimes labelled for being a bit scant with the food. 'Oh aye,' they would say, 'Stookie's wife's a bit bare wi the mait; ye wunna growe fat on fut ye get at Stookie's threshin.' Some of the wives were too lavish and overfed the men in an effort to please and earn some respect in the district, while others fed the men so heartily with second helpings of tattie-soup and dumplings that they dozed off in the straw of the barn after dinner and were scarcely able for their work in the afternoon. 'Enough is as good as a feast' as they say, but there were the two extremes. Our lady in question was a bit cannibalistic with her remark to the engine-driver to 'ate up stem-mull man, an ate up that ither stem-mull man an aa!' What she meant was that the fireman should also help himself to what was on the table, but in her enthusiasm she mixed up her grammar, and no wonder, for if anything would have gotten a twist in a woman's knickers, portable threshing days on the Buchan farms was the thing to do it, above all the other routine chores. (T)

ATHOOT: Without. 'Nivver a rose athoot a stob (thorn).' (B)

ATWEEN: Between. 'Atween ae thing an anidder.' Between one thing and another. 'Atween een anidder.' Between each other. 'Atween een an the idder.' Between one and the other. (T)

ATWEEN HAN'S: Between times. 'Chay loadit the corn atween han's sortin his nowt (cattle).' (T)

AUCHMACOY BUMMER: The Buchan Bumble-Bee. Why he is distinguished with the name of the oldest estate in Buchan still lived on and cultivated by its founders, the Buchan family, from the 13th century, is a mystery, but almost everyone of my own generation in Buchan knows what an 'Auchmacoy Bummer' is. 'Michty me, I wis jist loupin the dutch (ditch) at Meerton fin I got on the side o the heid (a whack on the side of the head) wi an Auchmacoy Bummer. He wis at some lick (speed), I can tell ye by the skelp I got!' Oor Auchmacoy Bummer hid been 'makin a bee-line' tae get somewye fast! May-bee he wis makin for his bike, for it is a fack that bum-bees hiv bikes, no not bicycles but bikes, a sort of nest in a turf dyke or woodland bank where they secrete their honey, wild-bees' honey, stored in small round balls or cells where the young bees are hatched, and woe-betide if you try to rob a wild-bees' bike while this is in progress, for they can sting like wasps, and even the young bee will sting if he is still inside the ball of honey you slipped into your mouth. Bumble-bee indeed, but certainly not humble-bee, and Auchmacoy Bummer describes him perfectly, jist the dunt! And his 'byke' is sometimes spelled that way. (T)

AVAA: At all. 'Nae bother avaa!' No bother at all! 'Neen avaa.' None at all. 'Nae neen avaa.' Not any at all. (The double negative is in use.) 'There's nae naebody here avaa.' There's nobody here at all. (B)

AWAA: Away.
HINE AWAA: Far distant.
HINE, HINE AWAA: Even farther distant.
HYNDIE FAR AWAA: Distant beyond description.
CAA AWAA: To keep plodding on; to carry on with the job.
FAA AWAA: To moderate (as of wind). 'The win'll faa awaa wi daylicht.'
FAA AWAA: To have a fainting fit. 'She'll faa awaa fin she hears the news.'
KEEP HER AWAA: Alter course to leeward.
KEEP HER TEE: Alter course to windward.
AWAACAST: (always in the negative) An insignificant sum. 'Ten quid the week? That's nae awaacast!' (B)

AWYTE: Indeed. 'A hunner cran? A fine shot (catch) awyte!' **WEEL AWYTE:** Yes indeed. The two words are customarily one complete expression and may carry a hint of sarcasm. (B)

AYONT: Beyond. 'Wullie herded the kye ayont the brae.' (T)

BAABEES: Money. 'Aal Bunchie fairly hain't the baabees, bit noo that he's awaa, the loons'll jist pish't up against the waa.' Old Bunchie fairly saved his money, but now he is gone, his sons will waste it all on drink. (T)

BAACHLE: A well-worn, down-at-the-heel shoe; a shoe twisted into the shape of the wearer's foot. (T)

BACCA BREE: The spittle, usually generous, ejected by those who chew tobacco. (B)

BACK DRAACHT: A spasm and involuntary holding of the breath during an attack of whooping cough. (T)

BACK O: Beyond; after; following. 'We're expectin the meenister at the back o nine.' (T)

BACK O BEYOND: Off the beaten track. 'I bocht it fae an aal crafter wifie up in Strathdon, awaa at the back o beyond.' (T)

BACK-SPEIRIN: Talking back; questioning in return. 'I didna catch his name the first time and I didna like tae back-speir im.' Deafness is sometimes an excuse for back-speirin but can be irritating in over indulgence to the extent of being told to 'muck oot yer lugs', and the good-mannered 'Pardon – I didna hear ye', doesn't always avoid embarrassment. (T)

BACKET: A joiner-made, three-sided, wooden box with hand-holes cut in the sides, useful for carrying peats or sliced turnips or potatoes. Latterly these were replaced with wire sculls or baskets that were lighter to handle. (T)

BACKLINS: Backwards. 'Ye look as if ye'd been trailed backlins throwe a hedge.' (B)

BAD USE'T: Abused; ill-treated; scorned. 'The lassie wis bad use't at hame; nae winner she ran awaa.' (T)

BADDER: Bother. (T)

BADE: Lived. 'Wullie bade awaa at the back o beyond.' **BADE:** Requested. 'The wifie bade the loon get doon oot o the tree.' (T)

BADGER: To torment. 'Peer aal Wullie, he wis aye gettin badger't by the kitchiedeem.' (T)

BAGGEREL: A shapeless female. (T)

BAICKIE: A short iron peg, hammered into the ground to hold a rope or tether for an unfenced animal, mostly goats. 'I say, Liza, ye'll hae tae shift the Billy's baickie – he's aetin aathin roon aboot tae the length o his tether.' (T)

BAILIE: A stockman, cattleman or water bailie. The municipal baillie is spelled with a double 'l'. (T)

BAIRN: A child. **BAIRNIKIE:** A small child. **BAIRNED:** Impregnated. 'Thon vratch o a loon, Tam Cardno, bairned oor Elsie.' (T)

BAITH: Both. 'We'd better baith ging for the milkan coos. It's a gey job gettin them across the main road.' (T)

BAKIT ROADIE: A trail of dried mud on the kitchen floor from the outside door to the fireplace, caused by the bairns running out and in on a rainy day. (T)

BALLANT: A ballad. (T)

BALL'T LEGGINS: Balled leggings. Knee-length, leather leggings shaped to the calf and fastened with straps. Fashionable with game-keepers and sportsmen but ploughmen also wore them before the rubber Wellington boot. The plain shorter type were known as 'Doos' leggins' or spats for doves, and in many instances replaced the traditional nicky-tams on the farms. (T)

BANDY: A small fish found in seashore pools. Most fisher boys would have a bandy in a jar at some time. (B)

BANTINS: Bantams. (T)

BARE: Raw; chilly. 'It's a gey bare win the day. Summer's nae here yet!' (B)

BARE SCAAP: A stretch of thin, shallow, stony, infertile ground; a poor farm. 'Yon's a gey bare scaap o grun that Roger bocht on the Hull o Jock. Ye could lash a moose throwe a girss park fae ae end tae the ither an nivver loose sicht o't for a meenit.' (T)

BARFIT: Barefoot. 'A bourachie o barfit bairns playin on the beach.' A group of barefoot children playing on the beach. (B)

BARFIT BROTH: Broth made without meat or bone. Vegetarian broth consisting only of barley and vegetables. 'Barfit broth the day Charlie, ye winna rin far on at.' (T)

BARK: A preservative for nets. In the days before man-made fibres were invented, herring nets were made from cotton, always brown in colour. The only known preservative was 'cutch', a product from a Burmese tree. All fishers called it 'bark'. At regular intervals, the nets were individually bundled and dipped in a tank containing a boiling hot solution of 'bark'. (B)

BARK AN BOWFF: A scolding. (T)

BARKET: Ingrained with dirt. 'Like a sharny, barket stirk.' Like a bullock caked in dung. 'Yer shins are barket Wullie, playin fitba. Ye'll hae tae get scrubber an soap.' (T)

BARM: Yeast. **REAMIN BARM:** Foaming yeast. (T)

BARRIE: A baby's flannel garment now out of date. It had a sleeveless bodice and wrapper attachment which was folded up at the feet for comfort. Used before the shortening stage. (T)

BARRITCHFU: Harsh. (B)

BARS: Rude jokes. The dirty stories told by farm workers at the hoe, one of the most wearisome and monotonous jobs in agriculture and the laughter lightened the labour and shortened the hours. The stories were the most hilarious I have heard anywhere, but because of their obscenity, must remain in personal oral transmission, which alas, has almost died in land depopulation and mechanisation, and reading them in print lacks the art of the bothy story-teller. Nowadays these stories would be labelled 'pornkisters'. (T)

BASS: A rug. 'Could ye but tramp on the basses there, I'm sure ye wid sink tae the cweets (ankles).' Also a canvas hold-all in which a carpenter carries his tools. (B)

> I like the toon o Peterheid,
> I like it's bonnie lasses,
> In tartan slacks an strings o beads,
> Shakin oot their basses. (T)

BAWDRONS: Pussycat. (B)

BEARDIE or BAIRDIE: To rub a child's face with the stubble of an unshaven chin. 'I gid yon impident quine beardie the nicht an it fair pat colour in er chiks!' (T)

BEATIN A HEUK: Using fine thread to lash a hook to a fishing line. (B)

BEDALL or BEDDLE: A chronic invalid, confined to bed. 'Ye'll mine on Davy, yon strappin chiel that eesed tae win aa the trophies at the Games? Weel he's jist a bedall noo; nivver gets oot avaa.' (B)

BEDDIES: Peevers or hopscotch. (B)

BEDDIT: Bedded. 'Hame at nine beddit by ten.' (T)

BEE-RUSKIE: A primitive type of bee-hive covered in ropes of twisted straw. **BEE-SKEP:** A wooden bee-hive. (T)

BEEF: On fishing boats certain superstitions are always observed. Butcher meat is always referred to as 'beef', bacon is always 'ham', and food is always 'mait' or 'grub'. The word 'food' is never used. (B) The word 'food' was never used on the farms either, it was always 'mait' or 'grub'. (T)

BEELIN: A sort of boil which is extremely painful as it gathers. The English word is 'whitlow', corrupted to 'futtlie', thus a 'futtlie beelin' is just an old-fashioned boil or festering sore. Not nearly so common these days, thanks to antibiotics etc. (B)

BEEN: Bone **BEEN MARRA:** Bone marrow. 'Prunin roses in widder like yon, the win wis caal aneuch tae freeze ye tae the marra!' (T)

BEESOM: A broom or broomstick. 'A new beesom aye swipes cleanest!' Referring to a new servant finding favour until the farmer discovers his faults. (T)

BEET: Need. **BEET TAE KEN:** Need to know. (T)

BEETS: Boots. 'It's fine tae hae tackets in the soles o yer beets; ye can fairly gar the sparks flee, slidin alang the pavement.' (B)

BEEZER: Something of extraordinary proportions. (T)

BEGICK: A shock; an unpleasant surprise. 'Sandy fairly got a begick fin he got the accoont fae the garage.' Note: stress the second syllable. (B) In the country we would say 'begeck'. (T)

BEGOOD: Began; begun. 'That year, we begood in early February.' 'It's time ye wis begood, my loon. The day's near deen!' (B)

BEGRUTTEN: Tear-stained. (T)

BELDIE: Isobel. (B)

BELLY-RIVE: Indigestion. 'Better belly-rive nor gweed mait spil't.' It's better to suffer indigestion than to see good food wasted. (B)

BEN: Through. 'Ben the hoose.' Through the other end of the house. (T)

BENE KAIM: Bone comb. This fine-toothed comb was used for removing head lice or nits and could be gey sair on yer scalp as ye sat wi yer heid bowed abeen a sheet o paper, listenin for the rattle o the beasties. This was a regular Friday night ordeal. (B)

BENMAIST: Innermost. **BENMAIST NEUK:** Innermost corner. (T)

BENNIN: A bend; a knot. The knot which joined two lines was the bennin (bending). 'A sure bend is a sure friend.' (B)

BENTS: Sand dunes. Locally pronounced 'bints'. 'A fine place tae rowe yer Pace (Easter) egg.' (B)

BEUK: A book. (T)

BIBBLIE-NIBBIT: Bubbly or wet-nosed. 'He aye his a drap at his nose an he's aye dichtin it on his sleeve.' 'Bibblie Jimmy' or 'Bibblie Wullie' were others, depending on the christian names, and if a nasal or chest infection developed, it was liable to be 'Snocherin Tam' or whatever. (T)

BICKIE: A young bitch collie dog. 'Caa in the bickie, Jess, it's ower caal tae leave her ootbye the nicht.' (T)

BIDDEN: Told. 'Erchie wis bidden tae dicht is sheen.' Archie was told to wipe his shoes (on the doormat). (T)

BIDE: To dwell; reside; remain. 'He's a country chiel though he bides in the toon. They say he nivver bides lang in ony job, aye shiftin aboot.' **BEDD:** Lived; dwelt. 'Aifter I wis mairried, I bedd wi the wife's folk, but I bide in my ain pairt o the toon noo. Back to my ain gate-end.' **BIDE:** An old Buchan name for a bed. Still in common use. (B)

BIDIE-IN: A live-in lover. 'The whalers could aye get a bidie-in up among the Eskimos.' (B)

BIELD: Shelter. (B)

BIG SHAK: The big shake. The wind that shaks the barley. Strong winds in harvest time can shake or thresh ripened grain crops before the farmer gets round to it. One gusty night can do it and 'the Big Shak' refers to one particular year in the 'sixties when it happened and nearly ruined some farmers waiting on a combine harvester on contract work. Barley is the biggest risk because the whole head falls off, whereas with corn, it is single ears. (T)

BIGG: To build. **BIGGIN:** A building. **BIGGIT:** Built. 'Sammy biggit a gless-hoose but the win blew it doon.' (T) **BIGGIT OOT:** Built out; having abundance of something. 'A gran summer this, for the fairmers. They're jist biggit oot wi grain an tatties.' (B)

BIGSY or BIGSIE: Proud and conceited. 'Damned bigsy thing,' folk said. (T)

BIKKER or BICKER: To sup or laugh heartily; to engage in something enthusiastically; a rapid noisy movement like running water; a bicker o brose. 'Steer yer brose wi the haanle o yer speen.' Also 'Nae tae be bicker't an lauchen at.' No laughing matter. (T)

BILIN: Boiling. 'A bilin o tatties.' A boiling of potatoes. A measure of potatoes sufficient for the family meal. (T)

BILLIE: A bill; a notice. When the herring fleet was in East Anglia, a report of the catches was sent daily to their home ports. This report was posted on a 'billie' in the sales office window. Swarms of loons would gather in anticipation of the billie's arrival, then run round the doors with the news, thus earning themselves a few coppers. This was known as 'rinnin the billie'. (B)

BILLIES: Chaps; fellows. 'Fellas, chiels, haflins, grouin men, loons, lads, laddies, the hale jing-bang o them.' (T)

BINDER: An unlikely story. 'Ye canna mind half o the binders he comes aff wi.'

Also used to describe something outstanding. 'That's a binder o a bike ye've gotten. It's a smasher!' (B)

BING: A large heap. 'A bing o saat in the layby for the slidder (ice) on the road.' 'Tashie's gaan tae be huddin on the lime, there's a bing o't coupit in his clean-lan park.' (T)

BINK: A hob. 'It wis jist an aal-farrant gratie, wi a binkie at baith sides.' (B)

BIRD ALONE: Utterly alone, like a bird on the deep. Fisher folk seem to think that this term is more emphatic than 'lief aleen', although it means exactly the same. (B)

BIRDIE'S EENIES: Bird's eyes. Used to describe sago pudding. 'I fairly like birdie's eenies wi aipples!' (B) In the country we called sago pudding 'puddick's eggs'. (T)

BIRKIE: A lively young fellow. (T)

BIRL: To whirl. 'The winmull's fairly birlin the day. A fine breeze for't.' (B)

BIRN: A load; a burden. **BIRN O DOOL:** A burden of sorrow.

> Some folk get the win in their backs;
> Theirs is a lichtsome birn,
> Wi nivver a flaw in the fine-spun flax,
> They draw fae the birlin pirn. (B)

BIRSE: Anger; temper. 'Dinna ging near the grieve the day – his birse is up.' (T)

BIRSEL: To roast. 'Hillie wis birselin his taes at the fireside, an nae even a cat kittlin, nivver mind a coo.' Back in the old days some of the cottar wives sat too near the coal or peat fires nursing their bairns or 'jist haein a hich heat' (warming their hips), and got their legs birsel't or mizzl't from the heat. (T)

BIRST: A slight stroke, caused by sheer excitement.

> Fin herrin seeks the Knowle gruns,
> They're like to hae a birst,
> An the war cry on their fivvered lips is
> 'Men wi gear first!' (B)

BITTOCK: A small bit. (B)

BIZZ : The buzz or hum of a bee. 'I wis jist new seatit in the kirk fin a muckle bum-bee cam bizzin roon ma lugs.' (T)

BLACK BREE: Mud. (T)

BLACK DRACHT: A most efficacious laxative, available on request from any local droggist. Reputed to contain liquid dynamite. It was consumed on the premises, always with the advice: 'Mak for hame at yer hardest!' (B)

BLACK SUGAR: Liquorice. In the days when sweeties were far less plentiful than they are today, youngsters would get a stick of hard liquorice fae the droggist. The liquorice was then broken into pieces and put into a lemonade bottle filled with water and shaken vigorously, the resultant black liquid being known as 'black-sugar water'. Nobody but bigsy, toffee-nosed folk ever used the word 'liquorice'. Black sugar also came in long straps, or in flat button-shaped sweeties. 'Come into my treacly oxter an get a black-sugar kiss' is a phrase used when playing with the bairn. (B)

BLACK VARNISH: A mixture of tar and creosote available at the local gas-works. Jist the verra dunt for tarrin a deck. (B)

BLACK YARN: Empty herring nets.

> At scalders, dogs, an bare black yarn,
> We've teen a proper scunner. (B)

BLAE: Pale; a cold grey-blue. **BLAE AN WIZZEN'T:** Pale and shrunken. (B)

BLATE: Bashful. 'Ging an spik tae the lassie, min. Dinna be sae blate.' (B)

BLAUD: To damage, spoil or disfigure something either by mistake or carelessness. 'Lucy blaudit the loon's tapioca. She pit saat in't instead o sugar. Nae winner he wis screwin up his face and couldna sup it. Hardly fit for a pig, stuff like that! Aye, she fair connached (wasted) the laddie's pudden.' (T)

BLECK: To exceed or surpass. 'Hughie's won the pools! That fairly blecks aathing.' (T)

BLEED: Blood. 'Bleed's aye thicker than watter.' **BLEED-REID:** Blood-red. **BLEED-JEELIN:** Blood-curdling. (T)

BLEERY EEN: Blood-shot eyes. (T)

BLEETER: A blether or gasbag; someone with the gift o the gab. 'Bandy Mutter's jist a bleeter; he wid argie-bargie till the back o a day, or even for a month o Sundays. Time an tide means naething tae Bandy. He's files nae verra weel, they tell me, bit there's nivver naething wrang wi's tongue, it's aye healthy aneuch.' (T)

BLEEZE: A blaze or fire. Also an indication to strike a blow, like a ball game with a bat or golf club. 'Lat bleeze at it, Jock! It's nae yer mither's heid yer hittin.' Also 'Lat skelp at it!', 'Lat flist!', 'Lat er rip!', 'Lat fung!' etc. (T) **BLEEZIN:** Blazing; in flames; rather highly intoxicated. 'The bairns fairly like to see the bonfires bleezin on Guy Fawkes nicht.' 'Sandy cam oot o the pub, fair bleezin, an fell atween the ship an the pier.' (B)

BLIBBER: To sup or drink a thin mixture or liquid. 'A blibber o soup.' A helping of thin, watery soup. (T)

BLIN-BRIDLE: A blind-bridle. A bridle fitted with blinkers or leather flaps to prevent a horse from seeing the cart or implement behind it. (T)

BLIN DRIFT: Blind drift or smoar drift is snow descending fast enough and thick enough to suffocate and obscure vision to a state of isolation and exhaustion and even death in exposed and desolate landscape where shelter is unobtainable and rescue unlikely. During a winter in the 'sixties, eight people perished in these conditions in one day in Buchan, one of them a local post-woman. (T)

BLIN LUMP: A blind lump. A lump which never comes to a head. (B)

BLIN ROADIE: A cul-de-sac. (B)

BLUE DOO: A failure, hoax or swindle. 'Ye didna miss naethin at the Gala; a blue doo as far as I wis concerned.' (T)

BLUE MOGGANERS: Natives of Peterhead. A moggan was originally a narrow leather tube which served as a purse or money-belt. As time passed, the word came to mean the contents of the sleeve, so that anyone with a 'gweed moggan' was a person who had a fair sum of money laid past. In the heyday of the herring fishing, when the fleet followed shoals around the coast, the gutting women followed as well, to process the herring. It was the custom for the women to work in 'bare sleeves' but on a particularly cold morning they would don their moggans, removable home-knitted sleeves, to keep out the cold. The Peterhead girls' moggans were always blue, hence the name 'Blue mogganers'. (B)

BLUFFERT: A squall of wind. (B)

BOAKIE: The old fisher term for a little boy. It has three syllables bo-ak-ie. 'The boakie's lowse (loose), he's got a touch o the back door trot (diarrhoea).' (B)

BOBBIN-JOHN: There is more than one claimant for the invention of the 'Bobbin-John', an instrument fitted with a perforated revolving drum for the sowing of turnip seed by hand, and it could be (and still is) used for vegetable seed. The Bobbin-John was replaced by the turnip or 'neep-seed barra', pulled by one horse on the drills, and later by the precision sower in the tractor age. Down in the Mearns they claim that Barclay of Ury was first with a Bobbin-John, while we in Buchan give credit for the invention to an Udny Laird of Udny in Formartine. When my first employer sent me over the ditch to 'By Chove', the neighbouring farmer, for a loan of his Bobbin-John to re-seed blank patches in our turnip drills I thought he must be joking, or sending me on a fool's errand (even in the month of June) like the loon who was dispatched to the joiner's shop for a tin of tartan paint, or the one who was sent to the smiddy for a docknail. I had never heard of a Bobbin-John and I had other ideas of what the name might imply. But 'Na, na,' said the fairmer, 'it's nae a joke, laddie. I could lose a lot o ma neep crap this dry wither. Jist ging ower tae By Chove an sic a len o his Bobbin-John an he'll ken fine fut yer needin!' And sure enough he did, without question, and I carried the thing on my shoulder home to my boss. (T)

BOCHT: Bought; purchased. 'I thocht I hid bocht a pig in a pyoke, bit na na, I've gotten a gweed aneuch bargain efter aa!' (T)

BODDAM COO: The fog horn at Boddam Head. Inaccurately called Buchan Ness. The old horn made a noise like the mooing of a cow. 'Ging forrit intae the stem an listen for the Boddam Coo.' (B)

BODDOM: Bottom. 'That waal's (well's) as deep ye can hardly see the watter at the boddom o't. Bonnie biggit, richt fae the foon. The vricht ees't tae cairry his watter in zinc pails on a yoke ower his shooder kis he hid farrer tae ging than we hid.' (T)

BODSY: Small and dapper. (T)

BOG O SWYTE: A state of perspiration. (B)

BOGIE: A two-wheeled, open wagon. (T)

BON or BIN: Humour; mood. 'Wullie's in richt gweed bon the nicht, he's surely won the pools!' Probably from the French *Bon-homie*. The Buchan 'bin' is probably regional slang for the original 'bon' in a much wider Scots dialect. (T)

BONE DAVIE: Artificial fertilisers mixed with bone-meal (crushed whale and animal bones from the slaughterhouses) came in the 1830's, when phosphates were discovered as best suited for turnip growing. The horse-drawn manure distributor followed and came to be known as 'bone davie', most likely from its use in scattering the bone-meal, lime and slag on the turnip fields, which had formerly been done by hand from a canvas hopper strapped to the waist and shoulders. (T)

BONNET-LAIRD: One who farms his own land. (T).

BOO BACKIT: Bent in the back; with a pronounced stoop. (B)

BOODIE: A scarecrow; a ghost; a trifling cause for complaint; dried mucus in the nose. 'Chaa the boodies! Fit a name tae gie a body! Wid that nae scunner ye?' Chew the bogies! What a name to give someone! Would that not sicken you? (B)

BOOL: A marble. (T)

BOORD: A board. (B)

BOO'T TWAA FAAL: Bent double. Where a Glaswegian might say that old so and so walked about 'like a half shut knife', a Buchan body would say that aal so and so was 'boo't twaa faal' or that he was 'fairly comin in ower noo!' (T)

BOREAS: Northern storms, from aurora borealis or 'northern lights'. (T)

BORRETT RICK: Borrowed smoke. Smoke with a waachy (stale) smell which had seeped through the wall or floor from a crack in a neighbour's chimney. Or it might have just drifted up the stair. (T)

BOSIE: The breast; to embrace; to cuddle to the breast. 'Come an get a bosie, quine.' (T)

BOSS: Hollow. 'He wis beddit boss.' He was sent to bed without supper. (B)

BOTHY: Farm workers cooked their own food and lived in the bothies, whereas chaumers (chambers) were merely sleeping accommodation, the men feeding in the farmhouse. (T)

BOURACH or BOURACHIE: A group of people assembled together; a cluster, numbers indeterminate. 'A hale bourachie o fairmers at the roup.' (B)

BOW-HOCHED: Bow-legged. Said to be common among long-serving sailors from trying to keep their balance on heaving decks. (T)

BOWE: A corruption of 'buoy'. A bowe is the float used in countless thousands by herring fishermen. These floats were originally animals' bladders. A pirn (cotton reel) was inserted into the neck of the bladder and firmly lashed in place. The hole in the pirn was ideal for the inflation of the bowe and could be easily plugged. Since these floats could not be fastened with rope, they were usually encased in strong netting which could be firmly attached to the upper rope of the net. I have seen hundreds of such floats in use by southern Irish fishermen about fifty years ago. The modern bowe is generally made of brilliantly fluorescent orange plastic. (B)

BOWIE: A barrel. **BOWIE WATTER:** Rain water collected in a barrel; slightly stagnant and disagreeable to the taste. 'Yer watter's nae gweed umman, it's bowie tastet!' (T)

25

BOWSEL: A barrel mole-trap; an iron hoop for binding cattle to a byre stall. (T)

BOWSTER: A bolster. (T)

BRAE: A hill; a slope. (T)

BRAID: Broad. **BRAIDSEA (OF FRASERBURGH):** Broadsea. The earlier part of Faithlie, later Fraserburgh, on the north shore and just inside the broad expanse of the Moray Firth. (T)

BRAK O SKY: The dawn of the day. (B)

BRANKS: Shackles. **COO-BRANKS:** Cow shackles. (T)

BRANNER or BRANDER: The grating on a drain. Also an old fashioned kitchen implement made from heavy wire, twisted into a grotesque shape, resembling a huge hand. This would span the fire in a grate, from bink to bink, like a crude grating, and was extremely useful in the roasting of fish etc. (B)

BRAW: Handsome; grand; beautiful. **BRAWLY:** Beautifully; well. 'She tied her hair sae brawly.'(T)

BRAZEN: Bold. 'A brazen loon, yon, speirin a len o ma Sunday briks.' (T)

BREE: Moisture; juice. Bree can also mean the consequence of someone else's carelessness. 'Jessie left the filletin knife on the table an the bairn got the bree o't (cut herself).' (B)

BREEM BUSS: Broom bush or wild Precos shrub, to give it its latin name. Bright gold flowers in summer and shooting pods in late autumn. On a quiet sunny day you can hear the pods splitting. A mild, sweet, almost whisky-tasting wine can be made from the flowers. (T)

BREENGE: A sudden, rather violent movement, requiring no finesse. You can 'breenge aboot in an ull teen.' You can 'mak a breenge' at something which would normally require careful handling. There is a mixture of haste and clumsiness in the word. (B)

BREER: Brier. (T)

BREET: One deserving sympathy, the opposite of brute. 'He's a peer breet Stoddie, mair need tae be peeti't than laachen at.' (T)

BREID: Oatcakes. Taken as a dessert in the Buchan farm kitchens, they were heated at the fire and crumbled or murled into a bowl of milk and supped with a spoon. Sugar and pepper were optional. Dr Johnson described oatmeal as 'Food for horses in England and for men in Scotland,' to which James Boswell his biographer quickly replied, 'But Sir, where will you find such horses or such men?' (T)

BREIST-STRAP: The leather holding the hames in place at the bottom of the leather collar on the breast of a horse. These were slightly bigger than the nicky-tams worn below the knee by the ploughmen, thus in the bothy ballad we read: 'When briest-straps brak there's naething like a pair o nicky-tams.' Obviously for repairing them. (T)

BRESS: Brass. 'Caal eneuch tae freeze the baas aff a bress monkey.' Which had a special significance when our eight-year-old son returned from the farmyard and told his mother what the weather was like – according to the foreman. (T)

BRIDAL: A dense gathering of excited gulls above a shoal of sand-eels or mackerel. A bridal is always on, or very close to the surface of the sea. 'Did ye see yon bridal the streen? Time ye had yer flies buskit!' (B)

BRIDDER: Brother. Brither is the variation of brother now more commonly used in Buchan, as is mither for midder, but fadder in preferred to faither. (T)

BRIERS O THE EEN: Eyebrows or eye-lashes. 'Saved by the briers o the een.' A narrow escape; a near thing; touch and go. 'Na, faith ye, bit it wis a near thing, and he jist got aff by the briers o his een fin yon ither lad took wi't (admitted it).' (T)

BRIKS: Breeks; trousers. The fishers aye wore hairback briks, wi the pooches at the front. (B)

BRITCHEN or BRETCHIN: Leather slings in harness which enables a horse to brake or reverse a cart and is carried behind the saddle and over the nares or hind-quarters. It is not required in plough harness. (T)

BROB: To prick, jab or pierce with a sharp thorn or instrument. 'I brobbit ma thoom wi the stob o a rose an I think it's gaan tae beal. I jist hope it disna turn oot tae be a futtlie bealin.' (T)

BROCH: A defence tower of stone built by the Picts to defend themselves against the Norsemen. (T) **THE BROCH:** The commonly used name for Fraserburgh, which was once called Faithlie. Brochers are natives of the Broch. (B)

BROCHT: Brought. 'I brocht a bottle o lang ale for ye for fear ye wis dry.' (T)

BRODS: Covers; boards of a book. (B)

BROKEN BISCUIT: That which was left on the baker's shelf at the end of the day (8.pm.). Youngsters from poorer families would be sent to the shop at closing time, when a great muckle bag would be filled for tuppence. (B)

BRONCAIDIS: Bronchitis. The term is still in general use. 'There's naebody taks the caal noo. It's broncaidis or some ither fancy disease that gars them hoast.' (B)

BROOK: Soot. Brook corroded on the links and crooks (chain and hooks) that hung from the swey (gantry) over the binks and the fireplace, on which the pots were suspended for cooking. The pots, pan, kettle, frying-pan and girdle were all corroded with the grime and soot from coal or peat-fires, coal being the worst for corrosion and these utensils had to be scraped periodically, perhaps once or twice a week to maintain them in a respectable condition. Coal-coom or coal-dust required frequent dusting from furniture and shelves where it lodged all over the kitchen, and also occasionally when fires were lit in bedrooms. Peat-dust or ase (ash) was less troublesome because it lacked the adhesive ingredient of the coal-smut variety, but could be easily air-borne when a draughty door was opened. 'Gyang an scrape the pots an pans lassie,' the mither or mistress would command, 'an ye'll mebbee hae tae gie the clear eens a scoor wi san (sand) tae brichten em up a bittie!' The 'clear eens' were perhaps stainless steel or aluminium, and enamelled tea-pots were also commonly used. 'Brookie' was a nick-name for the blacksmith because his clothes and skin were usually soiled with the soot and ash from the forge. (T)

BROSE: Oatmeal mixed with boiling water, salt and pepper, taken with cream or milk, sugar or treacle optional and milk may be substituted by stout or 'porter' ale. (T)

BROSY: Heavy, stout or well-proportioned. Someone who 'looks like his mait' or enjoys his brose. (T)

BROWDENT: Clinging. Refers only to a child. 'She's a richt browdent bairn, yon. She'll hardly lat her mither oot o her sicht.' (B)

BRUISED CORN: Pounded oats. (T)

BRUNT: Blame; fault; guilt. 'MacPherson took the brunt o settin fire tae the hedder bit there wis mair in't than him an they aa ran awaa.' (T)

BUBBLIE-JOCK: A turkey-cock. 'Sunie hid a face like a bubblie-jock. Fair roosed he wis, an like tae tak his jaikit aff. I widna like a skelp fae Sunie Merrlies fin he's in yon mood.' (T)

BUBBLIES: Paraffin torches. These came in various sizes. The smallest was about the size of a teapot, with a multi-strand wick protruding from the spout. It was used as a portable light on the steam drifter, and on motor boats too. Larger versions, as big as a large kettle, were used to illuminate the herring yards. The light produced was never very good, but the fire risk was horrendous. There was usually far too much paraffin in the containers. (B)

BUCHAN HUMLIE: A black polled (hornless) steer of the Aberdeen Angus breed. The pedigree also applies to most male members of the native population, which is nothing to be ashamed of considering the prize-winning reputation of the herd. (T)

BUCHANER: A native of Buchanhaven, once a village on its own, but now swallowed up in Peterhead. (B)

BUCHANIE: *'The Buchanie' The Buchan Observer.* Sometimes referred to as *'The Buchan Leear'.* Published by P Scrogie Ltd. of Peterhead.

> Noo last, not least, there's your Press,
> Thy famed *Observer* leaf –
> Wi hints on whaar tae buy oor dress,
> And aa the news in brief.
> Wha's stirks tae sale, or straw tae bale,
> And whaar they catched the thief! (T)

BUCHT: A primitive shelter provided for the shepherd's ewes at lambing time. 'The lambin bucht' it was called and could have been an old barn or extended outhouse or a big shed. The showyard at Inverness is called 'The Bucht Park', which is surprising because the Gaelic name for a shelter is 'bield', but 'The Bield Field' looks as meaningless in cold print as it would sound in speech. (T)

BUCKER: To delay or hinder. 'Dinna bucker aboot, min, get on wi the job!' (T)

BUCKIE: The whelk, which lives in a small round shell. 'Snug an asleep in her bed, curled like a buckie.' (T)

BUCKRAM: An English word that has been freely adapted into the Buchan dialect. A housewife, returning from her holidays to find her house plants dried out is apt to exclaim, 'Ma flooers are aa as dry as buckram!' The English definition is 'coarse linen cloth or goat's skin stiffened with glue.' (T)

BUDDICKS: Small, useless fish which used to be found in great numbers in practically every harbour. They were a source of great delight for little boys with fishing lines. I'm afraid pollution has decimated the buddick shoals. These little fishies were also known as 'geets'. (B)

BULFER: A heavyweight. 'Sic a bulfer o a chiel, I widna like tae be in his oxter.' (T)

BUMMER: Something very big indeed. 'Fit a bummer o a boat! She wid nivver get into Peterheid.' (B)

BUNG: To throw. 'Dinna bung an egg at me!' 'The loons hiv been bungin steens again.' Also the bung or stopper of the barrel where the tap screws in. 'The bailie's loon left the bung oot o the bowie an the neep shed's fluddit wi black trykle.' (T)

BUNGED or BUNG'T: In a sulk. Probably from 'Bung' or 'Bung-hole' (Stopper) because the mouth or bung-hole is firmly closed and no speech is forthcoming while the mood lasts. (T)

BUR: The tongue of a boot or shoe. (T)

BURN THE WITCHIE: To walk round the boat's deck with a blazing effigy (rags) on the end of a poker, to break a spell of bad luck. A pagan practice, long since discontinued. (B)

BURRY or BURRY THRISSLE: The Scots thistle, a giant of the species and the emblem of Scotland. (T)

BURSSEN: Bursting; over-heated. Almost at the point of collapse after some superhuman effort, particularly in hot weather. 'A body could be fair burssen shivvin a car that winna start.' (B)

BURSSEN ILE: Spent lubricating oil from the sumps of motor vehicles. If you see a herd of pigs with their backsides smeared with black stuff, you'll know that the farmer uses 'burssen ile' to soothe the painful cracks which can affect pigskin in that part of the anatomy. (B) Also used to prevent rust on farm machinery. (T)

BUSK: To dress or adorn. 'Lassie wi the yalla coatie, will ye busk an gang wi me?' To 'busk a ripper'. To fix fancy lures to the hooks. (B)

BUSS: A bush. A 'funn buss' is a prickly gorse bush. 'If ye dinna behave yersel min, I'll dab yer face in the nearest funn buss!' Some Scottish poets romanticise on the nostalgic smell of the reek (smoke) from kennel't funn (burning whin), in early spring. In summer the blossom sets the hills alight with gold. (T) **BUSS:** A dangerous submerged rock, of whose existence only inshore fishermen may be aware. (B)

BUTTERY: A morning roll or cookie, rich in butter and crisply browned. Not to be confused with the bap, which is a sooth-kintra abomination. (B)

BY-NAMES: Insults. 'Sticks an steens wull brak ma beens bit by-names wunna hurt me!' (T)

BYAAK: To bake. Seldom used nowadays apart from the saying 'His breid wis

30

weel byaakit lang, lang syne.' He made his money many years ago. (B)

BYORDINAR or BYORDINARY: Extraordinary; outstanding. 'Rab worked the odd pair o horse, off an on, when he wisna pooin neeps, usually a pair o raw colts that naebody else could handle. But Rab soon had them tamed wi his lang strides ahin the harras, or in the muckle steen roller that wis for crushin the clods, for they were byordinar at the Barnyards.' (T)

BYOUS: Exceptionally. (Used in strengthening an adjective.) 'They tell me the neep's ninety per cent watter. They could be richt, but it's byous gweed watter.' (B) **BYOUS WEETY:** Very wet weather. 'It's byous weety. If it rains muckle langer we'll need an Ark.' (T)

CAA: To drive, as an engine caas the propeller. To push, as in 'Caa tee the door, min.' Shut the door, man. To give a name to: 'Because his name wis Penny, the fisher loons caaed him "Copper".' To hammer: 'Caa the nails richt in.' Hammer the nails right home. To activate: Country girl, trying to explain to a visitor, in posh language, that the water-pump was seized up. 'The handle of the pimp won't caa.' To pierce: 'The rocks seen caaed a hole in the ship.' (B) **CAA CANNY:** Be careful. 'Caa canny wi the butter Tam, it's nearly aa deen, an ye canna expect the deemie tae churn twice a wik, surely!' **CAA CANNY AN FLEE LECH!:** Keep a low profile and don't boast. **CAA YER GIRD:** Get on with whatever you are doing. The way you used to whack your hoop or bicycle wheel or whatever you had for a gird that had to be driven with a stick. In biblical language 'Whatever thy hand findeth to do, do it with all thy might.' **CAAD AFF YER STOTTER:** Caught off your balance or upset by some interference with the routine. (T)

CAAL: Cold. 'Caal roch shooers.' Cold rough showers. 'The caal roch shooers that weet ither men, seem aye tae leave him dry.' (B)

CAALRIFE: Chilly; over-sensitive to cold weather; to feel the cold excessively. 'Oor meenister's affa caalrife. He's aye compleenin aboot the caal widder. He must be affa thin-bleedit.' (T)

CAANLE: A candle. 'Benzie wis burnin a penny caanle lookin for a bawbee (halfpenny).' In other words, Benzie was penny wise and pound foolish, or pouring good money after bad in a worthless investment. (T)

CACK or KEICH: To defecate. Both words mean exactly the same, and are of Gaelic origin. They are never used except in reference to bairns 'using the pottie'. 'Cack a heapie at the back o the doorie, an Mammy'll clean't in the mornin.' Reputedly said by a fond mother to her spoiled brat before the days of inside toilets. (B)

CADDEL'T EGG: Scrambled egg. A common supper in the farm kitchen if there were a lot of chipped eggs gathered in that day. (T)

CADDIS: Accumulated dust and fluff. 'It's that lang since I had a bath, my belly-button maun be full o caddis.' (B)

CADGER: A fish hawker. Cadgers, some with vans, some with pony and cart, would meet the early arrivals from the fishing grounds to buy a basket of herring which they would 'cadge' round the countryside. Terms strictly cash. (B)

CAFF: Corn chaff. For generations, the caff-saick (chaff-sack) was the recognised mattress for fisher folk and country folk alike. The great hessian bag was cased in a cotton cover, and made a very comfortable, cheap bed. 'Yon great clumsy clort o a quine has a body like a caff-saick tied in the middle.' (B)

CAIRT: Cart. **CAIRTIT:** Transported by cart. (T)

CAITHICK: Old Buchan name for the monkfish. Corresponds with the Moray Firth oof. (B)

CALFIE'S CHEESE: Cheese made from the first milk taken from the cow after it had calved. It was heated in the oven and sometimes sultanas were added. (T)

CALLER: Fresh. (B)

CANNY: Careful; easy. 'Ye hiv a fine canny job, I'm thinkin.' **CANNY LEETHE:** A cosy shelter. Anything which breaks the force of the gale provides a leethe, be it an island or a dyke. (B)

CANTRIP: A trick; a charm. (B)

CANTY: Cheery; pleasant; humoursome. (T)

CAPPERNYAAM: Extremely fussy and temperamental. The kind of person who is 'difficult'. Could there be some connection with Capernaum, from the Bible? (B)

CAPSHIN: A windfall; a first prize or reward; something really worthwhile. 'Fit a capshin for the fairmer fin he got first prize for his bull at the show.' (T)

CARENA: Care not. **CARENA A DOIT:** Do not care in the least. (B)

CARFUFFLE or CURFUFFLE: Confusion; disorder; mess; annoyance. 'That new roll o plain weir (wire) ye opened oot, Ewan, ye've fair carfuffled it. It's ravell't tae buggery. Ye open't oot the wrang end first.' (T)

CARGIE: Cargo. Cargo-ships are always cargie-boats, and a fishing boat with a really heavy catch is said to be cargie-load. (B)

CARK NOR CARE: 'Neither cark nor care.' Not a care in the world.

> Some hae aye the greet in their throat,
> Tho' they've neither cark nor care. (B)

The country word for cark is 'cauk'. 'Nae cauk nor care.' Cauk meaning carefree, irresponsible and unreliable. (T)

CARL: A fellow; a chap. (T)

CARL-DODDIE: Rib-grass. (T)

CARLERS: The heavy seaweed with the thick stalks and the broad fronds which may break the surface at low water, usually classed as 'tangles'. In some villages, these carlers are gathered into great heaps to dry. They are then collected and used in the manufacture of cosmetics and medicines. (B)

CARLIN: An old woman; a witch. (T)

CARPETS: Carpet slippers. 'Sittin by the fire wi their carpets on.' (B)

CARVEL BIGGIT: A boat built with planks edge to edge. (B)

CASSEN: Faded or changed colour, either from strong sunlight or washing. 'The peats are cassen.' The peats have all been cut for the season. If you 'hadna cassen a cloot (cloth or clothing) for the simmer,' you were 'still in yer lang drawers.' 'Cassen oot.' Cast out. When two friends have fallen out. (T)

CASSIE STEENS: Causeway stones; granite setts. For many years the popular medium in the paving of roads. 'His false teeth fell oot and gid skitin alang the cassie.' (B)

CATCH HER: The fisherman's term for getting to sleep. 'I've been in my scratcher (bunk) for twaa oors, but I hinna catched her avaa.' (B)

CAT'S DICHT: A brief wipe. Pussy wiping over his ears with a front paw which is considered insufficient ablution for the human face. 'Alec jist gied his face a cat's dicht afore he gaed tae the concert.' (T)

CATTIE'S TAILIE: A plaything made from odds and ends of knitting wool on a makeshift loom, constructed with a pirn and a few common preens (pins). Hours of pleasure for the quines. (B)

CAUK: To remind or challenge someone for repayment of a debt. 'I hid tae cauk up Jocky tae get my pound back.' (T)

CAUP: A wooden bowl. 'Brose caup an horn speen.' Brose bowl and horn spoon. Said to make the best flavoured mixture of oat-meal brose. 'A bool in a brose caup.' A bool is a marble, and to spin a bool in a brose caup was like the carnival death riders on their motor bikes flying round their giant barrel without going over the top. (T)

CAUR: Calves. 'I hiv caur in the trailer ahin the jeep!' 'There's fower caur for sale in the paper the day.' (T)

CEEST: To cast. (B)

CHAA: To chew. 'If things dinna improve, we'll sook mair than we'll chaa.' (B)

CHACKIE: A small bag. Back in the old days the chackie contained the chattles of the single farm worker and was slung over the shoulder on the long walks between his parents' home and the farm where he worked. It was abandoned early in the present century when the bicycle came within the grasp of the Scottish farm worker. (T)

CHANGIN-COLOUR: Mother of pearl. Also the vivid, multi-coloured streaks made by oil or petrol on a tarred road. (B)

CHAPPIT: Mashed. 'Chappit tatties.' Mashed potatoes. Once upon a time dates came in big wooden boxes, not wrapped at all. The contents would be set on the shop counter in the form of a great ugly slab, which simply fascinated the bluebottles. Anyone requiring a quantity of dates had to watch them being hacked from the mass, and, by the time that was done, the dates were 'weel chappit' squashed and bruised. 'I wis that mad, I could hae chappit him.' A hint of physical violence here. (B)

CHAUMER: A chamber; a sleeping chamber; sleeping quarters for farm workers. As opposed to the Bothy system, food was not partaken in the chaumer. Bothies were more common in the Mearns, where the men cooked their own food. In Banff and Buchan the workers were fed in the farm kitchens and slept in the chaumers. (T)

CHEIR: A chair. (B)

CHEP-JOHN: A Cheap-Jack; a con-man. Like the Chep-Johns at Aikey Fair or the Castlegate in Aberdeen. 'I eence bocht a jacket fae a Chep-John an it wis fu o moch (moth) holes!' 'They can tak baabees oot o thin air yon lads. They live by their wutts!' (T)

CHIEL: A fellow; a chap; a man. A human male older than a teenager. 'There's country chiels an fisher chiels an toonser chiels forbye.' (B)

CHILPIT: Chilled. (T)

CHINE: A chain. (B)

CHOUKS: The human jaw bones; the facial structure. 'Tam's chouks is affa swollen since he visited the dentist.' (T)

CHOWTER: A term of endearment, usually applied to children. 'Come awaa noo, my chowter. Come intae my bosie.' (B)

CHUCKIE STEENS: Granite chippings. Popular for covering driveways. The sort that crunch beneath your feet. (B)

CHUCKNIES: Young chickens. (T)

CHUDDERIN: Shivering. 'Chudderin wi the caal.' (B)

CHUMLA: A mantel shelf. This was immediately above the fire-place and usually bore the clock and a couple of brass candlesticks. 'Oh, she's a fool (dirty) midden (dung tip)! Her chumla's thick wi stue (dust).' (B)

CHUNNER: To murmur plaintively. (B)

CHUNTY: A chamber pot. In the days when outside toilets were the norm, this humble utensil was a necessity. It was commonly known as 'the dirler' but, if you were really posh, you called it 'the goesunder', since it was kept under the bed. (B)

CHYSE: To choose. 'Could I but pick an chyse again, I widna seek the sea.' (B)

CIRCUMSPECK: Respectable; presentable; in charge of the situation; all that one could hope for or expect. 'Robbie wis circumspeck an spoke weel for aabody concerned.' (T)

CLAA: To scratch. 'Claa yer pow.' Scratch your head (in perplexity). 'The poll tax? Man, that'll gar ye claa yer pow.' (B)

CLAACHT: To snatch or grasp hold of something quickly. 'I made a claacht at Elsie on the landin or she wid hae tummel't doon the stair.' (T)

CLAES-CAIRRYIN: The nicht afore the wedding, fin the bride's claes, her 'providing' (her bottom drawer) were cairried to the mairridge hoose. Since those who did the cairryin were young folk, the event was usually an opportunity for high jinks and horse play. (B)

CLAGGUM: Candy. **CLAGIELEERUM:** Sticky treacle toffee or chewing candy that was very popular with the bairns. 'I've seen bairns makkin a sweetie. Ye pit a pucklie sugar in a wee speen, stuck the poker in the fire till it wis reid-hot, then ye meltit the sugar wi the poker until it formed a wee ball o candy.' (T)

CLAGGY: Sticky. 'Better gie the cooker a dicht, my quine. It's aa claggy wi the jam bilin ower.' (B)

CLAIK: Gossip. It's strange that women are often called 'claiks'. Do menfolk never claik? That'll be the day! (B)

CLAITH: Cloth. 'Yon suit wisna made yesterday! Ye can tell by the claith.' Claith can also mean 'sufficient material'. 'I wid mak it a bittie bigger, but I jist dinna hae the claith.' (B)

CLART or CLORT: A sorry mess. 'Yon place is jist a clart o dubs.' 'A great clumsy clort o a loon.' As a verb: 'There's nae need tae be parteeclar, jist clart it on.' **CLARTIT:** Daubed in a messy way. (B)

CLATTERBEEN: The back end of a duck. (T)

CLATTERVENGEANCE: An uproar. (B)

CLAWIN POST: A scratching post for cattle, usually a stone in the middle of a field, like a monolith from a Druid's circle. (T)

CLEAN-LAN PARK: A field cleared of turnips and ready for ploughing. (T)

CLEW: A ball of straw-rape or coir yarn somewhat bigger than a football. Holding the end of the rope you threw the clew to the man on the ladder placed against the corn stack, who threw the ball down the other side and fixed the rape on the thatch with an edrin (pear-shaped clew) and the man on the other side tied in his rape and threw the clew back again to the man on the ladder, and thus back to you, where you tied in your rape and threw the clew again. With the rapes about a foot apart on the pyramid of the stack this went on until you reached the easin or shoulder, when the foreman descended from his ladder and carried it round to the other side and the performance was repeated, the crossed ropes forming diamond squares and securing the stack for the winter. (T)

CLICK: A large crochet-hook used for making a rag rug. 'Molly's clickin a rug for her aalest brother, he's gettin merried.' Sometimes refers to a shepherd's crook. (T)

CLINKER BIGGIT: A boat built with planks overlapping. Clinker comes from the sound of the 'clinking' of the copper rivets. (B)

CLIP: A smack. 'I'll gie ye a clip on the lug!' A long-handled gaff hook; a woman with a domineering tongue; a haircut. 'Fowerpence for a clip? Good grief!' An indeterminate measure of speed. 'That shippie's gaan at a fair clip!' (B) **CLIP:** A young horse; a gelding or mare approaching one-year-old. 'Tak in the clips, Hughie, afore it's dark. They'll be wytein at the gate for ye fin it gets caaler.' (T)

CLISHMACLAVER: Gossip; idle chatter. (T)

CLOCHER: To breath noisily as the result of a bad cold. 'He's fair clocherin wi the caal.' (B)

CLOCKIN HEN: A broody hen with the desire to hatch eggs and rear chickens, provided the eggs are fertile. (T)

CLOO O WORSIT: A ball of worsted knitting wool. 'That ull-trickit kittlin's (kitten's) awaa wi my cloo o worsit again!' (T)

CLOOD: A cloud. 'It's a cloody nicht, Fred. Nae a star tae be seen.' Clood was also a word used in Buchan horse cart transport, meaning half-a-load. When the moss road was in such bad condition that a full load of peats couldn't be carted out, half loads were toppled at the end of the road and later used to top up the half loads that followed. This was known as 'cloodin oot the peats.' (T)

CLOOER'T: Battered. (B)

CLOOK: To claw. **CLOOKIT:** Scratched. 'The bairn's han's bleedin. The cat clookit er. She'd been strokin the cat an he'd turn't on er; he's a nesty brute wi bairns and he's nae used tae them. Come awaa quinie, dinna greet, hud yer handie in aneth the caal watter tap, there's a lass!' (T)

CLOOT: Cloth or clothing. 'Ne'er cast a cloot or Mey be oot.' This was almost a proverb in the old days, but with our late century weather mixture under the greenhouse atmosphere and the perforated ozone layer it seems to have less effect or meaning. The supposedly vigorous May dew seems to be the same as that of November nowadays. The Gab o May also seems to have lost its bite, and the Teuchats' Storm in mid April, when I've seen the roads blocked with snow overnight, or in a few hours. The modern duffle coat or anorak and jeans with track shoes or trainers, and most of our women in trousers, seems a sensible answer to the vagaries of the T.V. weather man.

> Fin the mist comes fae the sea,
> Dry widder it wull be.
> Fin the mist comes fae the hull,
> Ye'll get watter for yer mull.
>
> Fin Mormond Hill pits on her cap
> The Buchan lads wull get a drap. (T)

37

CLOOTIE DUMPLING: A fruit pudding boiled in a cloth rather than a bowl. (T)

CLORTY: Sticky. (T)

CLOSS: Close. (T)

CLOSSACH'T: Enclosed. (T)

CLOUR, CLOOR or CLOUT: A blow or heavy smack. 'Fit a cloor in the lug I got fae yon quine's fadder for ruggin her hair. It gart ma een watter I tell ye, an the bells are aye ringin in my lugs.' (T)

CLUMP: A cluster. 'A clump o bonnie flooers.' (T)

CLYACK SHEAF: The last bound sheaf in harvest. Clyack is from the gaelic and means the end of the cutting season – not the end of harvest, which is called 'Winter' in Buchan when the last sheaves have been carted home. (T)

CLYTE: To fall or tumble heavily. 'Tam got an affa clyte fan he fell aff his bike on the sliddery road. I dinna ken fit wye he didna brak his neck.' (T)

COACH: A pram. 'Twaa bairns in the coach, anither twaa at her tail.' (B)

COAL-COOM: Coal-dust. A grimey coal dust from the fireplace that gathers on furniture, especially after a windy day. (T)

COCKLE EE: An eye with a squint.

> Ye mind, last year I took the flu?
> Weel, I'm only gettin the back o't noo!
> But it's teen a gey sair pick, ye see,
> For I'm lantered noo wi a cockle ee. (B)

COG: A wooden bucket made with staves and one of these extending above the rim served as a handle. The body of the cog was banded with iron hoops like a barrel. 'Cog the caur,' means 'Feed the calves from the cog.' Caur, like calves, is the plural of calf. Kye is the plural of cow. (T)

COGGIE: A small wooden tub into which the guttin quines would flick the herring guts. A larger wooden cask, for many years, was the only toilet on a fishing boat. (B)

COGGIT CALF: A calf fed with milk from a small wooden tub or coggie with an upright handle which was known as 'the calfie's cog'. (T)

COIR YARN: Light soft rope made from coconut hair and used for securing the thatch on corn stacks. It replaced straw-rape early this century, but was more expensive. (T)

COLE: A small, tapered, hock or stack of loose untrampled hay in the early stages of maturing for winter cattle feed. A process in hay-making now defunct with the advent of the modern round baler machine. (T)

COLLIESHANGIE or CULLIESHANGIE: An uproar or noisy dispute or animated conversation. 'Gweed sake! Fit a collieshangie aboot a roup. I thocht they wid hae the reef aff the barn afore they were throwe.' (T) To be as thick as thieves: 'He has a gran job wi the ile folk. They say he collieshangies wi Arab sheiks an the like.' (B)

COLLOGUIN: Gossiping. (B)

COMBINATIONS: The all-in-one undergarment which comprised semmit and pants. Sometimes called 'combs.'

> Oh! to Robbie's fite draars,
> Oh! to Robbie's fite draars.
> A hole in the middle
> For Robbie to piddle,
> A hole at the back
> For Robbie to cack.
> Oh! to Robbie's fite draars. (B)

COME AT: To damage something (accent on 'at'). 'See yon great dint in my car door? Somebody's surely come at it.' (B)

COME OWER: To befall. 'I thocht something had come ower ye, ye wis that lang in comin.' (B)

COME TIME: In due course. 'Jist hae patience, my loon, an come time, things'll be aa richt.' (B)

CONE: A black cone hoisted at Coastguard stations as a gale warning. Point upwards: Gales from North and West. Point downwards: Gales from South and East. (B)

CONNACH: To waste or destroy. 'Losh bi here Wattie, yer kitchiedeemie fairly connach't the denner fin she sung (singed/burned) the rice pudden. Bit the peer lassie mebbee couldna help it wi aa yon mous tae stap at a doon sittin.' (T)

CONTERMASHIOUS: Difficult to get on with; obstinate; contrary. 'He's a contermashious deil, a proper din raiser.' **CONTER:** Probably from contermashious. 'Their ilka thocht's clean conter to fit ye hear them say.' 'He disna like tae be contered.' He doesn't like to be contradicted. (B)

COOCH: Couch or settee. 'Sit doon on the cooch loon an lat's hear fit ye hiv tae say.' (T)

COONTER LOUPER: Doric slang for a shop-keeper, serving behind the counter before the days of self-service and the supermarkets. (T)

COOR: To cower, shelter, avoid or shy away. **COOR DOON:** To bend down in submission or to attempt to avoid a blow. **COORYIN:** Cowering. (T)

COORDIE LICK: A challenging blow dealt out amongst youngsters provoking a response. (T)

COORSE: Coarse. A multi-purpose word, with several shades of meaning, the most general being coarse or unpleasant. 'A coorse day' for the farmer means a day of heavy rain or snow. For the fisher, a day of strong winds. 'Yon wis gey coorse (unpleasant) stuff the doctor gied me.' 'Yon teacher can be richt coorse (unkind) tae the bairns at times. She micht try a mair kindly attitude.' 'Yon wis a richt coorse (harsh) thing tae say, an the man no there tae spik for himsel.' 'Watch yersel wi yon folk. They're coorse (rough and ready), man, coorse. They'd tak the een oot o yer heid an come back for the holes.' (B)

COO'S CLEAN: The cow's cleansel; the afterbirth. The embryonic sac in which the calf is carried during pregnancy and which is normally discharged after delivery. But there are exceptions. 'Watch the roan coo efter she calves, bailie, she's ull for atein er clean, keep it oot o sicht.' Mostly these were buried in the sharn midden. (T)

COO'S LICK: When the forelock on the brow looks as if it had been shaped by a lick from a cow's tongue. Buchan folk referred to the forelock on Hitler's brow as 'a coo's lick'. (T)

CORBIE: A crow. (T)

CORKIT: Constipated. 'It's time I wis back to the castor ile. I'm fair corkit.' (B)

CORNKISTERS: There was a corn kist or chest in the stable, one for each pair of horses and it contained the crushed oats for their feed. It was whilst seated on some of these stable kists that the farm chiels composed some of their famous bothy ballads, dunting out the tunes with their heels on the sides or ribs of the kist and taking the farmer to task in their lyrics. These ballads became known as 'cornkisters'. (T)

CORTERS: Quarters as used to describe oat cake baked over an open fire on a circular girdle and cut into four. 'It's fine tae get a corter o breid wi treacle.' Note: Oat cake is always 'breid'. Bread is always 'loaf'. (B) There is the story of the desperate hawker begging for bread, and the woman who gave him 'a corter o breid clortit (laden) with jam' and closed the door. The tinker went round the corner and licked all the jam from the oat cake and returned to the door. When the lady opened it he said, 'Thank e mistress for the laen (loan) o yer boord!' (T)

COTTAR: A married farm worker living in a tied cottage. The cottar's lease was for one year. 'Fae ear tae ear', as they used to joke or 'Fae lug tae lug!' (T)

COTTS: Petticoats or underskirts. (T)

COULTER: The turf cutter on the stem or beam of the plough. (T)

COUP: To topple or empty out. **COUPIT:** Overturned. 'The tinker coupit his cairt in the dutch an broke aa the dishes.' **COUP THE LADLE:** A see-saw on a plank over a barred fence or oil cask, one person on each end of the plank. (T)

COUPLES: Rafters. (T)

COUTHY: Homely; kindly. (T)

COVE: In Buchan a fella, a bloke or a chap, but could be alien slang. 'He's a gweed cove Alick, and aye ready wi a tip for the bairns.' (T)

COWER: To recover from. 'He had jist cower't the mirrles (measles) fin he took the kink-hoast (whooping cough).' (B)

COWK: To retch. 'The guff fae the aal tobacca pipes wis aneuch tae gar ye cowk.' (B)

COWT: A colt. (T)

CRABBIT: Short-tempered. 'Aye, a crabbit mannie, Cherles, bit he's a bittie like the mullert's dog, his bark is waar than is bite.' (T)

CRACK: Friendly conversation; news. 'Come awaa ben the hoose an gie's yer crack.' (B)

CRACK O DOOM: The crack of doom. The anticipated explosion on the Day of Judgment. (B)

CRAFT: A croft. (T)

CRAICHLY: Catarrhal. 'A Craichly hoast.' A catarrhal cough. (B)

CRAN-THE-NET: A good catch. The average fleet of nets in a drifter would be around eighty, so a cran-the-net would be good fishing, a 'fine strag'. Although that was quite common for a night's fishing, it was too much to expect that such good fortune could last for a whole season. There were always more misses than hits. (B)

CRANNY: The little finger; the pinkie. (T)

CRAP: A crop. 'The crap is naethin tae blaa aboot this year, there's been ower muckle rain.' (T)

CRATUR: A creature. Used in endearment or pity. 'The lassie had her purse stolen, peer cratur.' (B)

CREASH: Fat; grease; tallow. 'The fat soo's erse is aye weel creash't.' The fat sow's backside is well fleshed and rounded. Although rude and direct in its simplicity, this moral reflects a social injustice inculcated by the scriptural 'He who hath shall receive more,' indicating that the reward was unjustified considering the affluent circumstances of the recipient. (T)

CREEL: The basket in which fish wives carried their fish. Also a lobster pot. (B)

CREEPIN EEVIE: Someone who is incredibly slow and never makes much progress. 'Nivver oot o the bit.' (T)

CREESIT ILE: Creosote. (B)

CRIED ON: To have your marriage banns anounced in church. To be cried on in the kirk. (T)

CRINED: Shrunk; grown small by age. 'Aal Hughie's a bittie crined lookin nooadays, humphin aboot wi his staffie, he's like een o yon black snails snugglin back intae his shall (shell).' (T)

CRIVE or RIEVE: Hen-ree or netting wire enclosure for poultry. 'Hish the hens intae the crive, Rosie, afore we ging awaa, yer fadder said we hidna tae lat them on the fairmer's corn park, so awaa ye go an chase them intae the rieve!' (T)

CROCHLE or CROCHLY: Crippled; flat-footed. 'Mugsie's an affa crochle nooadays, scushlin his feet on the grun like an aal wifie wi rheumatism.' (T)

CROCKANESHUNS: Smithereens. 'Dyod wumman, gin ye cairry on like that ye'll hae aathing knockit tae crockaneshuns.' The word is sometimes spelled crockanition or crockanation and the 's' is added in speech to give it a plural sound. (T)

CROODS: Curds. 'Croods an fye.' Curds and whey. (T)

CROUP: To croak; whooping cough. (B)

CRULGIE DOON: Shrunk with age. (T)

CUDDY: A donkey. Donkey rides were a popular pastime for the kids at the beach on holiday. (T)

CUFFINS: Husks and hairs from the ears of corn but rougher than chaff. Something between sheelicks and chaff or the beard of the barley. (T)

CULLEN SKINK: A delicious soup made with smoked fish, onions and potatoes. (B)

CUNKER'T: Cankered. Used to describe turnips affected with canker of the root or club-root, a fungus deformity which was rampant in former days of organic farming. 'Fut wi tory-aetin corn an cunker't neeps an deein nowt, I'm nearly oot at the door.' (T)

CURN: An indeterminate number. **CURNIE:** A few. **A GWEED CURN:** A considerable number. 'A gweed curn folk in the kirk the day, surely?' 'Aye, fairly! An a curnie that I've nivver seen there afore!' (B)

CURRAN DAAD: The fancy cake which consists of sultanas, raisins or currants baked between two thin layers of pastry. Popularly known as a 'flee cemetery'. (B) Also known as a 'muck midden' or a 'mucker'. **CURRAN BAPS:** Currant buns. (T)

CUSHIE DOOS: Cushet doves, wood pigeon or ring-dove. If these greedy birds got a start on a newly planted field, they could almost devour everything. You needed a scarecrow to keep them away. (T)

CUT: A cut o worsit. A hank or skein of wool. In the old days, wool was sold by the hank or cut and had to be wound into a ball after purchase. 'I've jist bocht a cut o worsit and I'll get somebody tae hud it oot tae me this evenin.' By this she meant that someone would hold out the hank of wool for her over their fingers with arms outstretched while she wound it into a ball or cloo. It could also be done by placing two chairs back to back and hanging the skein of wool over them. (T)

CUTTANCE: Encouragement. 'Ye didna need tae gie Bell muckle cuttance. She kent aa the gossip and could spread it.' (T)

CUTTER: A small flask for whisky. (T)

CWEETS: Ankles. 'Better oot at the cweets than oot o fashion.' 'Ye wid near sink tae the cweets in yon gran carpet.' (B)

CWITE: A coat. But more generally an oilskin skirt with a bib, worn by women in the herring curing yards. 'It's a sair fecht for a livin, wearin a cwite an toppers (rubber knee boots).' (B)

CWYLE: A glowing ember. (T)

CYAARN: A cairn. Cyaarn is the Buchan term for a cairn, e.g. the Cyaarns o' Memsie, ancient burial mounds. Cairnmuir is pronounced 'Cyaarnmeer' for in Buchan a moor or muir is a 'meer'. (B)

DAACHLE: To hesitate; go slowly; loiter. 'Paddy nivver daachled fin he cam tae the burn, he jist gid plump in wi baith his feet at eence!' (T)

DAAD: A lump, pare or section of something of indeterminate size. A Buchan worthy was striding through Aikey Fair filling his pipe from a yard of Bogie-roll or black twist tobacco trailing behind him. Another farming chiel asked for a pipeful and the worthy said, 'Oh jist trump aff (trample off) a daad!' (T)

DAAVIT: David. Sometimes Dave or Davie. 'It disna metter fit ye caa me as lang's ye dinna caa me ower (knock me over)!' (T)

DAB HAND: An expert, one thoroughly experienced in his craft, but not necessarily a professional. 'Martin's a dab hand at baitin a hook for troot or salmon.' (T)

DAB-TEE: A mere touch. 'That wisna a richt kiss, Jock; that wis jist a dab-tee!' (T)

DABBIT: Dabbed; poked. (T)

DAFTIE: Someone who is mentally deranged. (T)

DALLIE'S CLEYSIES: Doll's clothes. Also soft silky seaweed which grows in shallow pools among the seashore rocks. It comes in two colours, green and red. Much loved by little girls in the days when bairns played among the rocks. (B)

DAM 'E BIT!: Damn the bit! An expression of mild surprise. The English equivalent could be 'You don't say!' (B)

DAMBROD: A draughtboard. Draughts or 'drafts' or 'the dambrod' was a very popular game in the chaumers and cottar houses in Buchan before the days of radio and television. Others were snakes and ladders, ludo, dominoes and card games, and most of the lads had a game of some sort in their kists. Card games were the most popular, including pontoon, snap, whist, three and pick the pack and the special favourite, Aal Maid, which was even more fun when played in the cottar hoose with female participation. The loser at Aal Maid was sent to the back of the inner door or the lobby, or fastened into a press, somewhere out of hearing of the other players who were still seated around the table discussing the penalties to be meted out for the unfortunate loser. In the case of a female the four kings of the pack were arranged on the table and each given a name identifying with some well-known character in the district; the local bobby or the doctor or minister, especially if these gentlemen were unmarried, and the list would also include someone who was present, perhaps the single foreman or the orraman, and of course the parish tink, Joe Meeks. Four individuals were selected and their merits or otherwise were discussed in secret and when all was ready the victim was cried on or released from the closet and returned to the table for sentence. She could do anything she liked with three of the men selected for her – drown, shoot or poison him or go to bed with one of them – but the fourth (though not in that order) she had to marry. And this was the exciting and laughable part of the game, waiting to see who the quine would marry, and if it happened to be Jock Pom (another tink), the laughter was hilarious, and if she decided on the handsome new schoolmaster she was congratulated all round and sometimes rewarded with a kiss or two. The same treatment was arranged for a male loser of Aal Maid, and perhaps the present kitchiedeem and certainly Meg Pom (Jock Pom's sister) were selected for his choice in wedlock. Great fun, nothing like it nowadays when our leisure hours are dominated by the parlour games on television. (T)

DAMMER'T: Dazed or confused as the result of a shock. 'He wis fair dammer't wi the faa. He's nae sae young noo, ye ken.' (B)

DANDER: To walk or amble, sometimes spelled 'dauner' or 'danner'. 'Tak a dander roon the waal (well) park, Percy, an coont the yowes an see there's neen o them on their backs.' This was an urgent request by the farmer to his part-time shepherd just before shearing time when the ewes were heavy with wool. If a ewe rolled on her back the wool formed a pad which clung to the grass and held her there. From bad circulation and lack of diet a few hours in this position could be fatal, and I have known them to die overnight. When assisted on to her feet again the ewe sometimes staggered and fell and had to be held in a walking position until she recovered. So the shepherd had to take a dander round the sheep with his dogs just before bed-time and first thing in the morning, four times a day in the last month before shearing time in midsummer, his busiest period. To say that a lamb was on its back is sheer nonsense, as it doesn't have the sticky wool to hold it in that position, and the same can be said of a hog or ewe that has been sheared of its wool. And by counting the ewes the shepherd could be sure that none of them were lying in a ditch. (T)

DANDY: Precisely what was required; the very thing. 'Jist the verra dunt, jist dandy.' (B)

DANDY BRUSH: A brush with hard bristles for grooming horses and cattle. (T)

DANGEL: To dangle; to suspend. 'The postie hanged imsel, he wis danglin fae the reef like a hingin lamp.' (T)

DANNY: A minor disaster. 'It's a danny fin the win gings oot at nicht.' (See 'wah, wah') 'The price has faan aa mornin, an oor herrin's nae sellt yet. I doot it's a danny!' Note: In Crosse & Blackwell's in Peterhead, damaged cans are 'dannies'. (B)

DARG: To dig. **DAILY DARG:** Daily routine. 'A sair darg yon drain, hard pan aa the wye aboot twaa feet doon. Ye need a shooder pick, a spaad wid nivver mark it.' (T)

DAUR: To dare. **DAURNA:** Dare not. (T)

DEAVE: To deafen. 'Fit a deave ye are.' What a loud-mouth you are! (T) 'I'm jist aboot deaved wi the din fae yon transistor radio.' (B)

DEE: Do. **DEEIN AWAA:** Doing away; progressing satisfactorily. (B)

DEECE or DEESE: A long wooden bench with arms at each end and a shoulder-high back. It wasn't upholstered. There was one to be found in every farm kitchen. (T)

DEED: To be 'the deed o't', to be responsible for something. 'Ye see that broken winda? I think I ken faa wis the deed o't.' (B)

DEEF: Deaf. (T)

DEEM: A member of the female sex. 'A richt sonsie deem, oor Jessie. She's a grand washer; she has airms like a Clydesdale horse.' Deemie is the diminutive and more affectionate term. (B)

DEEN: Done; complete; ageing; unfit. 'Is at aa't ye've deen?' Is that all that you have done? 'He's an aal deen mannie, yon.' He's an old worn out man, that. (T)

DEEVIL: A devil. **DEEVELICK:** A rascal. 'He's a deevelick o a loon fin he's oot wi his granda, kis he kens he'll wun aff wee't, bit he disna try't on wee's Grunny.' (T)

DEEVIL: A potato digger. (T)

DEID: Dead. **DEID-THRAA:** Death-throe. (T)

DEIL-MA-CARE: A carefree attitude. (T)

DEIL THE: Not a single one. 'Deil the word can ye believe. He's jist a born leear!' (B)

DEISTIN: Bumping. (T)

DEL: To delve or dig with a spade. The old horse ploughs couldn't reach into the field corners, so after the field was ploughed most conscientious farmers had the orraman dig them over and scratch in a handful of seed corn. But one farmer was a bit over anxious and became conspicuous because 'he had his neuks del't afore the park wis aa plooed.' (T)

DELEERIET: Demented. (B)

DEM: Probably from dam, to hold back or obstruct. 'A'm nae sickin velvet curtains, they'll jist dem the licht fae the windaes!' (T)

DENNER-TIME: The Buchan term for lunch-time. Lunch, in this airt, means to launch a boat. (B)

DEUK: A duck. **DEUK'S DISEASE:** Referring to a person of low stature. 'Wattie has deuk's disease. His erse is ower near the grun.' (T)

DEVAL or DEVALL: To stop, cease or leave off from something. 'The rain nivver devall't aa day, jist a steady poor fae morn tae nicht!' (T)

DEYDIE: Grandfather. May be shortened to Dey. 'My Deydie had a craa an its tail blew awaa, hine hine awaa, hine awaa.' (B)

DHAN: A marker buoy bearing a flag. Used by fishers world wide. (B)

DIBBER-DABBER: To halt between two opinions, to make a fuss. 'Lat's get on wi the wark, an nae mair dibber-dabber.' (B)

DICHT: To wipe. 'Dicht that dreep fae yer nose, min!' 'The aal folk hained (saved) the siller, but the loons'll gie't the dicht (spend it).' 'Celtic fairly got the dicht (short shrift) at Pittodrie last wik.' 'There wis as big a rowe that Muckle Davie wis gaan tae dicht the fleer wi Wee Tam if he didna hud is tongue.' (B)

DICKIE: A starched collar with front attached. (T)

DIDDIL'T: Confused or tricked. 'Thirty pee for a pint o melk? Ye wis diddil't!' (B)

DIDDLIN THE BAIRN: Bouncing the child. The mother is seated with the bairn on her knees, both are facing forward. She holds it by the hands and claps them together as she diddles her knees up and down to the rhythm of the lines she is reciting, much to the delight of the bright-eyed, smiling bairn.

> Clap clap handies,
> Clap clap away,
> A country school's a happy school,
> Upon a rainy day. (T)

DIDOES: Mischievous behaviour. 'Ony mair o yon kind o didoes an the teacher'll gie ye the belt.' (B)

DIN: Noise. **DIN-RAISER:** A hell-raiser; a trouble-shooter. 'He's a din-raisin brute thon, he shidna be in the union.' (T)

DIN-SKINN'T: Weather-beaten; sunburned; kippered; with a dark complexion. (T)

DING DOON: To throw down; to subdue. 'Facts are chiels that winna ding.' You can't alter the truth. 'An onding o snaw.' 'The win's as strong it could ding doon a soo o hey (huge oblong stack of hay)!' (T)

DIRD: A thump; a hard knock or blow; a stunning fall. 'The nickum (rascal) got a gey dird fin he fell aff the combine, bit of coorse, he shidna been there in the first place.' 'Yon's a big loon tae be aye at the skweel (school), an he gets a gey dirdy hurl on his fadder's aal bike, fleein aboot wi nae win in the tyres.' (T)

DIRDUMDREE: Routine. (T)

DIRL: To reverberate; to tremble. 'Kick ae erse in the village an aa the ithers dirl,' means they are a clannish lot. Offend one and you offend them all. Like birl (whirl) and skirl (scream), dirl is a doric word of such feeling and propensity it goes to the soles of your boots. (T)

DIRLER: A chamber pot. 'Dinna brush aneth the bed, Jean, in case ye coup (upset) the dirler.' (T)

DIRRUM DICHT: A more emphatic form of dicht (wipe). 'The aal man left a fortin, but the son fairly gied it the dirrum dicht (squandered it)!' (B)

DIRRY: The ash on top of a pipe. 'Keep yer dirry loon, keep it in yer lid or ye get yer pipe full't, syne pit it on the tap again, it'll mak yer pipe easier kennel't next time.' (T)

DIRTEN: Contemptuous. **DIRTEN GLOWER:** A contemptuous glare. (T)

DISNA MAK: It matters little; it doesn't count. 'Fit the public thinks disna mak. The strike'll go aheid.' (B)

DIS'T?: Does it? 'Dis't maitter if I dinna ging tae the kirk the morn?' (T)

DIV: Do. (B)

DIVERTIT: Highly entertained; fascinated. 'Yon wis a richt fine siree, the streen! I wis fair divertit wi the bonny singin.' 'The bairn's fair divertit wi her birthday present. There hisna been a myowte fae her the hale nicht!' (B)

DIVOT: A piece of turf. (T)

DIZZEN: A dozen. (B)

DOCK: To shorten. 'I mind fin the bairns were dockit (had their clothes shortened) at the age o sax wiks.' **DOCK:** Backside. 'If ye dinna behave, I'll gie ye a richt sair dock.' **OPEN DOCKS:** An old style of female underpants, which were simply two legs joined only at the waist band, or very near it. (B) **DOCK THE LAMB:** Shepherds 'dockit' their lambs by cutting off half the tail for cleanliness. (T)

DOCKEN: The dock leaf. Very cooling when applied to nettle stings. 'Roosty dockens.' Rusty dockens. In its latter stage, the docken goes all to length and turns a rusty colour. (B) 'Faa said "Nae worth a docken"?' (T)

DOCKET: A receipt, signed by the buyer, for a catch of herrings. 'Fourteen wiks athoot a docket, onward sailed the *Mary Jane.*' (B)

DOD: A pet name for George. (T)

DODDER: To totter. (B)

DODGE: To lie head to wind in stormy weather, with the mizzen sail set and the propeller turning slowly. You'll see the ducks on a pond at the same caper on a breezy day. (B)

DOG BIRDIE: The storm petrel, seen far, far at sea, fluttering along the troughs of the waves. (B)

DOITIT: Stupid. (T)

DOMINIE: A schoolmaster. (T)

DONS: The Dons. Aberdeen Football Club. (T)

DOO: The common pigeon. If the last doo in a race is termed the 'hin doo' is it related to Mahatma Ghandi? (B)

DOOBLE: Double. (T)

DOOK: A dip. (T)

DOON-SITTIN: A down-sitting. 'A gweed doon-sittin.' Marrying a well-to-do widow with house and furnishings provided. 'Jist haul in aboot yer cheir an sit doon.' (T)

DOON THE BRAES: On the sea-shore. 'So ye're gaan doon the braes tae play, are ye? Weel, if ye come hame here droon't, yer father'll murder ye!' (B)

DOOT: Doubt. In most instances it is the opposite of uncertainty and often emphasises a fact. It isn't 'I doubt if it will come to that', it is 'I doot it wull!' But there are exceptions like 'I hiv ma doots aboot at' or 'I hiv nae doots aboot at' and 'I doot it! I doot it!' which is actually an agreement. (T)

DOSE: A large number (nothing whatsoever to do with medicine). A dose o sweeties for a penny; a dose o coos in a park; a hale dose o cats in oor gairden etc. etc. (B)

DOSS: A bow, as in bow-tie. 'Tie yer pints (laces) in a doss, my loon. It keeps the ends tidy.' (B)

DOTHER: Daughter. **GWEED-DOTHER:** Daughter-in-law. (B)

DOTTER: To dither; to shamble about aimlessly. 'He's a dottery aal feel yon, jist follows his nose, he's like a dog withoot scint.' (T)

DOTTL'T: Confused, as in senile dementia. 'She's fair dottl't noo, peer aal cratur. She disna mind onything for mair than five meenits.' **DOTTLE:** The scrapings from a tobacco pipe. (B)

DOUCE: Quiet; gentle; well-meaning. (T)

DOUP: The buttocks. Also a nick-name for the village of Boddam. **DOUPS DOON:** Sits down. **DOUP SCOOR:** To fall on one's bottom. 'The aal dominie got an affa doup scoor fin he fell on the bairn's slide.' (T)

DOUR: Dull; hard; stern; determined; stubborn; humourless. The Buchan folk are supposed to be dour, which might imply obstinacy and determination; and they can be a trifle sullen at times, depending on the weather; and they can be a bit hard-hearted after a raw deal; but stern and sulky, no, and certainly not dull and humourless. They are a kindly, understanding and sympathetic class of people, a sentiment I feel will be endorsed by the emigrant English farmers who are settling in Buchan as their new neighbours. (T)

DOWIE: Dismal; dull; depressed; sad. 'Davie wis affa dowie fin he fun oot his new car hid been scratched. (T)

DOZENT: Dozing; half asleep. (T)

DRAACHT: Probably from the English draught which appears to have at least two meanings, and draacht in Buchan means two of something, like two cart loads of turnips, 'a draacht o neeps' or 'a draacht o peats', always in pairs, and 'a draacht o watter' is the same, two pails of water, but like the English 'draught' to describe wind in awkward places, the doric draacht also becomes singular in 'a draachty door', but I haven't heard the dialect equivalent for a budding author's first draft, but that's something you wouldn't hear in Buchan anyway. (T)

DRAFF HURLIE: A fairly large iron trolley on wheels which was pulled along the byre greep (floor) for feeding the cattle. It was mostly filled with draff (distillery offal) mixed with crushed oats, bran and maize and cattle cubes and was thrown into the feed troughs with a shovel. (T)

DRAIGON: A kite. 'A fine breeze the day for yer draigon, my loon.' (B)

DRATE: Defecate. **DRATE THE LINE:** Small useless fish caught on the line. (B)

DREEL'T: Hustled. (T)

DREENGED: (Probably from deranged.) Crazy; desperate. 'I'm jist dreenged for yon bookie aboot Buchan claik. I canna lay hans on't avaa.' (B)

DREEP: Drip or driblet. To drip dry a cloth that has been soaked in water. 'I left ma sheen on a steen tae dreep efter I fell in the burn.' We refer to so-and-so being a 'Sammy Dreep' or in modern terms a 'wimp'. 'He's a big Sammy Dreep yon chiel!' which is more impressive than the American 'Big Stiff'. (T)

DREEPIN PENNS: Sloping, concrete-floored, barred-fence penn or enclosure where newly dipped sheep were held for 'dreepin', or until all the surplus dip had drained off their fleeces and run back into the dipping trough. (T)

DREICH: Dismal; dreary. 'A gey dreich day this! The sun's surely droon't.' (B)

DREID: Dread; fear; apprehension; doubt. 'I dreid the thocht o gaan intae the hospital for ma operation.' (T)

DRESSER: An old-fashioned kitchen sideboard with a shelved back. (T)

DRIZZEN: Dull; foggy; misty and wet. (T)

DROCHLE or DROCHLIN: A short dumpy person. 'Ali's jist a drochle o a crater; he's nae eese for an unctioneer, ye can hear im bit ye canna see im for the crood o folk in the close.' (T)

DROGS: Medicine. Drugs for veterinary purposes. 'Here, Trootie, ye'll get a coo's horn in the crap o the waa in the shoppie, fess't ower tae the swineshoose an gie me a han tae drog the soo.' A pig would chew a glass bottle held in its mouth, thus the cow's horn. (T) **DROGGIST or DROGGIE:** The chemist. Only in recent years has 'chemist' been used. Most of the older generation still say 'droggist'. (B)

DROLL: Strangely eccentric; unpredictable; a serious jester. (T)

DROOKIT: Drenched. 'I'm jist like a drookit rat at the mou o a spatit drain!' (T)

DROON: To drown. **DROON'T:** Drowned. (B)

DROUTH: A strong thirst; an alcoholic. 'Oh mercy, I've an affa drouth.' 'Jock's jist an orra drouth noo. He's nivver sober.' (B)

DRUCHT: The drying effect of air. 'There's a gran drucht the day. A richt fine day for washin blankets.' Many country folk use the word 'force' for 'drucht'. (B) **DRUCHT:** Drought. **DRUCHTIT:** Dehydrated. **DRAPPIN DRUCHT:** A leaking drought; a spit in the wind; the rain's nae far awaa. (T)

DRUCKEN: Drunken; addicted to strong drink. 'Mary hisna her sorras tae seek, mairried tae yon drucken chiel.' (B)

DRUSH: Dross. Peat-dross was used to seal the sluice in the mill-dam after threshing. 'I say, Fergie, fin ye close the dam sluice, throw in a shuffle o drush.' A heap of peat-dross was always at hand on the dam bank for this purpose, especially in dry weather when surface water was scarce. (T)

DRY DARN: Constipation. 'The loon's been back at the black trykle bowie; he surely his the dry darn.' 'Is at so, Stan? Black-sugar (liquorice) is affa gweed for that they say, but maybe he needs a dose o salts or castor-ile tae gie him a richt blaa oot.' (T)

DRY STEEN DYKE: A low wall built without cement or mortar. Dry steen dykes are manifest in Buchan, enclosing the fields from the days of stone clearance. (T)

DUBS: Muddy puddles, as on a farm. 'Yon place is jist a sotter o dubs.' **SAPPY DUBS:** Really wet mud, beloved by bairns. (B)

DUFFERS: Natives of Macduff. (B)

DULE: Sorrow. (B)

DUMB TIT: A bairn's comforter or 'dummy'. 'Fancy a quine o that age still sookin a dumb tit!' (B)

DUMFOONER or DUMFOONER'T: Struck dumb; stunned; bewildered; mystified; flabbergasted. 'Roddy wis fair dumfooner't fin he wiz tellt he wid hae tae gyang tae the jile.' (T)

DUMP or DUMPS: To dump or thump down. 'Doon in the dumps.' Gloomy or depressed. (T)

DUNDERHEID: One who is very stupid. (B)

DUNGERS: Dungarees; working overalls. 'Biggin rucks in the corn yard wis affa hard on the dungers. The knees wis aye needin patched.' (T)

DUNT: To hammer or strike a heavy blow. 'Ye seldom hear the dunt o the souter's haimmer noo.' 'Geordie got a sair dunt fin he fell aff the cairt.' To 'get the dunt.' To sustain a loss or suffer a defeat. 'The verra dunt!' Ideal for the purpose. (B)

DUTCH: A ditch. (T)

DWAAM: A fainting fit. 'Rin an get the fuskie! My mither's teen a dwaam.' (B)

DWALL: To dwell. **DWALLIN:** Dwelling. 'Alister bides is leen in the dwallin hoose, there's naebody else there.' (T)

DWEBBLE: Feeble. (T)

DWINE: To pine or waste away; to fade, decline or wither, and no one can say it better than Flora Garry when reflecting on the maister o Bennygoak farm. **DWINE'T AWAA:** Physically deteriorated; faded away. (T)

> He bocht aal wizzen't horse an kye
> An scrimpit muck an seed;
> Syne, clocherin wi a craichly hoast,
> He dwine't awaa, an dee'd. (Flora Garry.)

DYKER: A native of Cellardyke. (B)

DYL'T: Toilworn. (T)

DYOD!: An exclamation of surprise. 'Dyod, the fairm o Braeside wis burn't doon yestreen!' (T)

DYOW: Dew. 'It's a dyowie mornin, Bertie, ower weet tae hairst (harvest). G'waa an ile the binder an spread the cloths (canvas elevators) on a stook tae dry or the day birsels up a bittie. Mind an sharpen the blade an pit a new ball o twine in the tow box an we'll be ready tae start.' (T)

DYSTE: To stamp or thump or drop something heavily. 'He jist leet the seck o coal dyste doon on the timmer fleer, nae winner it broke a boord!' 'He gaed dystin ben the Toon-hoose lobby like he wis the Laird o Cockpen!' (T)

DYTIT: Stupid; stupified; dazed. 'The dytit wye that he thocht an spoke, wid hae gart an angel greet.' (B)

EACH or EETCH: A carpenter or cooper's adze. 'Yon each is that sharp, it wid shave ye.' (B)

EARTH-CLOSET: A dry lavatory. (T)

EASIN: The eaves of a building or shoulder of a corn or hay stack. The inside wall head or ledge of the easin where the rafters or 'couples' rested was known as 'the crap o the waa', about two feet above the wooden floor in a corn loft, a favourite place for the rats to gnaw the wood, and the holes were often covered over with flattened out cocoa tins or similar material tacked to the walls. (T)

EASY-OZIE: Idle; easy going; languid. 'Man, the chiel had that little tae dee, he got intae an affa easy-ozie kind o wye, like suppin his brose in the mornin wi his spare haan in his pooch (pocket)!' (T)

ECHT or ECHTS: Ownership or possession; to belong to someone. 'Faa echts yon horse that wiz gotten in the kirkyaird amon the gravesteens? Naebody'll tak wee't!' 'I dinna ken faa echt it, Natty, bit it's fine for keepin doon the girss.' (T)

EDRIN: A skillfully made pear-shaped clew or small, pointed ball of straw rope or coir yarn for under-stitching or netting the ropes on a corn stack to hold the thatch in place. (T)

EEDLE ODDLE: Colourless in character. 'A gey eedle-oddle mannie, oor minister, I'm thinkin.' (B)

EEKSIE PEEKSIE: Six and half a dozen; both the same thing. 'Ae fairmer girns cos his diesel tank's half teem; anither fairmer's fine suited cos his tank's half full. They're eeksie peeksie, surely?' (B)

EEL: Completely empty. 'I'll need twaa hunner gallon! My tank's fair eel.' (B) 'The roan coo's fair eel (gone dry of milk).' (T)

EEMIST: Topmost. 'I'll tak the eemist ane, it's easier wun at.' (T) **EEMIST:** Eye-most; nearest to the eye. Thus a boat which is 'keel eemist' is actually upside down. (B)

EEN: One. 'Ony een o yon prizes wid dee fine wi me.' **EEN:** Eyes. 'Yon lad's ower nairra atween the een for my likin.' (B)

EENCE: Once. 'Eence we're throwe wi this jobbie, we'll hae oor tay.' (B)

EERIN: An errand. 'If ye run an eerin for me, I'll gie ye something tae yersel.' 'Did ye get yer eerin?' Did you get what you set out for? **EENCE EERIN:** Especially for that particular purpose. 'He came here eence eerin to get a fry o fish.' **EERINS:** Messages, usually groceries. 'There's nae message boys noo, tae deliver yer eerins.' (B)

EESE: Use. **EESELESS:** Useless. 'Daavit, man, ye're waar than eeseless, can ye nae dee naething richt?' (B) **EESE'T or EASE'T:** Accustomed or used to. 'He eese't work wi me yon lad, he's weel ease't at kind o widder!' (T)

EFFECK: Effect. 'Yon hairst ale hiz nae effeck on me. I could scoff a gallon o't an nae be neen the waur!' (T)

EFTERNEEN: Afternoon. (T)

EGG SHALLIES: Egg shells. 'Aa egg shallies the day.' Feeling rather fragile. 'The bairn's aa egg shallies the day; she's greetin at the least thing.' (B)

EIDINT or EIDENT: Industrious. 'Jock's a richt eidint chiel; aye on the go at some job or anither. (B)

EIK or EEK: To eik or add to as required; to eek oot something – the Buchan version. 'Lottie said there wisna aneuch o soup for the quines, so she hid tae eek it oot wi a beef cube an a wee suppie o watter.' (T)

ELBICK: The elbow or 'funny-been' (bone) is very sensitive to any awkward knock or sharp blow, which is more stupefying than painful in its paralytic effect. **ELBICK-GREASE:** 'It's elbick-grease ye'll need for that job lassie!' That was what the mistress of the Big Hoose said to the new maid when she was polishing the kitchen range, but it wasn't to be found in a bottle; what she meant was 'a bit more effort with the duster.' **ELBICK JAM:** Jam that has been made too thin and doesn't stop running till it reaches your elbow, then drops off on to your dress or suit. (T)

ELLON SQUEAK: The *Ellon Advertiser*. Published by Peters of Turriff. (T)

EMMERTINS: Ants. 'I didna enjoy the skweel picnic, Linda, I wis yokie wi emmertins!' (T)

ENTRY MORNIN: A dewless, sunny morning in harvest time when you could 'enter' the field and start work with the binder immediately. It was normally near noon before the corn crop was dry enough to harvest. (T)

ERSE-BREETH: Arse-breadth; a small expanse; something unimportant. 'A fairm did ye say? Yon's nae a fairm, it's jist an erse-breeth!' (T)

ETTLIN: Eager; anxious. 'Erchie arrived at the bar afore it wis open, ettlin for a dram.' (T)

EXLE: An axle. 'Mind an grease yer cairt exles loon, or they could be skirlin or ye be far fae hame!' (T)

EXTRY: Extraordinary; really special. 'A pair o new sheen, my quine? Isn't that extry, noo? Jist extry!' (B)

EYVNOO: Just now; for the moment; at the present time. 'Wis yon the Lifeboat gun I haard eyvnoo?' (B)

FAA: Who. 'Faa on earth tellt ye that?' **FAA:** To fall. 'Ye'll hae a gey faa ower there, my loon. It's a lang road doon tae the sea.' **FAA'N:** Fallen. 'Ye've faa'n an hurt yersel, hiv ye?' 'Faa Clyte.' To fall heavily. (B) 'Faa throwe the middle.' Break in two. 'Faa fae idder.' Fall apart. 'Faa oot o idder.' Fall to pieces. 'Faa tee again!' Get going again! 'Ye canna lie aboot at hame aa day deein naething. Na na lassie, ye'll jist hae tae tire (be fed up) an faa tee again!' (T)

FAAVER: Favour. 'For ony faaver!' For goodness sake! 'Gie's a meenit's peace, min, for ony faaver.' (B)

FADDER: Father. **FADDER'T:** fathered. (T)

FAE: From. (B)

FAIL DYKE: A low, turf wall. (T)

FAIR CHIEL: A redoubtable fellow. (B)

FAIR FORFOCHEN: Exhausted, breathless, usually after effort on a hot day. Often used to describe an exhausted ewe, heavy with wool. (T)

FAIR TAE MIDDLIN: Average; run of the mill; nothing out of the ordinary. (T)

FALDARAL or FALDARALS: Fancy, trendy, frilly adornments. 'Meggie wiz dress't tae the nines in aa her finery, and as mony faldarals on her hat it wiz mair like a flooer gairden.' (T)

FAN or FIN: When. 'Fan div ye think ye'll be ready? Fin I get my denner.' **FAN:** Fisher word for the propeller. **FANNED UP:** Having some obstruction in the propeller, e.g. rope. (B)

FANCY PIECE: A tea-cake. 'Nae mony fancy pieces in oor young day.' (T)

FANG: A large slice of cake or cheese. 'That's an affa fang o dumplin ye gaed me, there's aneuch here for twaa folk.' (T)

FAR BEN: Well versed. (T)

FARDIN: A butter biscuit, originally four a penny. Brochers call them 'tay biscuits'. (B)

FARLIN: A long wooden trough into which herrings were emptied on arrival at the curing yard. The quines would stand at the trough and gut the fish into tubs which were always behind them. The speed at which the fish were gutted and selected, all in the same movement, was simply amazing, especially since there was scarcely a backward glance. Very few herrings landed in the wrong tub, and even fewer on the ground. Herrings were divided into: small, matties, matt full, full, large full and spent (spawned). (B)

FARRA COO: A farrow cow. A cow in gestation but not giving milk, or dried off for butcher's meat. An eel coo or a dry coo or a farra coo. The story is told of the farmer who picked up the phone one evening and a strange voice enquired: 'Hiv ye ony dry coos, min?' The farmer, thinking there might be a deal behind the question, replied, 'Oh aye, I hiv a twaa three dry coos, so fit aboot it?' 'Weel, awaa an gie them a drink than,' the voice said, and some wag banged down the receiver in a phone box. (T)

FASH: Trouble; annoyance; worry. 'Ye needna fash yer thoom.' You shouldn't trouble yourself. (T) 'Dinna fash yersel.' Don't get excited. (B)

FASHIOUS: Pernickety; fastidious; hard to please. 'She's gey fashious, yon deemie; she disna ken fit she's seekin.' **FASHIOUS WIDDER:** Unsettled weather. (B)

FEART: Frightened; scared. 'I'm nae feart at the thunner, but I am feart at the lichtnin.' (B)

FECHT: A fight; to fight or struggle. 'It's a sair fecht for a livin.' It's a struggle to make a living. **FOCHT:** Fought. **FOCHEN:** Have fought. 'Brithers they may be, but they've fochen aa their days.' (B)

FECK: The most; the largest number. 'The feck o the traffic'll be bye efter the match has startit.' (T)

FECKLESS: Careless; regardless; incompetent. 'The feckless kitchiedeem bil't the tatties throwe the bree.' The careless kitchen maid boiled the potatoes until they disolved. (T)

FEE'D: Engaged to work on a farm, either at the feeing market or privately through the newspapers. The term of employment was six months for single men dating from 28 November and 28 May and a year for married workers, dating from 28 May. (T)

FEEDERS: Cattle fed for market. (T)

FEEL: A fool; foolish; silly; daft; unwise. **GING FEEL:** To lose one's reason. (B)

FEERIN: The first light furrow made as a guide before ploughing commences. 'Prop a feerin.' Dig up a sod every thirty yards or so in a straight line as a guide for the ploughman. (T)

FEERIOUS: Furious. (T)

FEERSDAY: Thursday in the old Buchan calendar. (T)

FEESICK: Medicine. 'Wullie gaed tae the droggist for his feesick.' (T)

FEINT A... : Not a ... (T)

FELL THOCHT: Reconsidered. 'I wis gaan tae flit, but I fell thocht an didna ging.' (B)

FENDER STEEL: A long, low, wooden stool in front of the fireplace. (B)

FERLIE: A wonder; something unusual or extraordinary. When something seemed impossible in Buchan they used to say, 'Ye mith as weel flee tae the meen (moon)!' Now it has been done. That is a ferlie. But of course, there are others of far less significance. (T)

FERLIFIED: Liable to exaggerate or slightly distort a story. Possessing a vivid imagination. 'If yon ferlified craitur tells ye onything, tak it wi a grainie o saat. She gies aathing hose an sheen, ye ken.' (B)

FERM TOUN: A group of farm buildings. (T)

FERN-TICKLES: Freckles. 'A lang teem whaup wi fern-tickles and a reid heid.' 'Ye couldna fart like at, min, withoot leavin fern-tickles on yer drawers!' (T)

FESS: To fetch or bring forward. 'Fess ben (bring through) ma glesses, quine, I canna see tae read the papers!' (T) 'The Grunny feesh (brought) them up; they nivver kent their mither.' 'They wir ull fessen up.' They were not properly raised. 'It's fill an fess ben, wi yon folk!' These folk have everything they want. (B)

FICH!: Same as Aliss! An exclamation of pain, like 'Fich aliss!' But fich applied mostly to burns, like burning your fingers on a clay pipe, and there was a small nipple under the bowl for holding it called 'the fich'. (T)

FICHER: To fumble or fiddle around with something. 'Dinna ficher wi things ye ken naething aboot.' (B)

FIDDLEY: A hatchway between the wheelhouse and the funnel on a drifter, giving access to the valves on top of the boiler. A fine cosy place for a yarn when the ship was head-to-wind. (B)

FIDGE: To fidget. **FIDGE AN PECH:** Fidget and puff; to be restless, puffing and blowing at the same time. (B)

FIE MAN!: An expression of mild denial or 'Choo-fie!' to the same effect. 'Fie man, div ye expeck me tae believe at, ye mith as weel tell me that the sea's geen dry!' (T)

FIKIE: Finnicky; intricate; complicated. 'A fikie job yon, sortin the watter pump at the Glebe.' (T)

FILE or FILIE: A while; a period of time. 'I hinna seen ye iss filie!' I haven't seen you for some time. **FILES:** Whiles; sometimes; occasionally. **FILIES:** Now and then. Sometimes pronounced 'noo-in-nan' or 'noon-nagain'. 'Fraser comes ower tae see me noo-in-nan, and noon-nagain I ging ower tae see him. Time aboot ye mith say, files ae wye an files the ither, and there's filies that we dinna see each ither for months on end, it jist depends on fit's agyaan (what's going on).' 'A fylie's ease.' A time of peace. (T)

FILE: To soil. **FIL'T:** Soiled. 'Ye've fil't aa ma fite claes wi yer coal stue (dust)!' (T)

FIN: When; to feel. 'Fin the factory's makin fish-meal, ye can fairly fin the smell.' **FIN:** To find. 'It sometimes peys tae keep yer ee on the gutter. Ye could easy fin a maik or twaa.' (B)

FINE: 'Fine div ee ken that.' You know perfectly well. **FINE THAT:** Most certainly. (B) **FINE SHUITIT:** Well pleased; satisfied; contented. 'The aal man wis fine shuitit in his airmcheir efter he full't his pipe fae his spleuchan (tobacco pouch) and it wisna lang or the hoose wis yoamin foo o rick (filled with smoke).' (T)

FINECHTY: Findochty, a village on the Moray Firth Coast. (B)

FINEERIN: Fancy work. 'Aa yon bonny fineerin must hae cost a hantle o siller.' (B)

FINNYFAAL: Whinnyfold, a tiny hamlet on the clifftop, south of Cruden Bay. (B)

FIR-YOWES: Fir-cones. The bairns used to collect them and use them as sheep for their toy farms. (T)

FIRE: To throw (usually a stone). 'He could fire a steen as far as the meen, he could haaver a tree in twaa.' (B)

FIRE FLACHT: Lightning without thunder. To 'get the flacht', to suffer loss or damage. 'The herrin men fairly got the flacht wi yon gale. They lost a lot o nets.' (B)

FIRE IN THE WATER: The beautiful phosphorescent light which flashes in sea water at times. Fishers don't like this because the fish can see the nets, which can look like a sheet of green fire. (B)

FIRL: A ferrule. A ring or metal band on the end of a staff to strengthen it. 'I nivver saw an umbrella athoot a firl on't.' (T)

FIRLIT: From the English 'firlot', a dry measure of $2\frac{1}{2}$ stone or a quarter of a boll of oatmeal (10 stones). A boll in the Doric is a bow, and a cottar got $6\frac{1}{2}$ 'bows o meal' in a year, delivered twice a year at the May and November terms when he got three bows and a firlit, three and a quarter bolls, which was emptied from the sacks into his girnal as part of his wages. If he couldn't use all his oatmeal perquisite, he would sell it to the grocer when he called with his van. (T)

FIRST FIT: The first person to set foot over the threshold in a Scottish home on New Year's morning. As a token of good luck in the coming year, the first footer was supposed to carry something black in his hand as a gift for the household, usually a small lump of coal, which could be substituted by a gill of Black Bottle Whisky. (T)

FISHIE: The village of Fetterangus, near Mintlaw. 'There's nae a herber at Fishie, min, it's ower far fae the sea.' (T)

FIT: What; which. 'Fit did ye say? I didna hear fit ye said.' 'Fit hoose div ee bide in, the first een or the second een?' **FIT:** Foot. There was the Aberdonian in the shoe shop trying to determine the correct shoe. 'Fit fit fits fit fit?' 'Which foot fits which foot?' **FIT WYE:** How?; Why? **FIT LIKE?:** How are you? A common greeting, to which the stock answer is 'Nae bad.' (B)

FIT A SAY AWAA: A harangue; a lecture; a somewhat boring declamation. 'Fit a say awaa aboot naething in partickler. My erse wis sair sittin on yon hard seat listnin tae the mannie!' (T)

FIT-AN-MOO: Foot and Mouth. A disease among animals of the cloven hoof, especially cattle, and the only known remedy is the wholesale slaughter of entire herds to stop the spread of infection. Formerly known as Renderpest, it got its name from the fact that it begins in the split of the hoof and is licked and absorbed internally by the affected animal. (T)

FITE: White. 'It's a richt fine day for the fite thingies (washing).' **FITE:** To whittle. 'Fite the pin.' Whittle the stick; to malinger. (B) **FITE HAAR:** White frost. **FITE-IRON:** Tin-plate. **FITE-WINKER'T:** With fair eye-lashes. (T)

FITEICHTIE: Whiteish; an off white colour. 'Jock's new car is a fiteichtie colour, nae like naething!' (T)

FITLESS: Not sure-footed. 'A fitless breet, oor Elsie; she wid trip on her ain shadda.' (B)

FITPAN: A rucked cotton bed valance which concealed what was on the floor beneath it; which, besides the dirler, could have been a box of seed potatoes to protect them from the frost. (T) **FITT PANS:** The valances on the old fashioned box-beds. These beds were often called 'bun-in beds' (bound-in beds). The term still applies to a bed in a recess. For many years of my own lifetime, the old folks called the valances 'bed pans', in sheer ignorance, of course, for very few of them knew what a bed-pan really was. (B)

FITTIE: Footdee, a district near the mouth of the River Dee in Aberdeen. (T)

FITTOCK: A sock with the leg cut off, handy for keeping the feet warm. Bairns liked to play around the lamp post in fittocks, if the weather was fine and dry. (B)

FLAGGIT: Made of flag-stones. 'The kitchie hid a fine flaggit fleer.' (B)

FLAISIN: Flattering, with a buttery tongue. 'Sandy fairly seems to get roon the weemin. It maan be his flaisin wyes, cos it's certainly nae his gweed looks.' (B)

FLAN: A heavy gust of wind, strong enough to shake the roof and drive the smoke down the chimney. (T)

FLANNEN BROTH: Saps; diced bread boiled in milk and sweetened to taste. 'Suppin saps wi a stob!' Impossible! A stob is a small gimlet for piercing screw-holes in timber. (T)

FLAP: A rest. 'A hare's flap.' A hollow in the grass where a hare has sheltered. 'I'll jist hae a flap abeen the blunkits or yokin time.' We used to spread a clean sack on the chaumer bed and lie on it with our working clothes and boots on. 'Come awaa in, freen, I wis jist haein a flap efter ma denner.' (T)

FLAUCHT: A flash. **FLAUCHT O FIRE:** A flash of lightning. (T)

FLECHS: A specimen of body louse that had the ability to jump from one person to another (a jumpin flech), especially in the crowded 'back street' cinemas that catered for the mass of working class audiences and earned the nickname 'Bug Palace' or 'Flea Pit', and some of the patrons said that when they got home, they had to 'change their sark' in front of the fire to get rid of the flechs. Main Street cinemas had flechs also, but they were considered somewhat more refined and milder in the bite than those in the slums. (T)

FLEE: A fly. **FLEE:** To fly. 'G'waa an flee yer draigon (kite).' (T)

FLEE-UP: An upstart; a show-off; not to be taken seriously. 'He's jist a flee-up o a mannie yon, ye'll nivver hear o im again. He's like a lot mair o them here aboot, jist a flash in the pan!' (T) 'G'waa an flee up!' Get lost! (B)

FLEED: Flood. **THE FLEED:** The flood tide. 'It took's a lang time to come North, borin the fleed.' (B)

FLEER: A floor. 'We're gaan tae be threshin for seed next wik, bailie. If ye hiv a spare meenit ye mith gie the laft fleer a swipe.' (T)

FLEET: To fleet; to regain position by steaming against the tide. (B)

FLEG or FLEGGIT: To scare or frighten. 'A beatnik ye say! A punk rocker! He's mair like a scarecraw wi a rig-oot like at on. He wid fleg the rottans (rats) fae a fairmtoon!' (T)

FLINDRIKAN: Flimsy; fragile; easily broken. 'That wis an affa flindrikan frock the kitchie deem hid on at the dunce. Ye could see richt throu't.' (T)

FLINT AN FLEERISH: During the Hitler War matches were almost unobtainable in mainland Britain, at least among the civilian population. With many others on the land I had to resort to 'Flint an Fleerish' (Flint and Flourish) combustion to light my pipe. Small flint stones with a sharp edge were easily picked up (or you could procure them from a flinty area) and the 'Fleerish' was a piece of iron obligingly shaped by the local blacksmith to fit your fingers like a knuckle-duster. This you struck against the flint to create a spark on a piece of brown paper previously soaked with salt-petre (but now quite dry – and supplied by the local chemist) which set it smouldering sufficiently to alight the strip of newspaper from your pocket, and with this you lit your pipe or fag, careful not to burn your fingers. Tapers were used at the fireside to save matches to light byre lanterns, but in the open, windy fields the flint and steel combustion was widely used by smokers, and one cigarette was lit from another whenever possible. In fact we were almost back in the Stone Age on the Buchan farms.

Foreign safety matches were more plentiful towards the end of the war, but lighter fuel was unheard of, even though you had a lighter; and with petrol rationed at two gallons a week, every drop went into the old banger, though very few people had a car, or even a motor bike, though a great many had push bikes. But despite the bicycles, the bus companies made a fortune and fleerished while we used the flint. (T)

FLITTIN THE DUMPLIN: Transporting the dumpling (a boiled fruit pudding) from one farm to another to feed all the workers. Mullies had two farms, and when threshing on both places with the hired portable mill, they would 'flit the dumplin', which must have been of considerable size to serve for two days among a dozen men. (T)

FLUCHTIT: Startled; panicked; in a state of excitement or annoyance. 'I wis a bit fluchtit jist afore denner time fin I took the butter oot o the churn. I hid been churnin aa mornin, ye see, bit fin I teem't the churn the butter wis saft, so I pat it in a pail o caal watter a filie tae firm a bittie!' (T)

FLUFFERT: A brief gust. 'A fluffert o snaa.' (T)

FLUKES: Flatfish. This term applies mainly to plaice (plashies). Lemon soles are 'lemons'. 'A fry o flukes' is usually a few dabs, the tastiest of them all. (B)

FLUSKS: Ink fish, sometimes called 'squeebs'. This is not the octopus type of inkfish. In shape, it resembles the fingers of a glove, with two triangular fins. The eyes and the tentacles protrude from the open end, from whence it can eject a stream of dense black ink. The flusk's body has no bones, simply a tapered membrane like tough, clear cellophane. Its flesh is just like white rubber which, cut into strips, makes a wonderful bait for cod. To see a box of flusks in the dark, is to see a box full of green, phosphorescent light. Flusks fetch astronomical prices now as they are regarded as a delicacy on the Continent. (B)

FLY CUPPIE: A sly cup of tea consumed between mealtimes. (T)

FLYPE: To turn inside out. 'The minister's wife's a gweed sowl, they say. A peety we couldna flype her, for she's nae muckle tae look at!' (B) 'Mind an flype at socks afore ye hing them oot.' (T)

FOBBIT YOWE: A ewe overcome by heat and breathing hard from exhaustion. Most unlikely after shearing. (T)

FOCHEN DEEN: Worn out with hard labour. 'Twaa hunner cran wis a rare shot awyte, but we wis fochen deen afore we got them inower.' (B)

FOGGIE BUMMER: A bum-bee. Nothing to do with Foggieloan. (T)

FOGGIELOAN: The Banffshire village of Aberchirder. Reputed to be named after the Gaelic for moss and loaning as 'an open space or pasture land', but supposedly named after the old tinker woman who slept one night in the fog while her companions rolled their tents and deserted her. 'I've been left in the fog alone', she lamented, thus Foggieloan. (T)

FOND: Foolish; silly. 'Ye wid be fond to pairt wi aa that siller!' (B)

FOO?: How?; why? 'Foo mony kinds o sexes are there, my loon ?' 'Three, sir. Saicks, pyokes an bags.' (B)

FOOL or FULE: Dirty. 'Yer face is fool, min. Time ye had a wash.' **FOOL:** Foul. 'I fell fool o Jake Birnie an couldna get awaa fae him.' (B) **FULE DARG:** A filthy dig. 'Houkin in a strang drain.' Repairing a urine drainage system from the byres, perhaps where there is a broken pipe. (T)

FOON or FOUN: Foundation, as of a house. 'If the foon's nae richt for a start, the hoose itsel'll nivver be richt.' (B)

FOONER'T: Foundered. 'A muckle traction-ingin o a thing that stinkit the barn an fooner't in the neep park an nivver did ony gweed at aa.' (T)

FOOSION: Energy; power. 'I'm a lot better noo, but I've affa little foosion yet.' (B)

FOOSTIT or FOOSHTIT: Bothered. 'I canna be fooshtit gaan tae the bingo, Ruby. The last time we wis there I lost a pucklie baabees an I'm nae gaan back.' (T)

FOOSTY: Stale; musty. 'Foosty aal fizzer.' A young person's perception of anyone over forty. (B)

FOOSTY STRAE: Straw that has mildewed and become unedible for cattle. (T)

FOR FEAR: Just in case. 'Tak yer jacket wi ye, for fear it rains.' (B)

FORBYE: Besides. 'A hoose an a huddin, an siller forbye.' (Logie o Buchan.) **NAE NAETHING FORBYE:** Nothing special. 'She's nae naething forbye to look at.' (B)

FORCE: This is the country word for the drying effect of air. The fisher equivalent is 'drucht'. 'Force' is also the country term for 'energy'. Fishers say 'foosion'. (B)

FORCEY: Eager. (T)

FORDAL: A store. 'A fordal o neeps.' A clamp or store of turnips for use in the winter. (T)

FORDALT: Well ahead. (T)

FORE-STAA: Fore-stall. The hake or manger or feed trough in a stable or byre. 'Clean oot the fore-staas loon, ye dinna like tae ate oot o a fule plate yersel.' (T)

FORENEEN: Forenoon. (T)

FORFOCHEN: Utterly exhausted. 'The first Buchan wis mate on Noah's Ark, but Noah haived him ower the side, cos he wis jist a proper girn. Buchan swam for a fortnicht afore he made the shore, sair forfochen, at Peterheid.' (B)

FORGETTLE or FORGETTAL: Forgetful; apt to forget. 'Madgie couldna mind her eerins athoot a list, she wis that forgettle.' (T)

FORHOOIE: To forsake. 'The aal hen forhooi't her nest.' The old hen forsook her nest. When the broody hen forsakes her nest all the eggs go to waste. A broody hen in Buchan is a 'clockin' hen, and when she is 'aff the clock' she leaves the coop and goes back on the roost. (T)

FORKIE TAIL: An earwig. 'I widna like een o that creepie-crawlies in ma lug.' (T)

FORRARD or FORRIT: Forward. 'Wasties wis aye weel forrit wi the wark so there wis aye a gweed chunce o gettin a half day aff on a Setterday efterneen in the simmer time.' (T)

FORTHOCHT: Not the same as forethought, more a change of mind or intention. 'Oor Annabel wis gyaan tae get merrite in the kirk, bit she forthocht, an noo it's gaan tae be a registrar affair.' (T)

FORTY FAAL: Forty fold; devious; deceitful. 'Dinna lippen ower muckle on yon chiel. He's forty faal, ye ken.' (B)

FOU: Full; drunk. **BLEEZIN FOU:** Extremely drunk. 'Dod cam hame bleezin fou an fell doon the stairs an didna get a scrat. If he hid been sober he wid likely hae broken his neck.' (T)

FOUSOME: Disgustingly filthy. 'A fousome place, yon water closet! It stank like aabody's business.' (B)

FRACHT: Two pails of water, carried from the well usually slung from a wooden yoke across the shoulders. 'Gyang tae the waal for a fracht o watter quine, the pails are baith teem.' (T)

FRAIKY: Friendly; flattering; pettish. 'Jock is gey fraiky wi the fairmer. He's surely expectin tae be socht tae bide for the neist sax months.' (T)

FRAISE: To pet or fondle an animal. 'Dinna fraise wi at dog Wendy, he'll bite ye.' **FRAISIN:** Ingratiating. (T)

FRAP: A predicament which may vary in seriousness according to circumstances. If your engine breaks down while you are on a lee shore, and the anchor fails to hold, you are in a frap, my loon. Weel awyte! (B)

FREEN: A friend or relation. This can be rather confusing at times. 'He's a freen o yours, isn't he?' He's a friend of yours, isn't he? 'He's freen to you, isn't he?' He's a relation of yours, isn't he? Note: The preposition 'to' involves relationship, however tenuous, and in no way presupposes friendship. If you are not a local, you can avoid possible embarrassment by using the words 'friend' and 'relation'. (B)

FREUCH: Fragile; brittle. 'She maks gweed breid, but fyles it's gey freuch.' (B)

FRICHEN: To frighten. 'The gamie pat a fite sheet ower his heid tae frichen the loon comin hame in the dark.' (T)

FROSTIT or FREESTIT: Frozen. (T)

FRY: A fry is the customary parcel of fish taken home by the fisherman for his own use. The term also covers the multitudinous free gifts of fish at the quayside. (B)

FULL BUTT: A fisher term for 'Full speed'. A relic of the drifter days. (B)

FUNG: To throw. **FUNG LEG:** A leg that has to be thrown forward on a crutch to enable a cripple to walk. The word is probably derived from the 'fung' or kick of a horse. (T) To 'ging fungin aboot' to give vent to one's frustration or temper by slamming doors or throwing things around. To be in a 'richt ull teen'. (B)

FUNK: A breath. 'There's nae a funk o win the nicht, so we winna see a herrin.' (Always in the negative.) (B) A sulk or huff. It is a selfish and childish state of indisposition but is sometimes practised by adults when they don't have their own way. (T)

FUNN: Whin. **FUNN BUSS:** A whin bush. The prickly whin or gorse bush with golden flower cups that vies with the broom to scatter the Scottish hillsides in mid summer with bright yellow cushions. **FUNN DYKE:** A whin dyke. (T)

FUPP: To whip; a whip; a whipcrack; a thong. 'Jenny hid her washin oot early this mornin. I could hear the fupp an crack o her sheets in the win!' **FUPP HAND:** The whip hand; an advantage, like having a good share of the trump cards at whist. (T)

FURL: To whirl or rotate. 'Ticket nivver made a skipper! Sookin bairn could furl a wheel.' (B)

FURLIEGORUM: A showy ornament. (B)

FURLIEMAFAA or FURLIEMIFAAS: A suspected slang word for the elaborate ornamentation, such as classical scrolls, rope and tassel and floral decoration in architectural stone carving. (T)

FURR: A furrow. 'Ye'll manage anither furr, min, ye're a bittie fae the dyke yet.' 'Furr up the tatties.' Cover the drills with more fresh earth. (T)

FURTH: Forth; outside; beyond. 'Gyang furth wi yer tooteroo an yer drums an nae domineer folk.' (T)

FUSKER: A whisker; a moustache. 'Ye'll hae tae shave aff yer fusker, Arthur, afore ye get a fee. It's bare-faced loons the fairmers are lookin for in the market wi risin wadges (wages). The loons are chep an the sicht o a mouser'll scare awaa the fairmers fin ye're needin mair siller.' (T)

FUSKIE: Whisky. 'He gey aften taks a dwaam (swoon), but it's aye ootside a pub. Handy for the fuskie, ye see.' (B)

FUSPER: A whisper; to whisper. 'Fit are ye fusperin aboot min? Spik oot an lat folk hear ye!' (T)

FUSSLE: A whistle; to whistle. 'They say aathing bit their prayers here an they fussle them.' 'G'waa an buy a penny fussle!' If someone doesn't believe your story or wants to be rid of you. (T)

FUTRET: A weasel or stoat. Characteristic of these creatures: sleekit, sly, cunning, crafty, shrewd. 'Yon lad up at the Reisk, yon futret o a crater that kens aathing.' (T)

FUTTLE: A short gutting knife with fixed blade, used by herring gutters. Also means to whittle. (B)

FYE: Whey. 'Croods an fye.' Curds and whey. (T)

FYAACH: To fidget. 'Fit are ye fyaachin aboot for, quine? Can ye nae sit at peace?' (T).

FYANG: A fyang o tow has no determinate length. It has been cut at random from the coil, and left in an untidy heap. (B)

FYOLK or FYOKE: People; kith and kin. 'A hantle o fyolk at the kirk, the day.' 'It's fine to be back amon my ain fyolk.' Most of the fishers in the villages north of Rattray Head use this word as a matter of course. (B)

FYOWE: Few. 'Fine days are fyowe an far atween eyvnoo (Just now). Fitivver is the warld comin til?' (T)

GAAN ABOOT HEN: A going about or walking about hen; a free-range hen. After nearly half-a-century of battery-caged hens a 'gaan aboot hen' is a welcome sight in the country, especially after the salmonella in eggs scare in the spring of 1989. It used to be thought that the yolks from battery produced eggs were less rich in colour and therefore less nutritious than those from free-range birds, but over the years, with improved and more selective feeding ingredients, the caged birds may be as well catered for scientifically as the free-range hen with her access to everything nature provides for her. The battery egg yolks may still be less rich in colour than those from the 'gaan aboot hen', but just as wholesome in nutrient value. But it's the system that's cruel and inhumane and it must be admitted that the factory farm has not been kind to the hen species of the poultry world. In the old days of portable hen houses in the fields, even when we induced more intensive egg laying with a condiment labelled 'Karswood Poultry Spice', and the farmers' wives preserved eggs in waterglass, I never heard of one single instance of food poisoning being traced to the eating of hen eggs. Not until the Egg Board took control did we ever hear of eggs gone bad, and the fact that they were too long in storage and distribution was blamed for this. I used to swallow a raw egg at a gulp and felt the better for it. (T)

GAB O MEY: The mouth of May. A stormy snap in the month of May lasting for about three days when the weather makes her gab (mouth) heard and felt by all who are exposed to her lashing tongue. Apart from this short spell, May is the darling of the year when the first buds appear and young girls wash their faces in the dew to keep them bonnie aa the year. (T)

GAE: Go. **GAED:** Went. **GEEN:** Gone. (T)

GAIMRIE: The village of Gardenstown. **GAIMRIE KNOTTIE (pronounce the K):** A nice biscuit to go with your fly-cup. Origin: Gaimrie (Gardenstown). (B)

GAIVLE: The gable end of a house. The end of a net. 'Jock cam oot till his gaivle end, an he leaned against the waa.' (B)

GALLUS: Bold; spirited. 'A gallus chiel yon; there's mischief in is een.' (T)

GALLUSES: Trouser braces. 'Cock-a-bendie hid his thooms in his galluses, raxin them oot like catapults, an chirpin awaa like a sparra on the shaft o a barra.' (T)

GANJIE or GANSIE or GUERNSEY: A home-knitted jersey whose title may vary from port to port. Also known as a 'maasie'. (B)

GAPUS or GAUPIT: Stupid. 'Sic a gapus o a chiel yon, it's a wunner he disna weer his sheen on the wrang feet, like he aye hiz his bonnet on the wrang wye roon, wi the snoot at the back. Fit a gaupit breet!' (T)

GAR: To force or oblige. 'He's a gran han at tellin a yarn. He can gar ye lauch an greet time aboot, jist fin he likes.' 'The crack o the lifeboat gun fairly gars ye lowp!' (B)

GARLAND: The Christmas decorations made by fitting one hoop into another, at right angles, and covering with tissue paper. The garland was usually hung in the window of the room (note the singular). If there was a Christmas tree at all, it would consist of one solitary branch. Very few people indeed could afford a proper Christmas tree. (B)

GARTEN: A garter, knitted in a long narrow strip. (B)

GATE END: 'G'waa tae yer ain gate end.' Go back to your own district. (B)

GAWK: To stare with open-mouthed astonishment; an idiot; a fool; one who gawks. 'It fairly gart him gawk fin he won a premium bond efter aa that years.' (T)

GEAR: Fishing accoutrements. (B) Property; possessions; wealth. (T)

GEDDER: To gather. (T)

GEESE: A geese = a goose. (B)

GEETS: Children. 'Aa yon squallachin (screaming) geets, aa yowlin at the same time, sic a mineer (din)!' (T) Also a name for small fish found in most of our harbours. (B)

GEY: Very; remarkable. 'It wis a gey caal nicht.' It was a very cold night. 'Yon wis a gey fecht at the fitba match!' That was a remarkable fight at the football match! (T)

GEYPIT: Affected, in a silly manner. 'Look at that geypit craiter showin aff.' (B)

GIE: To give. **GIED or GID:** Gave. 'I jist gid him the len o that buik but he's forgotten tae gie it back.' (T)

GIEINAFEN: Quite often. 'Jotty's gieinafen late efter he's heen a nicht oot!' (T)

GILLIEPEROUS: A fool; an irresponsible rough and ready person. 'Fit a gillieperous, he could a coupit the bus gaan roon corners at yon speed. He shid be lockit up!' (T)

GILP or JELP: To splash. Probably from 'gill' and applied to liquid. 'A jelp o bree.' A splash of beef or chicken stock. (T)

GIN: If. 'I'd climb yon hill, gin I wis young an feel again!' (T)

GING, GANG or GYANG: To go. 'Ging roon tae the chip shop, ma loon, an get me a pudden supper.' **GAED:** Went. **GAEN:** Gone. (T) **GING WORTH:** to become more or less useless. Commonly expressed as 'aa worth'. 'Dodie wis a strappin chiel, but at the hinner eyn his legs gid aa worth.' (B)

GIP ('g' as in gag): To break the neck of a fish by forcing the head backwards. Anyone receiving a blow to the throat, or having to wear a collar which is too tight, may be said to be 'jist aboot gippit'. (B)

GIRD: A bairn's hoop, seldom seen nowadays. Boy with broken gird, to blacksmith: 'Will ye sort my gird?' Blacksmith: 'Aye, surely, but nae the nicht, it's near lowsin time.' Boy: 'Dear me! Fit wye am I gaan tae win hame?' (B)

GIRDIN: The rope used to lash a load onto a cart. 'Ye'll get the jile if ye tak that load o hey alang the road athoot a girdin.' (B)

GIRN: To complain; to whine. Also a snare for a rabbit. 'He's jist a born girn; aye compleenin aboot something.' 'If ye set yer girns in the richt place, ye're sure tae catch a rubbit.' (B)

GIRNAL: An oatmeal barrel, usually with a hinged lid. A universal feature of country and fisher homes alike. The proper girnal was custom made, a real article of furniture, not barrel shaped at all. 'May the moose ne'er leave yer girnal wi a tear drap in its ee.' (B)

GIRSE or GIRSS: Grass. 'The girse is aye greener ower the dyke.' meaning things often look a lot better in someone else's patch. If you had visited someone and got 'girsie stibbles', you had been warmly welcomed and well treated. 'Girsie stibbles' is the stubble field where young grass is plentiful and thriving. (T)

GIZZEN'T: Warped; dried up. 'A gizzen't bowie (barrel) disna hud watter.' During a long dry summer, farmers sometimes had to soak their cartwheels in the mill dam to expand the wood and prevent them from becoming gizzen't and the iron hoops falling off. (T)

GLAAR: Mud; a pool of mud. 'Sic a kirn o glaar, Wullie, it's time ye hid the scraper gaan.' The scraper was an implement used to scrape the glaar into heaps for carting away. (T)

GLAIKIT: Stupid. 'A glaikit breet Danny yonder, ye could hardly trust him tae traivel for post holes!' Post holes were made in the ground with a spike for fencing and to suggest someone could or couldn't sell them was to deride them as stupid or glaikit. (T)

GLAISSERS: Glass marbles. These marbles were of different sizes and the colours were transparent, embedded throughout like lettered rock. (T)

GLEYED EE: A squint eye. Same as 'Cockle ee'. (B)

GLIT: Phlegm. A mucous discharge from the breast and throat during a severe cold. (T)

GLOAM: Sunset. (T)

GLORY HOLE: A cupboard to store odds and ends. 'There's a glory hole aneth the stair, bit dinna stan up in't cos ye mith rap yer heid. We ees't tae ging intae the glory hole fin we heard the Jerries comin ower tae bomb, the time o the war. A sair rap on the heid wis naethin tae the scraach o the air raid siren.' (T)

GLOWER: To glare. 'Grunnie gied Deydie and affa glower fin he gluffed the last o the dumplin.' (B)

GLUFF: To devour greedily. 'He has nae mainners avaa. He jist gluffs the lot.' (B)

GO-ASHORES: The fisherman's dress rig for going ashore at the week-end. This term was also widely adopted by country folk for casual wear. (B)

GO-BY-THE-GATE: (Always pronounced rapidly, as if it were one word.) A flighty, irresponsible, unreliable person. (B)

GOADSMAN: In the days of the twal-owsen pleuch, the goadsman was in charge of the team, mostly using a wand as a goad or whip. (T)

GOBBINFAE: A measure of grain scooped out with both hands cupped together. (T)

GOCK, GOWK or GYPE: A simpleton; a fool; a clown; playing the fool. 'He's a gocket breet, Donal, and ocht tae hae mair sense.' 'Donal's a gowk', or 'Donal's a gype', would mean the same thing. (T)

GOGS: A pet name for Gordon. (T)

GOLLACHS: Beetles. (T)

GOMERAL: A stupid, witless, ignorant person. 'Ye gomeral ye, ye've putten the anti-freeze in amon the ile instead o the watter!' (T)

GOOD-LIVIN: With a religious or highly moral approach to life. Those with such an approach never use the term 'good-livin'. (B)

GOOR: Nasty slime which may have an offensive smell. Usually from fish. 'G'waa an get yersel washen; ye're fair stinkin wi goor.' (B)

GOOSE IRON: A solid, flat iron, commonly known as a tailor's 'goose' for pressing garments. (T)

GORBLIN: An unfledged bird. 'Gape, gape, gorblin, an I'll gie ye a wormy.' (T)

GORGONZOLA: Cheese. 'A name like Gordon's College, and a smell like the skipper's feet.' (B) A pet name for a mottled blue and white breed of cow. (T)

GOVEY DICKS! or MY GOVIES!: An exclamation of surprise. 'My govies, boys, ye nivver saw the likes o yon!' (B)

GOWAN: A daisy. (T)

GOWDIE: The common gurnard, a fishie wi a heid as hard as a washin-hoose biler, a skin like leather, and fearsome stobs on his back, but a tastie fishie for aa that. The black-skinned ones are best. Once I had a shipmate who told me he had seen the Lord's Prayer written on a gowdie's bladder. I think he wis a leear!' (B)

GRAACHER: An extremely greedy person. 'Dod's a proper graacher! He widna gie ye a scare supposin he wis a ghost.' (B)

GRAAVIT: A scarf, usually home-knitted. 'Ye better pit on yer graavit, this caal mornin.' Note: It does not follow that 'gravity' means a little scarfie. (B)

GRAIP: A short, four-pronged fork with a cross handle for loading dung or carrying loose straw or hay.

> Noo wi a gun I'm little use
> As little wi a graip,
> But gie's a pen tae write abuse
> And faith I'll gar ye gape. (T)

GRAITH: Wealth; material; possessions. 'The plumber gaither't his haimmer, his wrench an aa his graith an pit them in his tool bag.' (T)

GRAIVEL: Gravel. (T)

GRANNY'S JOHN: A coddled boy, 'a richt granny's John' – somewhat effeminate and accustomed to getting his own way. 'He's a spil't loon yon, clean connached wi his mither an the wunt o a fadder!' (T)

GREE: To agree; to get on well together. 'Jock an Daavit focht an gree'd wi een anither aa their happy childhood days.' 'Brass screws an iron screws dinna gree in saat watter. The iron aye gets the dunt.' (B)

GREEN GAAR: The green growth seen along the high water mark on piers. The green growth on the walls of a house near ground level, especially on concrete. The green bile which is retched up from the stomach in the advanced stages of sea-sickness, i.e. the stage where a body thinks that life is no longer worth living. (B)

GREEN GARTENS: Green garters. When a girl gets married before her elder sister, she is supposed to have given that sister 'the green gartens'. The actual giving still occasionally takes place. (B)

GREEN SEA: Water which comes on board in a solid mass, as distinct from heavy spray. 'She wis takin the hale green sea ower the rail.' (B)

GREENICHTIE: Tinged with green; greenish in colour. 'I got a greenichtie mixter fae the doctor tae cure ma caal.' (T)

GREEP: A byre or stable floor. Applicable to byre and stable but never human habitation, except in jocular fashion or comparison. 'Yer fleer's as fule as a byre greep!' (T)

GREET: To weep or cry. 'Bathie wis born greetin an she's nivver managed tae stop, aye girnin aboot something. Bit there's nae muckle comin ower er fin aa's said an deen.' **GRAT:** Wept. 'The bairn grat for his fadder.' (T)

GREETIN FOU: The self-pity stage of intoxication. 'McGinty's pig managed somehow to get into the house where, in the pantry, it discovered a stock of whisky which it thoroughly enjoyed. (B)

> This pig wis greetin fou, an rowlin in the gutter,
> Till McGinty an his foreman trailed him oot upon a shutter,
> At McGinty's meal-an-ale far the pig gid on a spree.

GRIEVE: The foreman in charge of a farm; the gaffer. (T)

GRIMMY: A Grimsby boat or fisherman. (B)

GRINDIES or GRINDIE TOCHERS: The small greenish crabs found in seashore pools. (B)

GRINSTEEN: Grindstone. A huge, dressed, circular stone, hand-driven by an axle spindle on a trestle and usually outside the 'shoppie' or smiddy door on a Buchan farm. Mostly used for sharpening farm hand tools. 'Toby made sure that yer nose wis aye on the grinsteen wi plenty o wark!' (T)

GRIPPY: Tight-fisted; mean. 'A body has a richt tae be grippy wi their ain.' (B)

GRIZZIL'T: Greying. (T)

GROU or GROWE: To grow. **GROUTH:** Growth; weeds. (T)

GROUIN SHOORIE: Light summer rain after a dry spell to make the plants grow. 'A fine grouin shoorie. It'll swall the neeps an tatties an it's nae ower hivvy tae lay the corn crap.' (T)

GROUTH MIDDEN: A gigantic heap consisting of string-grass, knot-grass and other creeping weeds not of any use and left to decompose. **GROUTHY:** Good growing. (T)

GRUBBER: A heavy cultivator. 'Bide oot aneth at grubber hannle noo loon, if ye strik a fest (fast) steen wi a tyne it'll come doon an crack yer skull, an wi three horse pullin aginst ye, ye widna hae muckle chunce. Ye like tae work horse I ken, bit dinna say I hinna warned ye.' (T)

GRUBBIT: Grubbed or cultivated with a heavy implement. (T)

GRUE: To shudder with distaste. 'He drank the castor-ile an it gart im grue.' (B)

GRUGLE or GRUGLED: Creased or wrinkled. 'Yer suit's affa grugled, Grandad, I'll tak it tae the cleaners an get it press't for ye.' (T)

GRULSHICKS, GULSHICKS or GALSHACHS: The cheaper or inferior assortment of sweets that some children go for. 'Aa that grulshicks afore their denner. I widna lat the bairns aff wi that. They hiv mair need o a decent diet!' (T)

GRUMPIAN: Grampian Television. 'Switch on the telly, Ellie, there's a richt braw film on Grumpian the nicht.' (T)

GRUN: Ground; soil. 'A great skelp o grun. It taks me twaa days tae traivel roon aboot it throu the wik an hauf-an-oor on a Sunday.' (T)

GRUNNY: Grandmother. (B)

GRUNS: Grounds; dregs or sediment in liquid. 'My anti-freeze is nae eese, min, it's ower aal an there's gruns amon't.' (T)

GRUNT: Local pronunciation of 'grant'. By the same token we have bunk, tunk, wunt, plunk, hunk, thunks, swunk. A becomes U. (B)

GRUNTER: The fisher word for the pig. The word 'pig' is taboo to some fishermen who feel the name will bring bad luck. Certain fishers call it 'Sonnie Cammle (Sandy Campbell).' (B)

GRYTE LINS: Great lines. Strong, heavy lines with big hooks, for use in deep waters and on rocky bottom to fish for cod, skate, ling and halibut. A 'fleet' of gryte lins baited with herrings could stretch at least fifteen miles along the seabed and would take from dawn to dusk to haul. (B)

GUFF: A strong smell, usually unpleasant. 'The guff o waar.' The smell of rotting seaweed. Guff may also be an idle rumour. 'Fit a load o guff!' (B)

GULL: To gull or trick someone into doing something they didn't really mean to do. 'Dot wis gulled intae buyin yon shewin machine; she didna really want it an she'll nivver mak eese o't.' (T)

GUNNELS: Innards. 'Ye'll nivver get a drain doon ere min, ye're doon in the gunnels o the earth. If ye howk muckle deeper ye'll be in Australia!' (T)

GUNTIN: Yawning. 'Ye're guntin min, wis ye nae in yer bed the streen?' (T)

GURR: To growl. (T)

GUSHET: An insert in a garment to provide more space; an odd-shaped corner in a field. 'Willie Waddell, the Rangers winger, took that lang strides, he nott a gushet in his shorts.' (B)

GUT BARREL: Every gutting quine had to hand a small wooden tub or 'coggie' into which she would flick the herring offal. The coggies were teemed (emptied) into barrels. These barrels were themselves teemed weekly, and I can assure you that the guff from a teem gut barrel was unbelievable. (B)

G'WAA: Go away. 'G'waa an jump in the dock!' (B)

GWEED: Good; tasty; considerable. 'I thocht the soup wis byous gweed the day.' 'Ye'll need a gweed sup stuff to sair (serve) that big faimly.'
GWEED-FATHER: Father-in-law.
GWEED-MITHER: Mother-in-law.

GWEED-SIN: Son-in-law.

GWEED-DOTHER: Daughter-in-law.

GWEED ANEUCH: Good enough.

GWEED KENS!: Goodness knows!

GWEED PRESERVE US AA!: Lord preserve us all! (B)

GWEED-WULLY: Good-hearted. 'Gie the man his due, fut ivver his faats, he's gweed-wully and he widna see ye stucken for siller!' (T)

GWITE: A gully among steep cliffs. 'Watch yer step if ye tak the path along the tap o the cliffs. If ye faa doon intil a gwite, ye'll brak yer neck, for sure.' (B)

GYAAD or GAAD-SAKE: An expression of distaste or even revulsion, mostly regarding food. 'Gyaad-sake, mannie, I dinna like the taste o yer snails, an worms wid be waar. Gyaad-sake, the verra thocht o them gars me cowk (vomit)!' 'Gad' can also mean to travel frequently, to move widely, to gad about a lot. (T)

GYKE-NECKIT: When the head is held slightly to one side. Sometimes a permanent deformity but mostly of short duration caused by an involuntary contraction of the muscles. (T)

GYPE: To gape; a fool 'Dinna gype in at folk's windas.' 'Dinna be sae feel, ye great gype.' **GYPIT:** Affected; foolish. (B) **GYPERIE:** Foolish behaviour or idle frivolous talk. 'Fin a pucklie quines get thegither there's aye muckle laaching aboot naethin in parteeclar. Jist a lot o gyperie.' (T)

GYTE: Slightly mad; paranoid. 'Clean gaen gyte, she shid be lockit up!' (T)

HAAR: Coastal mist or fog. Country folk use 'haar' or 'mist'. Fishers never do, preferring 'fog', while their prime choice is 'thickness'. Thickness comes in varying densities: thick, smore thick, tar thick and thick as guts. Smore means to smother. (B)

HAAVER: To cut in halves. 'I wid need to be haaver't afore I could be in twaa places at ae time.' (B)

HABBER: To stutter or stammer in speech. 'He habbers that muckle, the words is rotten afore they get oot.' (B)

HACH: Phlegm from the back of the throat. **HACH AN PYOCHER:** A clearing of the throat followed by a cough. (T)

HACK: A cut. **HACKIT:** Chapped or cracked. 'Lang oors at the farlan an Maggie's haans were hackit wi the saat an the caal.' (B)

HACKIE: A very slight degree of variation, possibly from the hacks or notches on the tractor throttle. 'Can ye nae ging a hackie faster?' (B)

HAEN or HEEN: Had. 'He hisna heen a shave iss fyle, ye cwid nearly crack a spunk on is chin!' (T)

HAFLIN: A male teenager. 'Na na, oor Norman's jist a haflin, nae aal aneuch tae be foreman yet.' (T)

HAGGER'T: Hacked. 'A hagger't thoomb.' A hacked thumb. (T)

HAGGLE or HAGGLED: To struggle, argue or bargain. 'The twaa o them haggled for nearly an oor aboot the price o the binder.' (T)

HAIK: 'On the haik.' On the lookout. (T)

HAIMES: The steel frame with drag hooks that is fitted over a horse collar. It is not a permanent fixture and has to be adjusted every time the animal is yoked. (T)

HAIMMERS O HELL: A terrific and persistent domineering noise like a stone-crusher or a Jumpin-Jeck in a scrap-yard; demolition work, heavy lorries and motor traffic, trains, helicopters overhead and low-flying aircraft, a crash of thunder or even Top of the Pops on telly – all of these sounds in Buchan are aptly defined as the Haimmers o Hell or the Deevil's Foundry. 'Nae sleep last nicht, Jock. We hid the haimmers o hell in the back yard aa nicht. Thon din wid waaken the verra deevil imsel. If he can sleep throwe yon racket he maun be deid!' (T)

HAIN: To save; to be thrifty. 'I'll hae tae hain ma sugar ower the wik-en; it's nearly aa deen an the shop disna open till Monday.' (T)

HAIRBACK: A beautiful cloth from which the fishers' dress trousers were tailor made. There is a positive connection here with the East-Anglian village of Kersey. (B) The farm workers wore tailor-made kersey-tweed trousers. (T)

HAIRSE: Hoarse. 'I'm hairse roarin at yon bairns, but they jist winna listen.' (B)

HAIRST: Harvest. 'The hairst's naething nooadays wi they big combines an balers drettin aff (defecating) the strae aa ower the parks like rolls o tileit paper. It's a gey change fae my young day fin aathing hid tae be cut an bun an stookit an forkit an cairtit hame tae be thrashen. There's naebody could big a ruck noo onywye, or set a stook on the stibble for that metter, or cut wi a scythe.' (T)

HAIRST-FRAME: A harvest-frame. A wooden frame of considerable size and strength which can be fitted on to a horse cart to increase the loading capacity for straw, hay or sheaves. It was also used for cottar flittings before the days of the motor lorry. 'I'll gie ye a han tae pit the hairst-frame on yer cairt Lindsay, an we'll tak in a ruck o shaves for a thrash.' (T)

HAIRST MEEN: Harvest moon. The hairst meen is an Autumnal equinox phenomenon of natural light which assisted harvest operations and the mellowing colour was said to ripen the corn. While still crescent, the moon rose about the same hour every evening at sunset and never reached the zenith until it was full. Actually there were two of them but the first one was known as 'the Hunter's Moon'. Grieve: 'There's a hairst meen the nicht, lads. Wid ye care tae work an oor or twaa langer? Ye'll get yer tay fin we're throwe.' (T)

HAIRY-MOULDIT: Mouldy. 'We've keepit at cheese ower lang, mither. It's aa hairy mouldit.' (T)

HAIRY TATTIES: A hash made with potatoes and dried, salted fish. Very appetising with mustard sauce. In the poverty days of the past, many families must have been literally sick of the sight of it. But they couldn't afford meat. (B)

HAIVE: To throw. 'Dinna haive awaa yer smaa tatties, Sarah. I could use them for seed, or even bile them tae feed ma hens.' (T)

HAKE: A wooden frame, usually triangular, hung against an exterior wall with hooks attached, for the drying of fish. **HAKE:** A female who loves to roam the streets, without any apparent purpose. Not necessarily an immoral person. (B)

HALE AND HERTY: Whole and hearty. In good shape mentally and physically. (T)

HALE WATTER: A downpour; torrential rain. 'Ye canna ging hame on yer bike the nicht, ma quine. It's jist hale watter!' (T)

HALESOME: Wholesome. 'Nae neen o yer funcy stuff here. Jist gweed, aal-fashen't, halesome farin (food) like fit ma mither ees't tae mak. It's the belly that keeps up the back, ye ken, and ye need something tae stick tae yer ribs for a day's wark on the fairm.' (T)

HALF-HUNG-TEE: Doric slang for a disorderly, irresponsible person not to be trusted in a position of authority. 'Hector a foreman? Nae chance! He's half-hung-tee.' (T)

HALF-LIBBED: Half-castrated. When only one testicle had descended. (T)

HALF-NINE: In Buchan this means half past eight. The Dutch and the Germans agree! (B)

HALLY-RACKET: A frolicking boisterous person. 'Polly's a hally-racket bitch, nae cauk (no reckoning) nor care, an a heid like a hedder besom (heather broom). Ye wid think her claes hid been thrown on wi a graip (four-pronged fork)!' (T)

HAME-DRAACHTIT: Home-sick. No desire to leave home. 'I wis hame-draachtit for ma fadder's hoose, jist for the sicht o't, bit I couldna get hame, bit if I saw the lums I wis pleas't, and I ees't tae wave ma hand tae them, for I wis hert sick for hame.' (T)

HAME-OWER: Sociable; home-loving; natural; a family person. 'Oor doctor's a richt fine hame-ower chiel, nae palaver wi him, he jist comes in an sits doon like a neiper body, an ye can say near onything tull im, he'll news awaa, an he near aye kens fit's vrang wi ye jist bi lookin at ye.' (T)

HAMES: The iron frame fixed over the horse's shoulder collar with hooks for 'theets' or drag-chains. Showyard or ploughing match hames were polished steel with extended spikes on top known as 'Glasgow pikes', probably because these were worn by the cart horses in the city. (T)

HAMEWITH: Back home. (B)

HANGMAN CHEESE: Curds compressed in a gauze cloth, salted to taste, and hung to dry outside on a nail in the wall. It's much smaller than a kebbock of cheese, which is shaped and dried in a cheese press. (T)

HANLESS: Handless; clumsy-handed. The type of fella who will drop the dishes while he's drying them. (B)

HANLINS: Hand lines. Strictly for inshore use and mainly for pleasure. (B)

HANSELL: A gift or token of success for a new business enterprise. 'I wisna needin shortbreid, bit I bocht it fae the grocer tae hansell his new van.' (T)

HANTLE: A considerable amount or number. 'We aye thocht he wis peer, but he left a hantle o siller.' 'A hantle o folk at the Burns Supper.' (B)

HAP: To cover or conceal. 'Hap the thing wi a tarpaulin tae keep the rain aff.' 'The hale park's happit wi snaa.' (B)

HARD AS HAIKLE: An expression used to describe an extremely rocky part of the sea bed, suitable only for line fishing. (B)

HARD-VROCHT: Hard-worked. (B)

HARDIES: Butter biscuits. Also known as Fardin biscuits, probably because they were originally priced at a farthing each, four for a penny, and over the years farthing became the Buchan fardin. 'Breemies folk are surely gaan tae hae a pairty, the quine wis doon at the shop for tippence o fardin biscuits.' (T)

HARN: Hessian; sackcloth. 'Pit the best o the tatties in a harn bag, an haive the lave awaa.' (B)

79

HARNS: Brains. (B)

HARRA: Harrow. **HARRA-TINES:** The prongs fixed to harrows to cultivate the soil. Grubbers were also fitted with tines but they were much larger. There were also the 'Spring harras', not because they were used in the springtime, but because their tines were spring-loaded. Most of these implements have been replaced with the modern rotovator for cultivation. (T)

HARRIGALS: The entrails of animals and fowl or left-overs. 'By the time the butcher gets tae us he's clean oot o beef an there's naething left bit harrigals.' (T)

HASHIN: Hustling. (T)

HAUD or HUD: To hold. (T)

HAUGH: Flat ground on the banks of a river. 'The haugh wis a sea o watter fin the river burst its banks.' (T)

HAVERS: Blethers; jokes; nonsense. 'Yon lad his plenty tae say aboot aabody but its jist a lot o havers. He jist likes tae hear himsel spik.' (T)

HEARKEN: To listen.

> Hearken close, my bonny lass;
> Fit better could I tell ye?
> Tho moons an Junes awaa may pass,
> Ye ken I widna sell ye. (B)

HEDDER: Heather. **HEDDER COWES:** heather stems or twigs after the flowers have withered (T)

HEDDEREENGE: Hydrangea. 'Ye shid leave the deid flooers on yer heddereenge tae keep the frost aff the young buds in the springtime. (T)

HEEL-PIECE: U-shaped iron tab, nailed on to the leather heel of a tackety boot. 'Heels, taes an tackets souter, an patch at hole on the upper.' (T)

HEELSTER-GOWDIE: Head over heels. 'Sally gaed heelster-gowdie ower the soo's troch an landit amon the dubs wi her claes (skirts) abeen her heid. A sicht for sair een, I can tell ye!' (T)

HEFT or HAFT: A knife-handle. **HEFTIT COO:** an unmilked cow or goat, a cow with a bulging or inflamed udder for want of milking. The word is sometimes used in human terms like 'I'll hae tae gyang tae the Gents, Dick. I'm fair heftit for a rin oot!' (T)

80

HEID: Head. **HEIDY:** Clever. **HEID WIN:** Head wind; the wind in your face. 'He hid a heid win aa the wye hame on his bike, nae muckle winner he wis puggl't. (T)

HEIST: To lift something with great effort. (T)

HENNY-HERTIT: Soft; timid; dull; spiritless; faint-hearted. Afraid to say boo to the proverbial goose. (T)

HERD: To look after. 'Willie herdit a pucklie nowt.' (T)

HERRIE: To cheat or rob. 'Herrie a bird's nest.' Steal the eggs. **HERRIAL:** An extortion. 'The Poll Tax is a herrial amon peer folk!' (T)

HERRIN FIVVER: Herring fever. A peculiar, yet genuine ailment caused by a protracted spell of bad luck at the herring fishing, when one seems to be singled out to miss the shoals night after night. Self-pity and frustration take possession of a fella, so that he can actually become ill. There are two possible cures: A cran-the-net (a good catch) or else a six foot hole. (B)

HET: Hot. **HET FIT:** Hot foot; full speed; flat out; as fast as possible in an emergency. 'I jist cam ower het fit as seen's I saw baith yer lums reekin (smoking). My man said that wid be yer signal for the bairn bein born.' **HET SARK:** A hot shirt. A sweaty shirt from working in the heat outside or in the close stuffy atmosphere of barn or byre. (T)

HICH and HICHER: High and higher. 'Ye'll need tae be hicher up than at, Beldie, tae pit up the decorations; ye'll need the steps, and monkeys like tae be hich!' (T)

HID: Had. **HIDNA:** Had not. 'The shoppie hid plenty aal tatties but it hidna ony new eens.' (T)

HIDIE HOLE: A place of concealment, especially among the bairns when playing tackie, better known as hide-an-seek. (T)

HIGH TIME: Not before time; in the nick of time; almost too late. 'It's high time that Brucie hid yon park o corn cut doon or it'll be aa shakkin wi the win (threshed by the strong winds)!' (T)

HINE AWAA: Far away. **HINE DOON:** Far down. (B)

HING: To hang. **HING IN:** Hurry, get a move on. 'Hing in an hing oot yer claes, it's gyaan tae rain afore nicht.' (T)

HINGIN LUGGIT: Dismal; crestfallen. When someone is supposed to have the doleful expression of a Basset hound. 'Aye Wullie, ye're affa hingin luggit like the day.' Hingin luggit may have been derived from the luggit-bonnet, which gives the wearer a somewhat similar appearance when the flaps are down over the ears. (T)

HINMAIST: Hindmost. 'It's ilkie man for himsel, an deil tak the hinmist.' (B)

HINNER: To hinder. **HINNER'T:** Hindered; delayed. 'I wis affa hinner't wi yon insurance mannie. He wid news till the back o a day, and I ken as muckle aboot insurance as the bickie (collie dog) there kens aboot telaveeshin, and that's nae verra muckle, I can tell ye!' (T)

HIPPEN: A baby napkin. 'Can ye pit a hippen on the bairn, Johnathan?' 'Na, na, I leave that tae the wife. I wid nivver get the safety-preen fassen't athoot jobbin im.' (T)

HIPPEN TOWIE: The string or line hung across the mantel-piece for drying hippens. (B)

HIPPICK: Hiccup or Hiccough. 'There's naething tae beat a fleg tae cure the hippick, Donnie. I'll pit ye ootside wi yer bonnet on an I'll cry ye in bare-heidit!' (T)

HIPPIT, HIP-GRIPPET or SAIR HURDIES: Aching hip-joints and muscles. Like backache, the pain is often experienced after a lot of bending. 'I'm affa hip-grippet the day, wifie; I wiz getherin tatties ower the wik-en an I hinna cower't it (recovered from it) yet!' (T)

HIRED MAN: A deckhand who had no assured income. It was 'no fish, no money.' Actually he wasn't hired at all but he would have promised to sail with a certain skipper for a season. (B)

HIRPLE: To limp or walk with difficulty. 'He hirpled aboot like a bird wi ae wing.' (B)

HIRSEL or HIRSILL: A flock or herd of animals. 'I ken I'm late, bit I hid tae stop the car for a hirsel o sheep.' (T)

HIRSSLE: to fidget. (T)

HISE or HIZE: Friendly banter; verbal teasing; oral buffoonery. 'I think I'll awaa ower an hae a hize wi Geordie Broon aboot his turkeys, jist tae see foo mony bubblie-jocks (turkey-cocks) he his amon em. He's a bit o a bubblie-jock himsel, Geordie, bit nae an ull stock (not a bad lad) for aa that.' (T)

HISH: To shoo or herd poultry. 'Hish the hens intae the ree, Annie.' (T)

HIST: A good many. 'Ye're hardly startet yet an ye're baith young, aa the warld afore ye and a hist o geets; ye'll be feart tae throw a steen in ower a skweel dyke for fear o hittin een o yer ain!' (T)

HIST YE BACK: Haste you back; come again soon. The customary farewell to guests. (B)

HIV or HAE: Have. **HAE'T:** Have it. **HIZ:** Has. **HINNA or HIVNA:** Have not. **HISNA:** Has not. **HID or HEEN:** Had. **HIDNA:** Had not.

Dear Jenny,
If ye hiv at flooer I sent ye, ye can throw't awaa or gie't tae somebody. If Frances hiz yon yalla flooer I sent er she can gie't awaa tae somebody that hisna een like it, bit I hivna got that ither flooer wi the hingin beads that ye hinna seen since Frances hid it, and if ye hidna spoken aboot it, I widda forgotten that ye didna hae't.

Peggy. (T)

HIZ: Us. 'Gee whizz, ye nivver come up an see hiz!' (B) 'Div ye nae ken hiz?' Don't you know us? This is the sort of question that is asked by one of a couple who have met someone they know but haven't seen for ages and who doesn't seem to recognize them. Aikey Fair was the place for it, and if the stranger still seemed at a loss for identity the question would be followed up with 'Mind we used tae bide aside ye at Clockaben!' or wherever, 'next door in fack, an ye wiz jist new merrit at the time.' Shaking hands was taboo and the chiel would probably come out with 'Och aye, I hiv ye noo, bit man, ye're baith affa changed and I widna a kent ye if ye hidna spoken, neen o the twaa o ye!' Hiz or his is used in the plural as 'Don't you know us?' (T)

HOAST: A cough; to cough. 'A kirkyaird hoast.' A graveyard cough! A deep-seated cough that could have serious consequences. 'Bit mony een in the kirkyaird wid be gled o a hoast like at!' (T)

HOBBLE: A visible movement on the surface caused by something underneath. 'The strae wis a hobble o rats.' 'The loon wis a hobble wi lice.' But the 'hobble' here is imaginary. (T)

HOCH: In humans, the part between the thighs or buttocks. In animals, beneath the hind-quarters, 'the hin-hoch.' (T)

HOITER: An unsteady, stumbling sort of walk. 'Aal Geordie his a bittie hoiter aboot him the day. I doot he's been at the drink.' (T)

HOLES AN BORES: Nooks and crannies. 'Yon skipper kens ilkie hole an bore on the Wast Coast.' (B)

HOLIPIED: Riddled with holes. 'That's an affa holipied jumper ye hiv on, Meg. Hiz the mochs been at it?' (T)

HOOCH: To shout or ejaculate from the throat while dancing a reel. (T)

HOODIE: Hooded. **HOODIE CRAA:** Hooded crow. (T)

HOOEY'D: Chivvied. (B)

HOOF PARINGS: The small flakes whittled from a horse's hoof before fitting a shoe. It was mostly from the 'frog' of the hoof, the under sole. (T)

HOOF REEK: Hoof smoke. The smoke from a horse's hoof when the blacksmith fitted a red-hot iron shoe on to it to take the size. The smoke smelled slightly of roasted cheese. (T)

HOOICK: A small rick of corn or hay. **HOOICKING:** Trying to salvage corn in a rainy harvest, by building it into small or dwarf stacks to be handled again and stacked full size. Sometimes used to discredit a farmer's stackyard. 'That's nae a cornyard min, jist a puckle hooicks.' Another name for a hooick is a 'scroo'. 'Jist a puckle scroos, min.' (T)

HOOIE: To barter or exchange. **HOOIE-KNIFE:** A knife procured in a hooie, sometimes a blind hooie, when the pocket knife was concealed in a closed fist and you had to take your chance with what was on offer, like a child guessing what hand the sweetie was in. (T)

HOOLET: An Owl. (B)

HOOT AWAA WI: Down with. (B)

HOOZE: 'A yowe wi the hooze.' A ewe with fluke worm on the lungs which causes congested breathing and can be fatal. It also affects cattle. (T)

HORN EYNE, GUN EYNE or BUTT EYNE: The best room or ben-end of a butt and ben cottage. 'Oh aye, it wis a big funeral, the hoosie wis full o fouk and the gairden wis full and the minister gied his service jist ootside the door so that aabody could hear im. Bit the coffin wis in the butt eyne an they couldna get it oot at the door so they hid tae tak it oot at the windae. That wid a pleas't aal Geordie fine if he'd kent the chauve they waar haein wi his boxie; naethin pleas't im better than gettin aabody in a snorl, bit that'll sattle im noo, aye fegs it wull!' (T)

HORNY GOLLACH: A big black beetle. (T)

HORSE LANGUAGE: 'Hi' and 'Wish' was left and right for a plough horse in Buchan and 'Gee-up' and 'Whoa' for forward and stop. Most of them answered to these commands, so we must assume that the old Clydesdales knew their left front hoof from the right one, though I wouldn't go much farther than that, except to say that with the mouth bit they were very sensitive to rein control. Stable language consisted mostly of 'Hud ower min', or 'Hud ower quine', according to sex, or 'Stan ower lass', or 'Hud up yer heid lassie', and some of this was answered with a short nicher (neigh), as sometimes happened when you opened the stable door to feed them. Cattle on the other hand were unresponsive at feeding times, unless to give you a kick, or when you were late, and then they roared loud enough to be heard half-a-mile away. (T)

HORSE TROCH: A watering trough for horses and cattle, usually made of concrete or metal and sited conveniently in the farm close. If a haflin (teenager) failed to get out of bed for several mornings after being wakened by the foreman he was liable for a dipping in the icy cold water of the troch by other members of the farm staff. Another occasion for a dip in the troch was a 'feet-washing' before a wedding. The victim was then smeared with harness blacking and cart-axle grease. He then required a proper bath in a washing tub. 'I'll see ye bye the hens' troch!' was a favourite parting shot for a friend or neighbour who had visited in the evening, hinting jokingly that he might steal something if you didn't. (T)

HORSEMAN'S WORD: The horseman's word was revealed to initiates of a secret society of medieval origin which was strongly represented in the North-East of Scotland in agriculture during the 19th century. It had links with witchcraft and free masonry and The Horseman's Word was supposed to give its adherents an uncanny power over horses and women. Only horsemen were admitted to the society, and after a testing period of trial and suitability, an adherent was admitted to the initiation ceremony. Arriving with a bottle of whisky and a loaf of bread, the aspirant was blind-folded at midnight and led to the caff hoose (chaff house), the most secluded apartment on a farm steading, and in total darkness, handing over his gifts to the high priests of the society, he was allowed to shake hands with the devil, which is said to have been a calf's hoof on a broomstick. After swearing under oath never to divulge or share the secret of The Horseman's Word, under fear of death and eternal torment, the code word was whispered to him and he was set at liberty while the priests lit a lantern and enjoyed the whisky and bread. (T)

HOSE AN SHEEN: Stockings and shoes; exaggeration. 'He's won £10,000 aff the pools? It'll be £30,000 afore nicht. That kind o story aye gets hose an sheen.'
HOSE: To take the bait. (Nothing to do with stockings or piping.) 'The fishies micht hose a bittie better if ye tried a different bait.' 'I thocht I had gien him a richt gweed offer, but boys, he widna hose.' (B)

HOTTER: To boil. **HOTTERIN:** At boiling point, with the lid chattering. 'The kettle wis hotterin on the bink (hob).' (B) **HOTTERIN:** Seething. (T)

HOTTEREL: A festering sore; a seething, swarming or overcrowding. 'Sic a hotterel, it's time ye saw the doctor aboot at.' 'The cactus is fairly croodit oot; jist a hotterel wi young plunts.' (T)

HOVEN: Swollen. (B)

HOWDER O WIN: A bluster of wind. 'Aye wumman, yer claes are gettin a gey howder o win the day. That'll shak the wrinkles oot o yer sheets.' (T)

HOWDIE or HOUDI: A doctor or midwife, but the origin or meaning of the rhyme is a mystery.

> Roon an roon the Houdi's hoose
> Cullie chased the Deevil,
> Ridin on a bantam cock
> Pop goes the weasel! (T)

HOWE: A hollow; a valley. 'The howe o yer neck.' The nape of your neck. 'Dinna meeve, Wullie, or I get a skelp at im. There's a wasp in the howe o yer neck.' (T)

HOWK: To dig, as with a spade. 'Yon chiel's forivver howkin in is nose, the fool brute!' 'Thickness howks the sea.' Fog makes holes in the sea. This is an old fisher saying. It doesn't mean that fog makes swell in the sea, but if the swell or 'motion' is there before the fog comes down, the fog will definitely make the motion steeper, and the troughs deeper. Of course, the Met. men dispute this, but then they dinna ken aathing. (B)

HUD: To hold; to keep. 'That's aneuch tae hud's gaan.' That's enough to keep us going. (T) **HUDDEN:** Held. 'He's been sair hudden doon, peer stock.' (T)

HUDDERY: Rough; tousled. 'A huddery heid.' Hair that needs combing. (T)

HUD'S ON or HUD'S OON: Something that will help to avoid having to do something else. 'If ye phone or caa in by Rachel, that'll hud's on writin a letter till er.' or 'If ye buy a loff the day, that'll hud's oon bocht baps the morn.' (T)

HULL-RUN: Rough-and-ready; uncouth; outlandish. If applied to a man, he would probably be shabbily dressed and unshaven. 'He's a hull-run bugger, yon. I widna lippen (trust) im tae pare ma corns, he wid cut aff a tae.' (T)

HUMAN HAE: To hesitate. **HUMMED AN HAWED:** Hesitated; was undecided, couldn't make up his mind. 'Rab hummed an hawed an twirled his mouser.' (T)

HUMCH: To chew; a chew. 'Een o the muckle loons stole a neep an smashed it on a dyke. Aa the loons an quines gether't roon for a humch o the juicy swede.' Those were days of ignorance and bliss. (T)

HUMMEL-DODDIES: Worsted mittens without fingers. 'Ye'll need on yer hummel-doddies this mornin, loon. The neeps are caal an frostie.' (T)

HUMMLIES: Black polled (hornless) Aberdeen-Angus cattle of world-wide repute to the extent that the inhabitants of Buchan have adapted it for themselves. A breed apart and worthy of recognition in the highest places. There is also a flavour of modesty in being referred to as a 'Buchan Hummlie'. (T)

HUMPH: To carry laboriously. 'That peer aal wifie humphin her watter on a yoke fae a draa-waal (draw-well) nearly half-a-mile fae her hoose! The laird shid think shame o himsel. She shid hae pipeit watter, bit he'll mebbee get roon tull't some day!' (T)

HUMPH'T AN GLUMPH'T: Dithered. (T)

HUMPHY-BACKIT: Hunch-backed. 'Walk up stracht wi yer shooders back, Harry, or ye'll get humphy-backit.' (T)

HUNKERS: The hips or the backside. If ye're doon on yer hunkers, ye're in a squatting position. (B)

HUNKIT: Restricted in an overtight article of clothing, causing discomfort. 'Ma new jacket's affa ticht aneth the oxters, mither. I'm fair hunkit in't an I can hardly meeve.' (T)

HURDIES: Hips. In a sitting position you are on your hurdies. 'I wis oot getherin tatties aa day yesterday an I've affa sair hurdies. I'm hip-grippit wi sae muckle booin up an doon, nae bein eesed tull't.' (T)

HURL: A ride or drive; to ride or drive in a wheeled vehicle. Instead of paying for a taxi, you would 'seek (ask) a hurl doon the road' from a friend with a cart or a car etc.

> Fin I wis young and herty
> I hurl't in a cairty,
> The cairty bruk and I fell oot
> An skint aa my ersie. (T)

HURL IN THE THROAT: The audible movement of phlegm in the breast or throat. (T) Those who have difficulty with the letter 'r' and pronounce it in a guttural fashion are said to have 'a hurl in the throat'. (B)

HURLEY: A barrow with two wheels. 'A big crew aboard there, my loon. The grocer needs a hurley tae tak doon the grub. Naethin like sea air tae gie ye an appetite.' (B)

HURLEY BED: A low bed on castors, hurled (wheeled) underneath the box bed during the day, to be hurled out again at night when required. An essential in over-crowded housing. (B)

HURRICAN LUMP: A hurricane lamp or lantern. A circular type of wick lamp encased in windproof glass and protective wiring. Often used as rear-lighting on the threshing mills in transport after dark. 'Tak the hurrican lump, Jim, an ging oot an see if the mere's foalin.' (T)

HUSHEL'T: Huddled. (T)

HUSKLE: A Haskell; a golf ball. The delight of little quines as they played 'lairies'.

> One, two, three a lairie
> I spy Katie Clairie
> Sittin on a bumble airie
> Eating choclit babies. (B)

HYOWE: A hoe; to hoe. The hyowe is a small steel blade seven inches broad at the end of a six-foot wooden handle and used to single or separate turnip plants in the drills. (T)

HYSE: A romp; friendly banter. (B)

HYSTE: To hoist. 'When the hairber's closed, they hyste a black ball.' (B)

HYSTERGOWDIE: Head over heels. Sometimes heard as 'heelstergowdie'. 'Jeckie tummel't (fell) an gaed hystergowdie ower the steen roller. It's a wunner he didna brak a leg or somethin, bit na na, jist a bruis't knee an he's neen the waar o't!' (T)

HYTER: To walk with uncertain gait. 'See yon great feel hyterin aboot on stumperts (stilts)!' (B)

IDLESET: Idleness; sloth. 'Come awaa, noo, lads! Idleset winna get a frockie tae the bairn.' Idleness won't earn you any money to clothe your child. (B)

ILKA or ILKIE: Every. (T)

ILL-FAARED: Ill-favoured; not in the least handsome. 'Did ivver ye see sic an ill-faared boat? Neither shape nor form yonner.' (B)

ILL-FASHIONED: Inquisitive. 'Sandy's richt ill-fashioned. He wid speir (enquire) the guts oot o ye.' (B)

ILL-PAIRTIT: Unfairly shared out. 'The wordle's ill-pairtit; some has aathing – some has naething.' (B)

ILL SHOOKEN UP: Of rather poor physique. 'Ill shooken up an slack tied.' From the herring nets which had to be bundled and tied so often. There was a real knack to the bundling, or 'makkin up'. Some fellas could make a real tidy job, while others could only produce a really untidy mess. 'Silly made up' applies to a youngster who delights in impish behaviour. (B)

ILL-THOCHTIT: Having a suspicious mind. 'He's a richt ill-thochtit chiel, aye thinkin the warst aboot folk.' (B)

ILL-TRICKIT: Mischievous. 'A richt ill-trickit cratur, aye up tae something.' (B)

IMPHM: Yes or aye.

> That affa word Imphm
> That vulgar word Imphm
> That daft like word Imphm
> Ye ken it means Aye! (T)

INABOOTCOMER: An incomer. (T)

INCHIE: A small amount. 'This breid wid be neen the waar o an inchie o butter.' (B)

INCOME O DAYLICHT: The dawn of the day. (B)

INDRAACHT: Inhaling. (T)

INGLE-NEUK: A corner by the fireside. (T)

INHUDDIN: Intimate; condescending; currying favour. 'Slessor's affa inhuddin wi the mannie (the farmer) an tells im aathing that's goin on amon the ither lads. He gets imsel ull-likeit for at.' (T)

INKLIN: Inclination; a secret or slight desire. 'I aye hid an inklin tae shew an mak claes bit nivver pat ma mind tull't.' (T)

INTIMMERS: The inward parts of anything, including the human frame. (B)

IREN-EER: Rust sediment in water, perhaps an offshoot of the English iron-ore or chalybeate, or water impregnated with minute particles of iron rust. The water is slightly rust coloured with iron deposit and leaves a red slime on the banks of the stream. 'Dinna drink oot o at ireneerie ditch min, it's nae gweed for ye!' (T)

I'SE WARRANT: I guarantee. (B)

IVERLEEVIN GALLOP: Tremendously fast; flat out. 'The mannie and his horsie took oot aboot at the iverleevin gallop!' It could also refer to the postman on his bicycle. 'The postie took oot aboot like the iverleevin gallop an the dog efter im!' (T)

JAA: Jaw. This word can be used to curb a verbal onslaught with 'Ony mair o yer jaa an I'll gar the bells ring in yer lugs!' (T)

JAAD or JAUD: A pernicious, licentious, perverse or spiteful woman. 'Keep clear o yon jaad, Norrie, if ee say black she'll say fite an she'll dee ye an ill turn if she can get ye intae trouble.' (T)

JAAPIT: Thin; emaciated; sallow. 'Ye're affa jaapit-like Bryce, are ye aff yer mait or somethin? I did hear ye'd haen the flu.' (T)

JALOUSE: To suspect. 'Naebody wid jalouse ye wis stealin in braid daylicht, wumman!' (T)

JANDIES: Jaundice. Until recent years, those outside the medical profession assumed that the jandies was brought on by a 'scunner', a deep sense of revulsion. The sight of maggots, or even the sight of a really dirty cooking pot was supposed to be 'enough tae gie ye the jandies'. (B)

JANNER: Idle gossip. 'Menzie's hoosekeeper harkens tae aa the janner o the perrish that's agyaan.' (T)

JECK: To fit for size. 'I tried yon new seat on tae the rake bit it widna jeck, the bolt holes wis in the wrang place.' (T)

JEEL: To jellify. 'Poor the pottit heid intae the bowl an lat it jeel.' (B)

JEELY: Jelly or jam. **JEELY PIGS:** Jam jars. These big earthenware jars were used when the farming folk made a large supply of jam to last them for a year. (T)

JEETER: A glossy shine, like you might have on your shoes or your new polished car. 'An affa jeeter on yer sheen the day Ellis, did ye polish them wi the wife's tay cosy?' (T)

JELP: To splash. Jorum is similar but implies full measure in that 'the dish wis reamin fou!'

> Jean MacPherson maks my brose,
> And her an me we canna gree,
> It's first a mott an syne a knot,
> And aye the ither jelp o bree. (T)

JIBBLIN: Brimming; overflowing. (T)

JIMP: In short supply; scarce; inadequate. 'Ye've been a bittie jimp wi the seed, Hadden. There's hardly aneuch tae feenish the dreel.' And the answer might be, 'Dinna saw't sae thick an!' (T)

JING-BANG: 'The hale jing-bang o them.' Each and every one of them. (T)

JINK: To avoid; to escape. 'Wullie lay doon in the back seat tae jink the bobbies. He wis that drunk, he could hardly staan on his feet. If he'd been in the drivin seat an the bobbies had seen im, he wid a been up for the high jump.' (T)

JINNIPROUS: Spruce; well turned out. (T)

JIP!: What for! 'Jist ee wyte till yer father comes hame. He'll gie ye jip!' (B)

JOB: To jab; to prick, as with a needle. 'Sure as daith ye'll job yer fingers if ye dinna lay that needle doon.' **JOBBY NICKLES:** Stinging nettles. A real menace to loons who always wore short trousers. (B)

JOBBIE: A job; a chore. 'Ye'll be needin an easy jobbie efter yer operation.' (T)

JOCKTOBER: October. If it had been a wet harvest, folk would blame the weather antics of Jock Tober. (T)

JOCO: Jovial. (T)

JOHN GUNN: An outdoor water closet. (T)

JOOG: A jug. A jug is always a joog, but a mug is always a mug. (B) Also a pet name for Jessie: Joog or Joogie. (T)

JOOK or JOUK: To avoid; to dodge. (T)

JORUM: A generous quantity of liquid, usually alcoholic. 'Jist a wee drammie noo, Dod, kis ye ken I'm drivin. Nae a great jorum like fit ye gid me the last time I wis here or the bobby'll smell ma breath a mile awaa.' (T)

JOUKERY PAUKERY: Double dealing. Something akin to the modern cover-up or con-man transaction or political intrigue. (T)

JUMMLE: To jumble, mix up or confuse. 'Oh it wis a gran merrige hud awaa fae the speeches, an Geordie himsel wis warst avaa. He got the words aa jummel't up an ye widna a kent if it wis a merrige or a roup.' (T)

JUNT: A jaunt; a journey. On the farm it meant a break from the general routine.

'I'll get a junt tae the smiddy the day, ma cooter's broken!' (T)

KAIM: A comb; to comb. 'Kaim his pair.' Comb his pair of horses. 'Rab banged his steel kaim against the travis post. The wooden post wis poke-marked fae years o banging tae knock the stue (dust) oot o Rab's kaim.' The Dandy brush was also used on this occasion to smooth down the hair and get rid of the dust and hay-seed. Kaim an brush were also used in the byres to prepare the animals for slaughter. It gave them a better appearance to impress the butchers around the sale ring. (T)

KALE-RUNT: The stem of the kale plant, also known as the castock or castick. Also implies inferiority of stature or personality. 'Forbie wis jist a kale-runt o a cratur, nae muckle eese for naething.' If you feared the worst in punishment, you would be 'gettin yer kale throwe the reek the nicht!' (T)

KEEGER: A mess; a disorderly mixture; a muddle. 'Doreen, ma quine, sic a keeger ye've made mixin at dumplin, there's mair o't on the table than there is in yer bowl!' (T)

KEEK: To peep. (T)

KEELIN: A very large cod-fish weighing at least 2 stone. Not many of them left now. (B)

KENNLE: To kindle; to light. 'Chappin sticks tae kennle the fire.' Chopping sticks to kindle the fire. (B)

KENSPECKLE: Well known; familiar to nearly everybody. (B)

KEP: To catch. 'Pit a bucket aneth that leak an kep the dreeps.' (B) **KEPP:** To herd, catch or intercept. 'Kep the nowt, Gabby. Dinna lat them in at that gate; watch at black stott or he'll wun by ye. Nivver mind the dog, they're nae fear't at kye. Hiv ye nae a stick wi ye the day? Ye're nae muckle eese amon nowt athoot a stick!' (T)

KERSY TWEED: A coarse, woollen cloth used to make trousers. They were popular with farm workers before dungarees were introduced in the 1930s. (T)

KHAKISTAMACKET: Squeamish, having your stomach easily turned. 'He wis richt khakistamacket fin he saw the caterpillar on his piece.' (T)

KILLCRACKIT: Kiln-cracked. Minute cracks on the surface of old porcelain or on the face of a painting. 'Ye're nae buyin at thing, are ye? It's killcrackit, tho I will say it hiz a bonny picter on't.' (T)

KINABBERIE: A group of people, loosely related or of the same type. 'He's worth the watchin, my loon, baith him an aa his kinabberie.' (B)

KINCH: To wind. 'Kinch up a rope.' Wind a rope up in hand like a lassoo to keep it tidy. 'Kinch up the ploo rines (reins).' (T)

KINE: Cattle and swine. (T)

KINK-HOAST: The whooping cough. The cough which was such a scourge in former days. To see a bairn wi the 'kinker' was a very trying experience indeed.
Teacher: 'Why is your brother not at school today?'
Pupil (trying to speak 'proper'): Please, Miss, he has the hooping hoast, but I think he's a bittie better, cos he's nae hooping so muckle noo.' (B)

KIRK MOOSE: Church mouse. 'As hard-up as a kirk moose!' except on Communion Sabbath, when there was just the chance of the odd crumb of bread lying around after the communicants had left the building. (T)

KIRK OR MULL: Church or mill. 'I'm for naething tae dee wi yer transaction, ye can mak a kirk or a mull o't.' Inferring that the committee could do as they pleased with the affair suggested, but the speaker would take no part in it. (T)

KIRN: A butter churn; an unholy mess. 'Did ivver ye see sic a kirn o a place? A sotter o dubs aawye.' (B)

KIRSEN: To Christen. 'Kirsen the bairn.' Christen the baby. (T)

KIST: A wooden chest. The chaumer kist was used by unmarried farm workers to hold their belongings, everything from suits to tie-pins, hair-oil and money. The corn kist was in the stable, one for each pair of horses and contained the crushed oats for their feed. It was whilst seated on some of these stable kists that the fairm chiels composed some of their famous Bothy Ballads, dunting out the tunes with their heels on the sides or ribs of the kists and taking the farmer to task in their lyrics. (T)

KISTIT: Laid in a coffin. 'Sandy's deid an kistit, He's beeryin the morn.' (B)

KITCHIEDEEM or KITCHIEDEEMIE: The kitchen maid. 'The kitchiedeemie will be ower wi yer tay aboot three o'clock. I'll tell her faar ye're workin.' The kitchiedeemie sometimes had to walk half-a-mile, over dykes and through fences to the hairst rig, but she was always welcome with her basket of sandwiches, scones and rhubarb jam and a flagon of milk or a kettle of tea. If her lad was amongst the billies, she was always ragged about it by the other chiels. The introduction of thermos flasks in the late 'thirties saved the kitchiedeem a tiring journey. (T)

KITTLE: To tickle. 'If the palm o yer haan's kittley, ye're gaan tae get siller.' (B) Also to brighten up. 'We hinna the clean-lan led yet. The stooks are affa dump sittin sae lang on the young girss, bit if the widder wid kittle up a bittie, we wid throw them ower tae lat the sun get at the shear o the sheff and that wid dry them for leadin. We hiv shiftit the stooks aaready, bit it's been sic a lang time o drizzen foggy widder, a body canna get oot o the bit. **KITTLE UP:** To anger. 'Dinna kittle up yer fadder, or ye'll get Fa broke the hurley (What for).' (T)

KITTLIN: A kitten. 'Lat's see ower the cat's dish, Kate. I left a suppie brose melk in ma bowl for the kittlin. She likes a suppie warm brose melk in a caal mornin an she's fair thrivin on't.' (T)

KNABBLICH: Knobbly. (T)

KNACKERY (silent K): An animal offal factory where sick or elderly farm animals are humanely put down. (T)

KNAPDARLICH: A substance caked and hardened. Mostly refers to matted dung on the hind-quarters of cattle or sheep which has to be removed with shears or an iron-toothed comb. (T)

KNICHTIT: Delighted; overjoyed; pleased with oneself. 'Donzer wis fair knichtit wi imsel fin he won the raffle.' (T)

KNIPEIN ON (pronounce the K): Chappin on. Knipe is in *The Concise Scots Dictionary* but the origin is uncertain, and the definition is given as 'lad or chap' – 'chappin on'. We must therefore give credit to the Aberdonian music hall entertainer, Harry Gordon, 'the Laird of Inversnecky', for inventing the expression 'knipein on' when he recorded 'Hillie's Man' on the old 78 Beltona record label in 1928. It was top of the charts all over Buchan and far beyond for more than a year, and almost everybody was knipein on like the verra deil trying to emulate Harry. It became almost a personal greeting among the farm chiels, and after the customary 'foo are ye deein?' (how are you doing?) the rejoinder inevitably became 'Oh, jist knipein on', and the salutation lasted for many years. (T)

KNOTTY-TAMS (pronounce the K): Oatmeal brose made with boiling milk instead of water. A once-a-week supper in the Buchan farm kitchens. (T)

KNOWE: A brae, mound or summit. 'Ye canna see the ither en o yer feerin (first furrow) fin it's at the ither side o the knowe.' (T)

KNYTE (pronounce the K): A big lump of something. 'Michty, Andy, that's an affa lump o cheese ye've gotten. It'll be comin oot at yer lugs or ye get aa that aetin. Naething like a knyte o hame made cheese, beats aa yer bocht stuff ony day!' (T)

KWINTRA: Country. 'Gane are the days fin ye could spot a kwintra chiel in the toon.' (T)

KYACK: The village of New Pitsligo, near Rosehearty. It comes from the 'kyackers', a local name for the workers who were engaged in the process of lace-making, for which the village was famous in the nineteenth century. (T)

KYARD or KYARDIN: A woman with a waspish tongue. To be lashed with such a tongue would be 'a kyardin', a telling off, in no uncertain terms, a severe reprimand. **KYARD-TONGUED:** Vile-mouthed. There is a saying 'Kyard tongued, yet sometimes blessed with longevity.' and the popular epigram: 'There's a lot o killin in a kyard.' (T)

KYE: Cattle. **KYE TIME:** Cow time; milking time; time to get the cows in. (T)

KYPIE: A hollow. (T)

KYSIE: A small cowrie shell, to be found in remarkably few places. The search for it is a great exercise in patience. Known also as a 'Johnny Groatie', or a 'calfie's mooie' (calf's mouth), to which it bears a strong resemblance. (B)

LAADIEDA: Palaver; pretence; airs and graces. 'Sic a laadieda. Her wi a fur coat an nae draaers.' (T)

LABSTER: The general fisher term for lobster. 'Faa caaed ye partan face, my lamb, an you sae like a labster?' (B)

LAD O PAIRTS: A versatile, well-educated fellow who can turn his hand to nearly anything. (B)

LADE: A narrow canal which carries water to a mill. 'The mull-lade at Newton wis nearly a quarter o a mile lang an it gaed throwe aneth the main road.' (T)

LAFT: The north-east term for loft. Old photographs show the harbours more or less surrounded by sail-makers' lafts. With the disappearance of the sail boats, these lafts fell into disuse and were then used as stores for all sorts of gear for the steam drifters. However, many herring fishermen who had a share of nets (though not necessarily a share of the vessel), preferred to store and mend their nets at home, where their wives could do the mending. This required an attic or a spare room, but where such a luxury was not available, outhouses were adapted for the purpose. With the demise of the old style herring fishing, the mennin lafties (mending lofts) disappeared too. (B)

LAGAMACHIE or LAMGABBLICH: A long rambling discourse or rigmarole. 'Fut a say awaa aboot naething. I cocket ma lugs a filie tae hearken tae the mannie's lagamachie, bit ma erse gaed dottel't (numb) sittin on yon hard cheir, an I wis sair needin a smoke.' (T)

LAICH: Low lying. **LAICH-IN:** Quietly; secretly. **LAICHY-BRAID:** Low and

95

broad; short and broad; stocky; obese. 'Malcolm's jist a butter baa: he wid as ready rowe as rin – a laichy-braid like his mither's folk, they waar aa like at!' (T)

LAIR: Peat moss. The area in the peat moss where the peats are spread to dry. Also to sink or get bogged down. **LAIRY:** Soft; marshy. (T) **LAIRED:** Bogged down, as heavy farming machinery may well be after a spell of wet weather. 'He begood tae hairst fin the grun wis ower weet, an the combine wis laired afore ye could say "Jake".' (B)

LALLAN: Lowland. (T)

LAMBIKIE: A little lamb. (T)

LAME EGG: An imitation egg made of porcelain or clay and placed in a nest to tempt a hen to lay beside it and thereby stop her from laying astray. If this happened, it was known as 'a hen layin awaa', perhaps in a hedge or bush where the truant eggs were difficult to find. (T)

LAMES: Fragments of broken crockery which little girls played with, in the days when youngsters had to make their own amusement. (B) Lames were broken down into crumbs for the hens to eat, helping them to form their egg shells. (T)

LANG ACRE: The grass verges on the roadside. 'Shinnies sometimes ploughed down a sole o tassled clover that mony a crofter lad would have been glad tae graze on. Aal Snorlie fae Swineden had tae tether his horse at the roadside, and sometimes herd a coo or twaa, on the 'lang acre', as he called it, kiz there wis nae girse in his parks, naething bit steens an thistles, an there wis only a steen dyke atween him an Shinnies.' (T)

LANG ALE: Lemonade, ginger-beer or American cream soda. Perhaps it was the shape of the bottle that gave these soft drinks the name. (T)

LANG EE: Long eye; attraction for. 'Jessie hid a lang ee at big Tam.' (T)

LANG-HEIDIT: Long-headed; intelligent; enterprising; experienced. 'He's a lang-heidit chiel, Birnie, and he disna mak the same mistake twice. His heid is screwed on the richt wye.' **LANG-LEGGIT:** Long-legged. **LANG-NIBBIT:** Long-nosed; nosey; prying. (T)

LANG WESKIT: The long waistcoat. Literally a leg-pull or trying to take advantage of a situation. 'Ye're tryin on the lang weskit wi me noo, Tam.' Meaning that Tam was trying to make the speaker believe something that wasn't true and that by wearing the lang weskit figuratively, like the robe of a judge or the frock of a priest, he was in some position of authority. (T)

LANGER: Langour. 'Tae keep ye oot o langer.' To keep you from being bored.

'It's fine to hae a jobbie in the hoose at nicht tae keep ye oot o langer.' (B)

LANGSOME: Wearisome; monotonous. 'A gey langsome job wi twal-oor shifts.'
THINK LANG: To long for. 'I'm thinkin lang for hame, noo.' (B)

LANTER'T: Left in the lurch. 'Jeannie's lanter't wi the bairns noo, since yon tink o a man ran an left her.' (B)

LAPPER: To freeze. (T)

LAPPER'T: Clotted. Lapper't cream or soured milk. Clotted cream. 'The bailie's cat's surely been amon the lapper't cream, Jessie. Jist hae a gweed look at her fuskers!' (T)

LARRICK: Larch; a larch wood. 'There's naething better than a larrick post if ye wunt a gweed pailin. A bittie dearer mebbe, bit they're worth it. Inverlestin ye mith say an they fair hud a stepple.' (T)

LATCH: A door fastener. (T)

LATCHIE: Late. 'Ye're latchie iss mornin, Ivan. Did ye faa asleep again efter the alarm an miss the bus?' (T)

LATTEN: Allowed; given permission. 'I wisna latten tae the dunce, I hid tae bide at hame.' **LATTEN BE:** Left alone. 'Sorrie wid behave imsell aaricht if he wis latten be, bit they're aye tirmintin at im. Fit else cwid ye expeck fin he hiz in a dram?' **LATTIT BE or LAT IT BE:** Let it alone or leave it alone, but 'Lattit be' has an undertone of 'Let sleepin dogs lie!' or some such sterner language. (T)

LAUCH: A laugh; to laugh. **LEUCH:** Laughed. 'The quines leuch at Geordie, peer orra-like thing.' (B)

LAVE: The remainder. 'Ye dinna hae tae sup aa that broth if ye're nae able for't, I'll throw oot the lave o't.' And there is the title of the old Scots song 'Whustle Owre the Lave o't!' There is also the lavin-pan, a bowl-shaped zinc or tin pan with a handle for 'lavin (scooping) watter oot o the biler in the washin hoose', but it was a handy little pan with many other uses. (T)

LEADING-IN: Carting home the sheaves at harvest time. Now discontinued with the advent of the combine harvester. (T)

LEAL-LOVED: Well-loved. (T)

LEAN-TEE: A lean-to shed; a shed or hut of three walls using the wall of a house as the fourth wall with an outward sloping roof. 'Na na, I couldna affoord a richt hen-hoose so I jist biggit a lean-tee shed wi backs (bark fringed boarding) and sheet iron at the back o the hoose.' (T)

LEAR: Learning; education. (T)

LEDDER: Leather. 'Ledder beets an pints.' Leather boots and laces. **LEDDERIN:** A leathering; a thrashing. A ladder is also pronounced 'ledder' in Buchan. (T)

LEE SHORE: A shoreline which provides no shelter because the wind is blowing directly on to it. **WEATHER SHORE:** A shore which provides splendid shelter, because the wind is blowing off-shore. Do not anchor too close to a weather shore; it may be a lee shore by morning. (B)

LEEAR: A liar. 'Ye canna believe a word, he's jist a leear!' **LEEIN:** Lying. (T)

LEEFULANE, LEEFULLANE or LEEFALEEN: Quite alone; isolated; on your own. 'Aa his leefulane for a hale oor or the bobbies cam tae lat im oot. He'd been ower lang in the loo an wis lockit intae the pitch efter the match wis by.' (T)

LEEPY: A dry measure of crushed oats for horses. A small, home-made, square, wooden box was made to hold around four or five pounds of oats and kept in the stable corn-kist for convenience. 'Jist gie the new mere a half leepy o corn, Jimmy. She's a bit kittle in the yoke, so we'll keep er short a filie.' (T)

LEERUP: A skelp or smack. A sharp blow from an unexpected source. 'Michty Eke, the factor got an affa leerup fin he stood on the gairden rake. It fairly gart his een watter or he cam tull imsel an I thocht he wis gyaan tae greet.' (T)

LEETHE: 'I'll get intae the park in the leethe o ye.' I'll gain admission through your influence. (B) **LEETHE SIDE:** The sheltered side of a dyke, bush etc. (T)

LEFTS AN RICHTS: A soup made from neeps an tatties, boiled with a marrow bone or boiling beef. Very nice too. In the days of the big families, sheer economics decreed that dinners be 'supping' dinners, meat being a luxury. (B)

LEN: A loan or to loan. 'Aal Lumlie socht a len o ma puddick (heavy sledge) tae haul steens aff his clean-lan park (after turnips) an he forgot tae geest (give it) back. The neist time I saw ma puddick it wis for sale at Lumlie's roup an I wis a bittie timpit tae pit in a bid for't tae buy back ma ain. Bit ach, I jist leet im gyang wee't!' (T)

LEYS: Grassy fields. (T)

LIAR: Lawyer. 'Keep clear o the liars, my loon, or ye'll be reetit aathegither.' Note: An actual liar is a 'leear'. (B)

LICHTLIFY: To treat lightly. (T)

LICHTSOME: Lightsome; flimsy. 'Aat's an affa lichtsome jaicket for a caal wintry day. Ye'll get yer daith o caal.' (T)

LICK: The word lick has two meanings in Buchan, and while it still has relevance to the tongue, like 'coo's lick' and 'saat lick', it can also be used to indicate speed, or terrific speed, when prefixed with the superlative 'gey'. Therefore, a 'gey lick', means faster than ever. **A LICKIN:** A thrashing for some childish misdeed. (T)

LIFT: The sky. 'The lift's a bleeze.' The sky is ablaze. (T)

LIKE: The word like is sometimes added at the end of a question or sentence where a reply is requested to confirm what has been stated. 'So ye're gaan tae cottar, like?' which is as much a statement as a question but needs confirmation from the recipient. 'So ye'll be gettin merrite, like?' If suicide was suspected the question might be 'So ye wid jump in the herbour, like?' or 'slide doon a kirk reef (roof), like?' or 'jump aff a cliff, like?' And it is hoped that by this time, like it or not, the listener would have changed his mind. (T)

LIMMER: A bold, unmannerly young woman. 'Yon receptionist deem's a brazen limmer. It's a winner she keeps her job.' (B)

LINGEL: Length. 'Aat's an affa lingel o string tae tie a wee parcel!' (T)

LINNER or LINDER: A flannel sark (shirt) with the dubious virtue of being capable of absorbing sweat. 'Fin he taks his briks doon, the tail o's linner flaps like a flag.' (B)

LINTIE: A linnet. Some of the old fishermen would have a lintie in a cage. 'A bonny singer, yon lass. Jist like a lintie.' (B)

LIPPEN: To trust. 'I widna lippen tae yon chiel. He'll lat ye doon.' (B)
LIPPEN: Brimming. 'A lippen peel.' A brimming pool. (T)

LIRK: To crease. 'His briks (trousers) wiz lirkit up his legs like Nora Batty's stockins.' (T)

LITTLE BAILIE: On the bigger farms there were two cattlemen or bailies: the heid bailie who was in charge of the fattening cattle; and the second or little bailie, who might have been a loon or a haflin, and was responsible for the younger or store cattle until they reached the fattening stage. The story is told of the farmer who was showing the gentleman stranger round the steading when out from a door and over the close goes a great strapping chiel, a handsome six-footer by any standards. 'By Jove,' said the stranger, 'but that's a fine figure of a man. Who might he be?' The farmer listened to the iron heels of the lad on the causey stones and he says, 'Man, that's oor little bailie!' 'Good heavens!' the stranger gasped,

'If that's your small cattleman I should certainly like to see the big one!' (T)

LITTLIN: A little one; a baby; a small child. 'Hud the littlin, Jock, or I get pooder for his doup.' (T)

LIV: The palm of the hand. 'If ee hud at hairy wullie in the liv o yer han or I coont ten I'll gie ye a saxpence tae yersel.' (T)

LIVERING: A shot (catch) of herring was never discharged or landed. It was always 'livered'. In the boat's hold two crew members filled the herring into baskets using scoops or sheils. The baskets were then hoisted ashore, one at a time and emptied into wooden kits, one basket to the kit. As the herring were being 'cowpit' into the kits, they received a liberal dose of salt. The kits were made by local coopers. The baskets were stoutly made to a fixed pattern, and each was branded with the Crown brand of the Fishery Office. A level basket was reckoned to weigh seven stone, so if four baskets made a cran, a cran would be twenty eight stone. That is three and a half hundredweights. I know nothing about kilos. A rough and ready guide was to reckon five cran to the ton. The baskets were never level, always full and running over. (B)

LIVROCK: The laverock. (T)

LODESTEEN: A magnet. (T)

LOE: To love. (T)

LOO-WARM: Luke-warm. 'Gie's a suppie loo-warm watter in a basin, Netta, tae wash the bairn's face.' (T)

LOON: A boy. 'He's a gweed loon at, he'll ging a lang road.' He's a good boy that, he'll go far. (T)

LOOT: To let. 'Loot the cat oot for the nicht, Wullie.' (T)

LOSHTIE BE HERE! An exclamation of surprise. (T)

LOSS: To lose. 'Pit at thermis flask in yer piece-bag, Hosie, or ye'll loss it on the road.' (T)

LOUP: To leap or jump over something. 'Jessie loupit the dubs tae keep her feet dry.' (T)

LOUR: To become cloudy and darken. 'I dinna like at lourin cloods aa roon the eesin (in this case horizon) Pheelip, I doot we'll get rain.' There is also Lourin Fair, held annually at Old Rayne in the Garioch. (T)

LOW DOOR: Nothing to do with the height of the door itself, it simply means an entrance at ground level. (T)

LOWES: Flames of fire. **LOWEIN:** Glowing. To 'sweer blue lowes', to swear vehemently, loud and long. (B)

LOWN: Mild. (T)

LOWRIE: A long, heavy, steel hook for handling heavy fish, or for dragging boxes of fish along the market floor. (B)

LOWSE: To unfasten, as of a rope. **LOWSIN TIME:** Time to stop work. 'It's time tae lowse, lads, it's five o'clock.' (B)

LOWSIN SHOOER or LOUSIN SHOOER: A heavy shower of rain that was likely to put a stop to all outdoor work on the farm. But as the old hard-bitten grieve used to say, 'It'll tak a gey shooer tae lowse me, laddie!' Which meant he would persist in the rain (unless he was harvesting or hay-making) and he was blamed for 'puddlin his men', who were nicknamed 'The coated regiment', because they were working in the fields on days that were only fit for 'deuks an mullarts' (ducks and millers) providing a puddle for the ducks and water for the miller's wheel. (T)

LOWSS: Loose; suffering from diarrhoea. (B)

LUCK PENNY: A discount. 'That's an affa price tae pey for a cassette player, Bessie, I hope ye got a luck penny wee't!' 'Dinna be daft, it's on tick! Ye dinna get luck pennies on the hire purchase, it's jist sometimes if ye pey cash.' (T)

LUCKY: The old fisher term for 'granny'. 'Come to Lucky's bose, my quine, an tell her fit's wrang.' (B)

LUIT or LEIT: To give permission or consent. 'Knowie luit the foreman gyang tae the market tho he wiz bidin on again.' 'Lizzie leit the quine awaa hame afore dark kiz she hidna a licht on her bike.' (T)

LUM: A chimney. Putting a sod or divot on the lum to smoke someone out of his hovel was a favourite splore or prank in the old days. (T)

LUMP OF WATER: A great mass of water, usually the top of a breaking sea, which comes charging on board with tremendous weight and awesome force, sweeping all before it. This is the fisher's worst enemy. (B)

LUMPERS: Fish porters; workers who handle fish on the market floor. (B)

LUMPHANAN: A village on Deeside where MacBeth is said to have taken refuge in a house with a fallen chimney. Hence the name, 'Lum-fan-in'. (T)

LUNTREN: A lantern; a byre or stable lamp. 'Ye'll hae tae pit paraffin in the byre luntrens, quine, an clean the glesses.' **LUNTREN CHAFTIT:** Lantern faced; horse faced; long-jawed. Could even refer to a face with high cheek bones. (T)

LYING HOLES: Patches of corn or barley flattened by heavy rain and liable to choke the binder. It had to be cut by scythe and bound by hand. (T)

LYKIE DOON: A little lie down; a short nap. 'I like a lykie doon efter my denner on a Sunday.' (B)

LYTERIN: Loitering. 'Tak langer strides, min, ye're lyterin.' (T)

LYTHE: Shelter. (T)

MA LEEN: Alone. 'I'll ging tae the toon ma leen.'(T)

MAA or MYAAVE: The common gull is known by several names which differ from port to port in Buchan. Buckie: A gow. Gardenstown: A pule. Fraserburgh: A myaave. Peterhead: A skurry. (B)

MAASIE: A jersey. This term for the fisher 'ganjie' is from the Macduff/Whitehills area. (B)

MAGGIE RENNIE: 'A different Maggie Rennie.' A different kettle of fish. 'Ye'll hear folk complainin aboot the siller the fishers are gettin. If they were at the job themsels, 'twid be a different Maggie Rennie.' (B)

MAIK: A half-penny. **MAIKST:** A half-penny worth. 'A maik for a woodbine? That's profiteerin, surely.' **MAIK WATCH:** A half-penny watch. 'She's gey smaa beukit (slightly built) yon quinie. Her facie's like a maik watch.' (B)

MAINS O BACKCHINES: Mains of Backchains was a fictitious fairmtoon invented to discredit a haflin (teenager) and take him down to size if he got a bit larky and dared to put his thumbs in his armpits after getting a fee in the market. Some bogie-chewing heavy was sure to collar him and remark 'Aye aye, laddie, so ye're gaan hame tae Mains o Backchines tae riddle hens' dirt', which usually took the puff out of the youngster's sails and left him completely adrift. Some of the bigger farms had a reputation of superiority and being asked to engage with one of these was really a feather in your cap and no one would dare to question your enhancement. A Laird's Toon or Home Farm for instance, as compared with a one-pair croft (two-horse farm) was considered to be of some standing, or one that had a smoke stack or a reputable name in the district, or where the farmer had a motor car; anything was preferable to the common 'Acht (eight) day place', where you were supposed to work an extra day a week, which would certainly earn you the title of being the foreman at Mains o Backchines. Wages were also important, and 'big toon – big siller' didn't always comply, but at least pride of place would raise you above the level of ridicule. The backchain was used in the saddle crup to carry the shafts in a horse cart. (T)

MAIR: More. 'Mair than likely.' More than likely; almost assured. 'Mair than likely we'll get a batter o rain efter yon fite frost, it's gieinafen (mostly) the wye o't. (T)

MAIST or MAISTLY: Most or mostly. 'Maist o folk wis throwe wi the hyow (hoe) jist afore Aikey Fair.' 'It's maistly aaler folk on this side o the street.' (T)

MAIT: Food in general, not meat precisely. On some Buchan farms you could nearly tell the season of the year or the day of the week by your diet. Yaval broth on Monday (left over from Sunday) and a helping of boiled, cold beef and dumpling from the same source. Tuesday, tatties and skirlie; Wednesday, lentil soup; Thursday, chappit-tatties and size (chives); Friday, tattie soup; Saturday, stovies, and Sunday back to barley broth again. Dessert was usually semolina or cremola, rice, sago or sago and rhubarb or milk and breid (oat cakes), yerned milk or new cheese if a cow had calved. Tea or supper as we called it, was usually porridge or milk brose (oatmeal brose made with boiling milk instead of water), kale or cabbage brose, neep brose, milk broth, and peasmeal brose. At antrin times ye got kippers or yalla fish or sausages, saat herrin an peal-an-ate tatties, hairy-tatties (hard, dried fish, boiled and mixed with chappit tatties and mustard sauce), mealy dumplin, boiled or fried eggs (hen and duck), the odd stewed rabbit or hare, loaf, scones and bannocks, butter or margarine and plenty of tea or skimmed milk. Breakfast never varied, brose every morning but on some farms porridge on a Sunday morning and jam instead of treacle for your bread. Meat was the scarcest item on the menu. There were certain farms where the mistress endeavoured as far as possible, to feed the single men on what grew on the farm. There was Elsie Wabster at the Dookit Fairm for instance. 'Feed the men on what grows on the place', that was Elsie's motto. Self-sufficiency, and but for a few triflin thingies, like saat, spice, sugar and treacle, Elsie's scheme was verra nearly fool-proof. Dyod aye, gin there had been a troot in the mill-dam as there were hares in the parks, Elsie had naethin tae learn aboot feedin the five thoosan. Spik aboot a Shepherd's Calendar! – a Bothy Calendar wis nearer the mark. Elsie had a menu tae beat aa! In the simmer fin the eggs were cheap she preserved them in waterglass, and ye ate them in the winter fin the fresh eggs were dearer tae sell. That left mair fresh eggs tae sell at the richt time. Dyod aye, and when the butter wisna sellin she made saat butter, an ye got that and margarine when the price rose again. Sell butter and buy margarine, sound economics in those days when the price wis sae muckle agley. And Elsie laid the table hersel, tae mak sure the men didna get ower muckle, a wee bittie o butter aboot the size o yer thoom-nail, a wee ballie or twaa that wisna near aneuch; and the jam wis the same, a wee spoonfae that wad hardly stick a flea, and ye nivver saw the honey, na faith ye, that gaed intae the sale o work in the kirk hall or ben the hoose.' (T)

MAITHES: Maggots. 'The maithes wis workin aa roon aboot the lammie's backside.' (T)

MAK A BAN: Make a band of straw for binding a sheaf. Deftly and swiftly done by twisting two strands together at the ears end of the stalks. The 'Yankee Band', supposed to be an American method, was the slickest of them all, done in an instant by splitting the strand at the ears and throwing one half of it over the forearm. It required slow motion for the learner to follow. (T)

MAK DOON: Make down; to alter an adult garment to fit a youngster. 'Mak doon a frock o yer ain, wuman, for een tae fit the quine.' (T)

MAK NOR BRAK: Make nor break; neither help nor hinder. 'The price o the yowie (ewe) wunna mak nor brak ye, Soldie.' Not of any great consequence one way or the other and not likely to cause bankruptcy. (T)

MAK ON: To pretend. 'He's nae sleepin, ye ken, he's only makkin on.' (B)
MAKKIN ON: Getting older. 'Aal Wullie's fairly makkin on. Eighty-fower his nixt birthday.' (T)

MAK SICCAR: To make sure. This announcement was immortalised by Sir John Kirkpatrick, a supporter and friend of Robert the Bruce after the future King of Scotland stabbed the Red Comyn in the church in Dumfries in 1306. Emerging from the kirk, Bruce sheathed his dagger and said, 'I doubt I've slain the Comyn!' On hearing this, Kirkpatrick said, 'I'll mak siccar!' and with dagger in hand went into the kirk and finished off the dying Comyn. (T)

MALAGROOSE: To injure or administer severe punishment. 'I could malagroose yon game-keeper chiel for takin ma cat in a snare.' (T)

MALLIE: The fulmar, which nests on cliffs at Peterhead but lives far from land. Should it inadvertently land on a boat's deck, it is immediately sick, and cannot take off without assistance. (B)

MANEER: A manoeuvre; a fuss. 'Fancy her huddin sic a maneer aboot naething. I nivver haard the like.' (B)

MANGIN ('g' as in 'hangin'): Longing desperately for something. 'I'm jist mangin for a saat herrin. I hinna seen een for years!' (B)

MANT: To stammer. Other variants are stutter or hubber. 'He's a hubberin brute, Bendie. Ye wid files think he wis gyaan tae choke on the wirds, he's got sic a mant.' (T)

MARL'T: Mottled; blotched; variegated. 'Her stockins wir that thin ye could see her marl't legs throwe them.' (T)

104

MARLESS SHEEN: Unmatching sizes in shoes. The farmer's son who had to go to school wearing his mother's shoes while his own were being repaired, remarked, 'Ye've nivver haen tae dee that, hiv ye? Ging tae the skweel wi yer mither's sheen on? I wis near greetin aboot it in front o aa the ither loons, and then I saw anither lad wi his mither's sheen on, and then I didna feel sae bad. At least my mither's sheen werna marless.' (T)

MARRA: A match; an equal. 'Aye, my loon, ye fairly met yer marra the day!' (B)

MARRIT: The Peterhead name for the Guillemot. (B)

MARTINGALE: A nickle-plated harness decoration worn on a leather strap. Similar to the Rosette. (T)

MASELLY: Myself. (T)

MASK: A single mesh in a net. 'That net's ower nairra in the mask. Ye'll get the jile.' Also 'Mask the taypot.' Infuse the tea. (B)

MAUN: Must. **MAUNNA:** Must not. 'Ye maunna claa yer doup, loon. It's nae nice.' (T)

MEAL AND ALE: A Harvest Home celebration, originally named after the oatmeal and corn husk used in the fermentation of sowens, a porridge and liquor preparation partaken during the festivities. (T)

MEALICK: A crumb of bread or oatcakes. 'Mither dichtit a mealick aff o fadder's waistcoat afore they gaed awaa tae the kirk, bit a kirk moose wid a been gled o't in a pew!' (T)

MEASLEY: Greedy; tight-fisted; grudging. 'He's a measley hun, Cowie. Fin the foreman tore his new waldies wi pikeit weir Cowie gid im an aal deen pair baith for the same fit. At's nae muckle eese til a body.' (T)

MEGGINS ALIVE! An exclamation of surprise. (B)

MEEN: The moon. **MEENLICHT FLITTIN or MEENLICHTY FLITTIN:** A moonlight flitting; a flitting in the dead of night. 'Oh, the Braxie folk jist took a meenlichty flittin. Naebody kens far they gaed; bit ah think they wid a been affa in debt aa roon aboot.' (T)

MEER: A moor or muir. (B)

MEET THE CAT: To undergo a spell of bad luck.

I'm thinkin that we've met the cat.
She's surely been a bummer.
At scalders, dogs, an bare black yarn
I've teen a proper scunner. (B)

MEEVE: To move. 'Meeve ower a bit, min, I hinna room tae meeve. I'm like a sassige in a sanwich.' (T)

MEGGIE MONYFEET: A centipede. 'If at lad wis a fitballer, he wid hae somethin adee tae change aa that beets (boots)!' (T)

MENEER: A fuss. (T)

MERCH BOUNDARY FENCE: The march fence, dyke, hedge or ditch dividing or separating one farm from another. Sometimes there are double fences and every farm has strict geographical boundaries. (T)

MERE: A mare. When Jamie Fleeman (the Laird of Udny's fool) met the minister one day, Jamie was carrying a horse-shoe. Holding up the shoe in passing, Jamie asked the minister if he knew what it was. 'Of course I know what it is, you fool. It's a horse-shoe!' 'Oh!' Jamie sighed, smiling gleefully in the minister's face. 'Ae! Sic a blessin as it is to be weel learned! I couldna tell if it was a horse's shoe or a mere's ane!' (T)

MERRY DANCERS or NORTHERN LIGHTS: The Aurora Borealis in the northern hemisphere. 'It's the sun shinin on the ice-bergs in Greenland.' That was what the old folk in Buchan thought, but now we know that the phenomena is caused by eruptions or explosions in the sun and that the debris or minutae is attracted to the earth's poles and becomes fluorescent in the sun's rays. 'The Northern Lights of Old Aberdeen' was the song composed by the late Mary Webb of London and popularised by the voice of Robert Wilson. (T)

MIDDEN: A tip for cattle excrement. **MIDDEN BREE:** Moisture drained from the midden. **MIDDEN PLUNK:** This was a strong wooden plank which enabled the cattlemen to wheel a barrow-load of dung from the byre onto the midden or into the loose cattle court. 'The midden plunk's a bit slippery this mornin, efter the frost, Jeck. Ye'll hae tae throw a pucklie san on't tae hud yer feet.' (T)

MIDDER: Mother. Mither is more common nowadays and the old-fashioned Mammy is seldom heard. Mither is synonymous with the best in everything in contrast to the masculine gender: the Mither Tongue, the Mither Tap (Bennachie) and Saddam Hussein recently enlisted her emblematic hierarchy for his 'Mither of all Battles' which never materialised. (T)

MIDDLIN: Of doubtful quality. 'A gey middlin kind o chiel, yon.' **MIDDLIN:** Meddling. 'Middlin in ither folk's affairs.' (B)

MIDGICK: The Scots midge or midgie, which has such a sharp bite. (T)

MIDS: Half-way; in moderation. (T)

MILDYOW: Mildew. (T)

MILKERS: Milk cows. (T)

MILKIE: The milkman, just as the postman is the postie. (B)

MINT: Meant; intended; aimed. 'Aye, Michael, bit Doddie nivver mint tae knock doon the dyke; it wis the tree he wis cuttin doon that fell on't.' (T)

MINITY: A minute. 'You bide here, Erchie. I'll be back in a minity.' (T)

MIM-MOUED: Tight-mouthed; prim or shy in speech; restrained in manner or behaviour and seemingly afraid to speak out; reserved and shy in company and most notable in the fair sex. Similar to the English 'mealy-mouthed' apothegm which lacks the pursed mouth physical almost visual impression of the Buchan words where we can picture the fastidious creature primping over her food with fork and knife in the search for the pearl in her oyster. 'A mim-moued sparra yon, ye wid think butter widna melt on er chiks (cheeks).' (T)

MIRKY or MIRKIE: Merry; bright and breezy; cheerful. 'A gey mirky lad Sanders, aye in gran yumour.' (T)

MIRRLES: The measles. Always 'the' mirrles.

> In coorse o time,
> Like ither folk,
> The aal man met his death.
> Some say it wis the mirrles,
> But I think 'twis want o breath. (B)

MISCA: To miscall, slander, scandalize, speak ill of, like the local minister who upbraided Jamie Fleeman with a remark on his vagrancy, and was rebuked by Jamie's biting retort: 'Ah weel, Reverend, but I dinna hae tae misca the deevil tae mak a livin!' Which we may assume put the minister in his place, and may have given him a new slant on religion. (T)

MISCOMFITTIT: Upset; annoyed; angered. 'Ernie miscomfittit Dites wi yon fule story. He hisna been the same since!' (T)

MISHAACHL'T: Deformed; ill-shaped. 'The peer loon canna help bein mishaachl't. He wis born that wye.' (B)

MISHANTER: A mishap, accident or disaster. 'Yon's a gey mishanter that Toby Baird hid wi his car. It furl't roon on the icy road an hit a tree an coupit Toby intae a ditch.' (T)

MISTEEN: Mistaken; mistook. 'I misteen a burry for a meikle thistle an nearly broke ma scythe.' (T)

MITH: Might. 'Ye mith a tellt me ye wis gaan tae the roup, Morgan. I wid a gaen wi ye.' (T)

MITHER or MIDDER: Mother. **MITHER TONGUE:** Mother tongue; native language. (T) **MITHER WIT:** Plain common sense. 'He's maybe nae affa clivver, but he has plinty o mither wit, an maybe that's better than bein clivver.' (B)

MITHNA: Might not. (T)

MITTEN: To grab something in an unmannerly way. 'He mittened the packet afore onybody else could get a chance.' (B)

MIZZEN: The sail at the rear end of a boat. The mizzen was an essential in the days of drift-net fishing. It kept the ship head to wind while lying at the nets, and acted as a sort of rudder during the hauling process. It was a great asset in stormy weather, keeping the ship's head to the gale, while the engine kept turning 'slow ahead'. There was no need to touch the helm at all. Modern boats don't have mizzens, but it is my humble opinion that they would be all the better to have them. But, you see, the place which a mizzen would occupy is taken up with hydraulic power-blocks and the like. It is interesting to note that with the disappearance of the mizzen, at least ten words have also disappeared; e.g. the yard, the boom, the sheets, the hylerts (halliards), the peak, the throat, the parles, the toppin-lift, the doon-haul and the oot-haul. (B)

MOCH-AETIN: Moth-eaten. 'Oh mercy, my best briks an they're aa moch-aetin!' (T)

MOCHIE or MUGGLIE WIDDER: Drizzen, foggy weather. 'Gey mochie widder, Paul!' 'Aye, man, ye could ging doon tae the sea an get lost in the fog and nivver be miss't!' (T)

MOLESKINS: Trousers of thick cotton. (T)

MOO-BAG: A mouth bag for horses, mostly of canvas or leather and slung over the head behind the ears on a strap and usually containing crushed oats and bran or maize. A lady's handbag is sometimes called her 'moo-bag' because it contains her lipstick. (T)

MOOCH: To scrounge; to obtain by stealth, cunning or flattery. 'Dites wis weel kent for moochin a drink at the bar.' (T)

MOOSE WOB: A spider's web. 'Tak the lang shaftit brush, quinie, an knock doon that moose wob in the crap o the waa.' (T)

MOOSIE'S LUG: A mouse's ear. 'Nedderton maistly aye startit the hyowe (turnip hoeing) as seen as the leaves on the plants were the size o a moosie's lug. An startin at that early stage maks sure they (the crop) dinna get the better o ye.' It makes sure that you can keep up with the speed of growth in the plants, which means easier hoeing. (T)

MORTAL: Alive; living. In Buchan it is used comprehensively, 'Aa mortal thing.' 'There's aa mortal thing in iss shop, aa that a body wid be needin.' (T)

MOTE: A tiny speck. 'A mote in the meen', a slight imperfection in an otherwise perfect scene i.e. something seen by nit-pickers. 'Ye say ye nivver saw me? Weel, I'm sure I'm nae a mote!' (B)

MOU or MOO: Mouth. 'Netta nivver open't her mou bit she pat her fit in't.' Netta spoke at random, without much thought, and sometimes annoyed or embarrassed folk. She was outspoken without realising it and a lot of people avoided her company, unless they wanted to hear the latest gossip, for she was a walking, talking scandal sheet. Quite the opposite of Netta would be someone who was 'mealy-moued', or smooth of tongue and reluctant to give offence or hurt anyone's feelings, the modest condescending type who is always anxious to keep the peace almost at any price. **MOU O HAIRST:** The mouth of harvest; on the verge of harvest, the corn ripe and ready to start. 'Ready tae redd roads roon the corn parks.' Ready to scythe a swath round the corn fields as a path for the binders. The combine harvester cuts its own way round the fields. (T) **MOUFAE:** A mouthful. (B)

MOUDIEWARP: A mole. (T)

MOWSE: Safe; reliable; believeable. (B)

MOWSER: A moustache. (T)

MUCK: Dung. (T) **MUCK THE LINE:** To remove from the hooks of a baited line, the bait which has become putrid while waiting for the weather to abate. Not a pleasant job. (B)

MUCKLE: Large; much. **MUCKLE FURTH:** The great outdoors. (T)

MULDOON or MULDOAN: The basking shark which could wreck such havoc among herring nets. These creatures would utterly destroy a fleet of nets by swimming through them, in and out, like a skier doing the slalom. Some of the old fishermen thought that it was to rid their bodies of lice that the beasts behaved like this. (B)

MULL: A meal mill or threshing mill. 'I wid like a drink o lang ale (lemonade) mither!' 'Ach, geet (child), ye can tak a drink o watter. It's gey strong stuff an caa's (drives) Newton's Mull.' 'Charlie's been throwe the mull; he kens fut it is tae live!' Meaning that Charlie has had his share of troubles and knows what existence is all about. Mull can also mean a tin-can or canister or a container for snuff a 'snuff mull', or matches, a 'spunk mull', or 'jist an aal roosty mull', a rusty tin-can that wee Jockie was kicking down the street, although you wouldn't say nowadays that 'wee Jockie was kickin a mull doon the street' in the belief that it was a threshing mull, nor would you talk about a 'mull o beans' or a 'mull o soup' in the supermarket. (T)

MULLERT or MULLART: A miller; a corn grinder. When the Laird of Waterton speired at Jamie Fleeman where he could safely cross the Ythan river on horseback, Jamie directed him to the deepest pool in the area, where the Laird plunged in and was soon up to the waist in water. He clambered up the opposite bank where Jamie was waiting. The Laird was soaked and furious. 'You damned fool,' he cried, 'I could have drowned in there, just wait until I see your master.' But Jamie knew there was no love lost between Udny and Waterton and he calmly replied, 'Weel Sir, I've seen the mullert's deuks (ducks) cross there hunners o times an I thocht your horse hid langer legs than them.' (T)

MUMMLE: To mumble. 'Spik oot, min – fit are ye mumlin aboot?' (T)

MURLIN: A basket made to fit precisely into the top of the fish-wife's creel. This served as an extension to the creel so that a bigger load might be carried (e.g. peats), but the main purpose for the murlin was to provide a space wherein the 'trock' (butter, eggs, cheese etc. which were really barter) might be kept separate from the fish. 'And muckle luck attend the boat, the murlin and the creel.' (B)

MYAAKIN: A hare. (T)

MYOWE: To mew. 'The cat wis myowin at the door tae get in.' (T)

MYOWT: A sound. 'Nae a myowt.' Not a sound, not a whisper, especially of complaint or protest. 'And yer bairns, Mrs. Lunan, are they asleep as weel?' 'Aye they are that. I beddit them aa doon and I hinna heard a myowt fae them since then.' (T)

NAB: To grab, snatch or grasp very quickly. Perhaps the word is best described in the last verse of 'The Puddock' (a frog or toad) by J M Caie.

> A heron was hungry an needin tae sup,
> Sae he nabbit the puddock and gollup't him up;

Syne runkled his feathers; 'A peer thing', quo' he,
'But puddocks is nae fat they eesed tae be.' (T)

NACK: Knack; expertise. 'Louie fairly hiz the nack o shufflin the cairds.' (T)

NACKET: A knick-knack; a miniature ornament; tidy; small; compact; neat. 'That's a richt nacket o a thing. It'll look fine in yer cheena cabinet.' (T)

NACKETS: Small children. (B)

NAE or NA: An almost negative 'No' and sometimes both can be used in the same expression like 'Na, ye're nae are ye?' When the incomer novice installed himself in a Buchan croft he had occasion to visit the local garage. Trying to be polite and hoping to impress the mechanic he announced his presence with 'I'm Mr Throgmorton from Rora!' The busy mechanic, taken by surprise and at a loss for words retorted: 'Na, ye're nae are ye?' in a riot of derisive laughter from the village standabouts. For months afterwards they greeted each other and the mechanic with a mocking, 'Na, ye're nae are ye?' and several announced themselves as 'Mr Throgmorton!' But it taught that gentleman to be somewhat less pompous in his approach to the Buchan laity. (T) The word is very often used in the double negative. 'I hinna been weel iss fyle.' 'Foo lang hiv ye been nae weel?' 'I hinna been weel since I saw ye last.' 'Oor Davy's been the same. Jist nae neen weel avaa.' 'Wid it be aal age, think ye?' 'Weel, if it's aal age, he'll seen get the back o that!' (B)

NAE AHIN TIME: A very common misuse of 'Not before time.' 'The pension's gaan up, did ye say? Weel, it's nae ahin time.' (B)

NAE BAD!: Not bad! 'Nae sae bad avaa!' Not so bad at all! Certainly not constructive criticism. 'Nae bad!' is perhaps the most commonly used expression in the everyday Buchan dialect. It is an evasive negative criterion that is non-committal in conversation and serves its purpose in the dour nature of Buchan word economy in any given circumstance. A favourite instance is the opinion of Aberdeen expressed by the earth-bound farm worker who had gone to the city by train and was asked next day what he thought of it. 'Oh nae bad,' says he, 'a gey place, but aa covered wi gless,' indicating the fact that he hadn't found his way out of the railway station. And the inevitable: 'Aye aye, fit like?' 'Oh nae sae bad, foo's yersel?' (T)

NAE GREAT DELL: No great deal; not up to much and might refer to dealings with others. 'Na, the concert wis nae great dell.' or 'Na na, Fiddes made the hood (cab) for yer tractor. It's nae great dell; it'll seen faa tae bits an ye'll be losing it on the road. Naething tae hud it thegither, min. Nae great dell a wyte!' **NAE UP TAE MUCKLE:** Another variation of the same. (T)

NAE GURR: No energy, drive or spirit. 'I've nae gurr aboot me, doctor, I'm fooshionless!' And the mannie understood. Gurr could also apply to the angle of the bonnet, a bit to one side, and a sharper tilt might be greeted with, 'An affa gurr in yer bonnet the day, Jock. Fit's up? Awaa tae the tug-o-war or something?' (T)

NAE MISSIN NAETHING: Not missing anything. 'Hiv ye nivver tasted oor cook's Irish stew? Weel, ye're nae missin naething.' (B)

NAE MOWSE: Risky; uncanny, even dangerous. The modern phrase would be 'It's nae real!' 'We ran the Pentland Firth in the dark o a richt coorse nicht. Good grief, boys, yon wis jist nae mowse!' (B)

NAE NICE: Not nice; rather vulgar. 'He's nae nice, yon lad, aye tellin fule (dirty) stories.' (B)

NAE NOTT: Not required. (T)

NAETHIN: Nothing. 'Nae naethin?' Not anything? 'No, nae naethin avaa.' No, nothing at all. (T)

NAEWYE: Nowhere. 'I lookit aawye for Pam, bit she wis naewye tae be seen. She could a been in the loo mind ye, bit I couldna ging in there lookin for her, naewye – fit div ye tak me for – a secks meniyack?' (T)

NAITER: Nature. (B)

NAMMLE: Enamel. Nobody would say 'An enamel pan.' 'A nammle pan' is better. (B)

NAPHTIE: Strong drink. 'He's ower fond o the naphtie for yon lassie tae look at him.' (B)

> **Ode tae a Dram.**
> Get awaa fae me I hate ye,
> Come back tae me I love ye,
> For aft ye've made me pawn my claes,
> And aft ye've made my freens my faes,
> But seein ye're sae near my nose,
> Ti Hell, here goes! (T)

NAVES: Hubs. The spoked wooden hubs of farm cart wheels fashioned by the local vricht or joiner. (T)

NEAR HAN: Near hand; nearbye. 'Near aneuch han.' Near enough hand. 'Clive's near aneuch han tae be a neeper jist ower the pailin (fence). If he wis muckle nearer, I could spit in his face. Fut mair wid ye hae?' (T)

NEEBRA: The village of Newburgh on the River Ythan near Ellon. The skippers of the old cargo steamers always said: 'Neebra is in Aberdeenshire, Newburgh is in Fife.' **NEEBRA WATTER:** The Ythan estuary. (B)

NEEN: None. 'Neen the waar.' None the worse. 'Altho her feet are flat, she's neen the waar o that!' (B) 'No, nae neen avaa.' Absolutely none. 'Nae neen the wiser.' Not any the wiser. (T)

NEEP: A turnip. 'Neeps man neeps! As big as yer heid up here, nae neen o yer smaa dirt!' **NEEP LUNTRIN:** A turnip lantern. A fairly large turnip was cut in two and the flesh scraped out to the skin which was shaped on one side to form a face with eyes, nose and mouth cut out and a string attached for carrying. A candle was lit inside, and when the halves were fixed together, the face was illuminated on a dark night at Hallowe'en or All Saints Eve. (T)

NEEPER: A neighbour. 'Foo am I gettin on? Speir at my neeper – he'll ken better than me.' Also refers to the other fellow. 'If ye get neeper's fare, ye'll hae naething tae girn aboot.' Or a partner. 'If ye're thinkin aboot tryin the pair trawl, ye'll need a neeper. Ae boat canna dee the job.' **HALF NEEPER:** A close acquaintance, possibly related. (B)

NEIST: Next. 'Jock neist door has a score o cran, but yer father hisna neen.' **NEIST WIK:** Next week. (B)

NEP: Hirsute; hairy. 'If my heid wis as nep as my chest, I widna be beld.' (B)

NERRA-NECKET: Narrow or thin-necked. 'Kirriemeer ye say, a nerra-necket toonie yon. I couldna get an achteen-inch collar tae fit me in aa the toon, and the causies (streets) are jist as bad, aabody rubbin shooders tae get by among the horse beasts and their cairties and the scaffies swipein up the dirt. Aye faith, a nerra-neckit placie yon!' (T)

NEUK: A nook; a corner. (T)

NEW-FANGEL'T: Newly invented; up-to-date. 'Aa that new-fangel't machinery in the showyard, I dinna ken fit it's for, it looks like somethin oot o *Doctor Who* on the telly or somethin fae ooter space. I nivver saw naethin like yon contraption on a fairm fin I wis on the grun. I wid raither work a spaad than drive een o thon things ony day.' (T)

NEWS: To exchange news; to chat. 'The wife's been oot for a lang time. She'll be newsin wi somebody, I expect.' 'I've heen a richt fine news wi Sandy, the day.' (B) **NEWSY:** Talkative. 'Aye, aal Forbie hid aye plenty tae say an there wisna muckle gaed by him. He took taik (notice) o aathing an he hid aa his wits aboot him! Fine an newsy he wis.' (T)

NIB: A nose or beak. (B)

NICE: Fastidious; possibly prudish. 'I'm nae nice, sittin here listenin to sic language!' 'She's ower nice for oor kine o folk!' (B)

NICK: To successfully impregnate a woman. 'Donald had waited fower year for a bairn an he wis ower the meen fin Katherine laid her hands on her belly an smiled at him an he realised he had nicked her.' (T)

NICKUM: A rascal. Almost a pet name for 'rascal' and mostly used in reprimanding young loons with 'Ye wee nickum' or 'Ye're a nickum, min!' for some minor mishap and could scarcely be regarded as chastisement. (T)

NICKY-CLOOTS: The devil. (T)

NICKY-TAMS: Also known as Waal-Tams. Leather straps with buckles worn under the knee by farmworkers. These were fashionable before the days of the welly-boot and kept the trouser legs out of the mud. If an inquisitive stranger had asked a farmworker what they were for, most likely he would have replied, 'Oh jist tae keep the stue (dust) oot o my een.' But apart from decoration, they were also a symbol of manhood. (T)

NIEVES or NIVS: Fists or closed hands. The latter were sometimes used when presenting a small gift to a child to see if he or she could guess which hand contained the present. There is a four line verse which accompanies the procedure.

> Nievie nievie nick nack
> Fit han will ye tack?
> Tak een, tak twaa,
> Tak the best een o the twaa. (T)

STEEKIT NIEVES or NIVS: Clenched fists. (B)

NIP: To pinch as with the finger and thumb. 'Nip his backside, that micht waken him up.' To smart or sting: 'Yon ingins fairly maks yer een nip.' 'To get nippit', to be caught in the act. (B)

NIRL'T: Shrivelled. (T)

NIVVER EEN: Not one; not likely; most certainly not; that'll be the day! 'Fit? Me wear a kilt! Nivver een, freen, nivver een.' (B)

NOCHT: Nothing. 'Five year in the Royal Navy, aa for nocht.' (T)

NOO AN NAAN or NOOS AN ANS: Now and then, periodically. 'Oh Harold jist comes tae work here noos an ans. Ye widna think he hid a steady job. He jist

114

comes here fin he's in the yumour (humour) o comin, that's oor Harold.' (T)

NOTT: Past tense of the verb 'need' or 'require'. I nott a hurl hame. I wis that tired, so I order't a taxi. **NOTT NA:** Shouldn't have. 'Ye nott na deen at, min. I wid hae gien ye a hurl hame for naething!' You shouldn't have done that, man. I would have given you a lift home for nothing! **SAIR NOTT:** Sorely needed. (B) **NAE NOTT:** Not required. 'There's plenty helpers at the thrashin mull the day so Charlie's nae nott. But he micht be nott the morn.' (T)

NOWT: Cattle. 'A great hantle o nowt at the mart the day.' (B)

NOWTS' BINNIN: Cattle binding. A strong chain fixed to a byre stall for holding cattle by the neck. It was fitted with a swivel under the neck to prevent choking and the other end of the chain worked on a perpendicular slide fixed to the travis post, enabling the animal to move its head up and down. 'Gyang tae the smiddy, loon, for half-a-dizzen nowt's binnins an sik twaa-three split-links fae the smith. They're affa handy for mennin broken eens!' (T)

NYAAKET or NYAAKIT: Naked. 'Fancy him lyin half-nyaaket sunnin himsel on the green on a Sunday an aa the kirk folk gaan by. Some folk hiv nae affront.' (T) **BARE-NYAAKET:** Even more naked, if that's possible. (B)

NYARB: A discontented person; someone who is never satisfied. 'A nyarb o a cratur, Trudy. Nivver pleas't, aye compleenin aboot something.' (T)

NYATTER: To natter or nag. 'She's a nyattery cratur, ma brither's wife. I widna like tae hae merrite yon deem.' (T)

OCHT: Ought. 'Fit's at? Muggie Jean's loon broke his leg, did ye say? Weel, he ocht tae hae kent better than try tae jump oot o ae teem (empty) bowie intil anither een. It's a winner he didna brak baith his legs!' (T)

OCKA: Ochre. An orange or red pigment used as a mixture for painting house walls instead of using wallpaper. It rubbed off on clothing and was supplanted with a liquid mixed with size known as distemper, mostly green fast colours that couldn't be erased without water. Nowadays we use emulsion or gloss paint. (T)

OD!: An exclamation. (T)

ODDS: A difference, but with the emphasis on improvement. 'Sic an odds a lick o paint maks.' or 'A stock cube maks an odds tae yer tin o soup.' 'Dis't mak ony odds tae you?' Does it make any difference to you? 'No, nae odds avaa.' No, no difference at all. **ODDS AN ENS:** Odds and ends. (T)

OH ME!: My goodness! (T)

OILIE: A fisher's oilskin frock, made from canvas treated with linseed oil. Not very efficient and long since superseded by plastic. (B)

ONDING: A heavy and continuous fall of rain or snow. 'I nivver saw sic an onding. It's nivver devaalt the hale day.' (B)

ONGAUN: Activity. (B)

ONYWYE: Anyway. (T)

OO: Wool. **OO MULL:** A woollen mill. (B)

OOF: The Moray Firth name for a monkfish. The Buchan counterpart was 'caithick'. (B)

OOH ME!: Oh my! 'Ooh me! That's richt sair.' (B)

OOLT: Cowed. (T)

OONCHANCY: Dangerous; not safe to meddle with; unpredictable. (B)

OONSHAVEN: Unshaven. Oon in Buchan means to avoid, 'Tae hud me oondeen something' is to save or prevent me doing it. 'Tae hud me oonshaven I'll grou a baird.' or 'I'll grou a baird tae hud me oonshaven.' Oon is a sort of Buchan prefix for un. (T)

OOPIE UP: An expression used when lifting a bairn into one's arms. (B)

OOR: Hour. (T)

OORLICH: A miserable creature. (T)

OOT: Out. **OOT AHIN:** Out behind. **OOT AMON'T:** Over the top; in excess. **OOT-BYE:** Outside. **OOTCOME:** Outcome. **OOT-GAAN:** Out-going. **OOT-HOOSE:** Out-house. **OOT O HAN:** Out of hand; beyond control. 'Yon spreckil't (speckled) mere (mare) at Backhill is jist clean oot o han: the foreman his tae brob (jab) her on the nose wi a bit funn buss (whin bush) afore he can get her tae back (reverse) a load o neeps intae the shed and she jist loups oot o the cairt at lousin time. Nae eese avaa yon cairry on. She's jist oot o han.' **OOT OWER THE DOOR:** Outside the door. **OOTSIDE-IN:** Outside in or inside out. **AN OOT-IN-OOT DAY O RAIN:** Lashing down rain. (T) **OOT THE DOOR:** Facing ruin. 'If things dinna improve shortly, some o the fishers'll be oot the door.' **OOT WIN:** Wind from off the sea. 'Oot win, caal wi the threat o rain.' (B)

OOTLIN: An alien; the odd one out. One who seems to have been behind the door when the blessings were dished out. One who is never fully accepted. (B)

OOTS-AN-INS: Hair pins. 'Get a packet o oots-an-ins for oor Meg's hair.' (B)

OOTSIDE LOFF: Outside loaf; the loaf at each end of the oven batch. 'I can mind fin a half-loff wis fowerpence-ha'penny, bit I eenst got an ootside loff for thrippence.' (T)

OR: Until; before. 'The bus is awaa! Ye'll hae to bide here or the morn.' 'Hiv ye lang to wyte or ye get yer holidays?' (B)

ORALS or ORRILS: Scraps; left-overs. 'I'm nae for yer orals. I'm nae gyaan tae lick oot yer soo's troch.' (T)

ORRA: Shabby or untidy in appearance. 'Ye dinna expect tae see the doctor as orra as that!' **ORRA DROUTH:** A drunken rascal. **ORRA LOON:** An odd job boy; a beginner on a farm. **ORRA PAIL:** A slop bucket. **ORRA TROKE:** Debris. **ORRA WARK:** Menial tasks. **ORRA WYES:** Unmannerly ways. 'Orra wyes aboot them.' A low standard of conduct. (B) **ORRA-BEASTER:** The man who worked the odd horse on a farm. **ORRA-MAN:** The 'Orraman' was an iron frame, shaped like a fireguard and fitted with hooks for holding a sack upright while you filled it with corn from a bushel or scoop. (T)

OWER: Over (T)

OWERCOME: Overcome. 'The owercome o their sang.' The burden or message of their song. (B)

OWERGAAN: A reprimand; a telling off; a chastisement. 'In oor young days she wid a gotten an owergaan for lyin in the back green wi hardly a stitch o claes on an aa the men folk glowerin at her fae the windaes. She ocht tae be black affrontit o hersel!' (T) Also a close examination, as may be given to a net, to ensure that there are no holes in it. An overhaul; a thorough check, as for an M.O.T. (B)

OWERHEID: Overhead; self-willed, with an inclination to flout authority. 'She's an owerheid kind o quine. She'll hae her ain road fitivver ye say.' **OWER YER FITT:** To twist your ankle. 'Geordie's nae at his wark the day. He gid ower his fitt the streen.' (B)

OWERMIST: Offside; the one furthest away. 'I'll tak the owermist een. I think she's the best yowe o the twaa.' (T)

OWSEN: Oxen (T)

OXTER: Armpit. **TO OXTER:** to embrace. 'He oxtered the deem in front o aa the folk. She wis fair affrontit.' **OXTER POOCH:** The inside pocket of a jacket. 'It's as dark as yer oxter pooch the nicht!' (B)

117

PAAL: A mooring bollard. 'Ye'll nivver mak a livin wi yer rope fast to the paal.' (B)

PAAPS: A kind of sea anemone found among the rocks only at low water with an exceptionally low ebb. This accounts for the fact that they are rarely seen. The size of a small potato, mottled red and yellow, they make a splendid bait for cod in the winter time. Of course nobody is interested in them these days. The term also applies to sickly-looking sea anemones found clinging to debris (particularly coal) dredged from the bottom by a trawl or seine net. Duffers (Macduff men) call them pluffs. (B)

PAAPS O CAITHNESS: The mountains of Caithness, seen from the Banffshire coastline. (T)

PACK MERCHANTS: Small clouds flying before the wind. 'I doot we're in for a gale. See aa yon pack merchants in the sky?' (B)

PADDY HAT: The old fashioned trilby. (B)

PAE-WAE: Sickly; unwell; emaciated. 'The souter (shoemaker) wis gey pae-wae the last time I saw him. Nae muckle tae ride the watter on. A gey peer thing, picket tae the been like a skeleton.' (T)

PAILIN: Fencing. 'The loon tore his new briks on the pikie weir comin throwe the fairmer's pailin on his road hame fae the skweel. He wis takin a short-cut, ye see, bit it's a gweed job there wisna a bull in the park.' (T)

PAIR TRAWL: A very effective method of fishing, when two boats tow one trawl between them. (B)

PAIRTIN: Sharing things out; dividing the spoils. Commonly used to describe the sharing out of the deceased's personal effects, a potential cause of 'bleed an hair'. (B)

PAITRICK: A partridge. (T)

PAMMER: To hammer about with noisy feet on a wooden floor; to stamp about aimlessly. 'There wis somebody pammerin aboot half the nicht up the stair. I couldna get tae sleep for the din!' (T)

PAN-LOAF or PAN-LOFF: A Scotsman making a poor attempt to speak proper English and making a hash of it. Radio and television have improved the Scotsman's mastery of the English language, but before then, anyone from a Scottish working class family trying to speak English to the gentry was considered 'pan-loaf', or as the English themselves would say, 'putting on airs and graces'. When the Buchan farmer was 'caain oot muck', his kitchiedeem informed an enquiring toff in knicker-buckers that he was 'caaing out ding'. (T)

PANJOTRIL: A cooked dish consisting of leftover pieces of meat. (T)

PANSHITE: Panic; predicament; confusion. 'Tosh wiz in an affa panshite fin his briks fell doon.' (T)

PAP: A teat. (T)

PARTAN: The common, reddish, edible crab caught in creels (lobster pots) in inshore waters. (B)

PEAT BARRA: A flat-leafed, wooden barrow with a broad wheel to prevent it sinking at the peat bogs. **PEAT CREELS:** Slatted wooden extensions fitted on to a box-cart to accommodate a bigger load of peats or potatoes. **PEAT SPAAD:** A peat spade. A long, cross-handled spade with a small lug attached to the blade for shaping the peats. 'Gie the peat spaad a cloart o grease, Wull, afore ye pit it by. It'll hud it oon roostit for nixt ear.' It will prevent it from rusting for next year. (T)

PECH: To pant with effort. 'If ee shiv, I'll pech, an we'll seen get the thing shiftit.' (B)

PEEKIN EEVIE: A discontented girl. 'She's a proper peekin eevie. Aye on the girn aboot something.' (B)

PEEL: A pool. (B)

PEEL-AN-ATE TATTIES: Potatoes boiled in their skins and peeled just before eating. Commonly served with boiled salt herring. (T)

PEELIE-WALLIE: Delicate looking; lacking spunk or energy. 'Jessie wis affa peelie-wallie like, nae lookin weel ataa .' (T)

PEELS: Pills. 'Ye nivver get a mixter fae the doctor noo, it's peels for aa.' (B) 'Peels peels, I'm rattlin like an aal can.' (T)

PEEN: Pane. 'I'll hae tae pit in a new peen o gless. The loons his kicked a baa through the windae again.' (T)

PEER: Poor. **PEER-MAN:** Poor man. The peer-man was a long, narrow, steel lever fitted with a vice-grip wedge and used for tightening fencing wire with pressure against a strainer post. It went out of fashion with the introduction of the ropes and pulley system, also used from the strainer posts, and this again has been replaced with the modern ratchet wire-stretcher, which can be adapted for mending a broken wire in the middle of a fence without resorting to the strainer posts at each end. But in the old days the farmer would say 'Tak the peer-man,

Robbie, an gyang doon tae the rashie howe an sort yon broken weir in the pailin faar the yowes are brakin oot. Ye'd better tak the peat barra an a rowe o weir wi ye an a post or twaa, an the mell hemmer an stepples, jist in case.' And Robbie would know exactly what was required of him. (T)

PEERIE: A small spinning top, kept rotating by means of a whip. (B) We call them 'totems' in the country. (T)

PEERSHOOSE: Poorshouse. The last resort and abode of the poor before the days of Income Support or Social Security. There was at least one peershoose to every parish and a Poor Inspector was appointed to deal with the worst cases of poverty and hardship, including the protection of children. (T)

PEESIE or PEESIEWEEP: The peewit or lapwing, more commonly known as the teuchat. The peesie or peesieweep has a weepy, eerie call that brings such sweet sadness to the heart of every exile. (T)

PEETY: Pity. 'That's a peety noo.' (T)

PENNY-WOBBLE: Something cheap and inferior, flimsy or unreliable. 'That's a gey penny-wobble o a bicycle ye've bocht, loon. The spokes are hingin oot o the wheels.' (T)

PERJINK: Fastidious, tasteful, discerning. Mostly smart and neat in appearance. 'He's affa perjink, Donlie. Nae a hair oot o place and he his aye a flooer in his buttin-hole.' (T)

PERNICKETY: Ill to please; fashious. 'He's a pernickety aal sod, likes tae see things richt deen. But, mind ye, he taks a richt pride in his wark.' (B)

PERNURIOUS: Possibly from the English penurious but the meanings are somewhat different. While the English word refers to penury, the Scots pernurious implies bad temper, fussy about food and attentive to detail. 'A pernurious vratch yon, picks ower er mait like a skechan hen. If she wiz richt hungry she wid be gled tae ate.' (T)

PERVOO: To desert or abandon, as when a bird leaves her nest and eggs. 'Oor clockin hen pervoo't her settin o eggs and gaed back on the reist (roost).' (T)

PESS: Easter. (B)

PEYED THANKLESS: Most ungrateful. 'Ye're a peyed thankless vratch, for aa that yer mither's deen for ye.' (B)

PHAETON: A four-wheeled horse carriage which mostly ran on solid rubber tyres. With bigger families, it replaced the gig or governess cart, which was a lower, smaller type of gig probably dating from the days when the lairds employed a governess and used it in transporting her with the children. (T)

PICHER: Trouble; bother; agitation. 'Sic a picher the traffick warden wiz in fin the wifie's keys widna open the car door. His fingers wir aa thooms.' (T)

PICK MIRK: Pitch dark. (B)

PICKIESAE: A deerstalker type of hat sometimes worn by gillies and farm grieves (gaffers) as a symbol of authority which entitled them to a 'pickiesae' or influence on the running of the place, limited of course for the farm grieve in that the farmer was master, though some of them were in complete charge and insisted on these conditions. 'I see oor Angus is weerin a pickiesae noo since he got on for gaffer.' (T)

PICTER: A picture. **PICTERS:** The pictures; the cinema. (T)

PIGS: Earthenware jars; stoneware. 'Oh, there's mealy pigs an jeely pigs an pigs for huddin butter. Aye, but this pig wis greetin fou an rowlin in the gutter.' (McGinty's Meal an Ale.) Note: The word 'pig' is taboo on fishing boats. One must say 'Grunter' or 'Sonny Cammle' (Sandy Campbell). (B)

PIK: A terse, pointed saying of restricted use but can be applied to pitch black as 'pik dark', 'pik thank' or to 'tak a pik' at somebody (a dislike). (T)

PIKE: To pierce or penetrate; a sharp piece of iron. 'The dumplin at Drimmies wis that hard that fin they threw't oot the hens couldna pike it.' **PIKE-THANK:** Thankless; ungrateful; ill-mannered; discourteous. 'Pike-thank brute at! It's like throwin pearls afore swine.' (T)

PINER: Enfeebled; frail; delicate; emaciated. **PINER STIRKIES:** Cattle in poor condition, yet the saying was, 'There's a lot o killin in a piner', which implies hardihood and the ability to survive difficult circumstances. Stirkies is a diminutive for half-grown cattle or stirks, castrated and female. (T)

PINS: Clothes pegs. (T)

PINT: A point; to point. 'They say that Wimpey gies ye a pick wi a richt sharp pint.' 'Dinna pint yer finger at me like that!' **PINT:** (rhymes with lint) Paint. 'Come up and see my hoosie, it's aa pintit blue.' **POODER-PINT:** Powder-paint. **PINTS:** Boots or shoe laces. 'Tie yer pints in a doss (bow); it keeps the ends tidy.' (B) **PINT:** Pronounced as a 'pint' of milk. 'Tatties an pint.' Potatoes and point, which was potatoes only and anything else on the plate was imaginary. (T)

PIPSYLILLS: A pretended illness; a frivolous or trifling excuse for being off work. 'Myra's nae at her work the day, she hiz a dose o the pipsylills.' (T)

PIRLIN: Rippling. (T)

PIRN: A cotton reel. 'Ye canna get a pirn o strong threid nooadays.' **PIRN-TAED:** Pigeon-toed. (B)

PIRR: Motion. 'A pirr o win.' A slight breeze. (T) **PIRR:** 'On the pirr', having made a start. 'Noo that ye're on the pirr, ye micht as weel feenish the job.' (B)

PIT ON: Put on. One who assumes airs and graces. 'A proper pit-on, yon deem! Lady muck! She fairly scunners me.' (B)

PIZ: The collective word for peas. 'They're like piz in a pod, they're that like een anither.' **PIZ MEAL:** Pease meal. (B)

PLAIDS or PLEYDS: An old fisher term for blankets. 'A mairrage present? Fit better than a pair o plaids?' (B)

PLAIKS: Children's toys. 'Watch an nae trump on the bairn's plaiks. They're lyin aa ower the fleer.' (T)

PLASHIES or PLASH FLUKES: Plaice, as distinct from soles or dabs. (B)

PLEITER: To work outside in wet weather. 'Pleiterin oot an in like a drookit rat at the mou o a spatit drain.' Some farmers objected to bad weather working because of the horses, and one of them said to his foreman on a rainy day, 'Ye can tak a spaad (spade) an ging ootside an del neuks (dig field corners where the plough couldn't reach) if ye like, bit ye're nae gaan tae pudddle my horse.' Horse was meant to be in the plural – a pair of horses. The other extreme was the farmers who were supposed to take their tattie-boodies (scare-crows) inside from the wet and ignore the servants. (T)

PLEUCH: A plough. **PLEUCH STILTS:** Plough handles. 'Ye hinna suppit aneuch o brose yet, min, tae wun in atween the pleuch stilts. Ye need tae be able tae stammack yer brose for a job like at.' (T)

PLOOK: A pimple. 'He wid look better if he hidna sic a plooky face.' **SAAT WATTER PLOOKS:** Before the introduction of modern plastics, oilskins chafed both neck and wrists, tearing out small hairs and setting off infection, which resulted in a crop of ugly, very painful boils. One preventive measure was the wearing of red flannel bandages round the wrists (it had to be red flannel). This was only a temporary remedy, for every crew member had his own bandages, and these were apt to get mixed up, when hung up to dry. Thus did the infection spread. The use of a communal wash-bucket didn't help any, either. The recommended treatment was to drink a vile concoction of Epsom Salts and Cream of Tartar. Not exactly efficacious. Penicillin spelt the end for the saat-watter plooks, and modern materials dealt with the root cause. Seldom will you see a fisher with plooks now. (B)

PLOTT: To soak in boiling water, such as a hen before plucking to make the job easier, but with the risk of tearing the skin. 'Tak time tae pluck at hen, quine – nae ower fast or ye'll tear the skin.' (T) **PLOTTIN:** Sweating. 'Get somebody tae open a windae – we're jist fair plottin in here.' (B)

PLOUT: A whack or blow with the hand. 'He leet plout at me fin ma back wis turned and I didna get a fair chance tae hud aff o masel.' I didn't get a fair chance to defend myself. (T)

PLOWT or POTTED HEID: Jellied meat made from the boilings of a cow's head, or part of a head. Butcher's shops sold it, as did countless corner shoppies. It was usually sold in little bowls, but many a mother with a large family preferred to make her own. Then enamel ashets and pudden dishes came into use. A great slice of mother's own make, along with Champion tatties, made a really first class meal. (B)

PLOWTER: To play around; to fiddle about. 'We're plowterin aboot here in the dark. Wid we nae be better to wyte till daylicht?' (B)

PLOY: An adventure; a caper. 'Lang fine days wi their happy ploys, an bare feet rinnin free.' (B)

PLUNK: A plank of wood. Also means to conceal, with every intention of recovering. 'The thief plunkit is swag in the boot o yon aal car, but the bobbies wis wytin for im fin he cam back for't.' (T)

PLYTERIN: Messing about in the wet. (T)

POM-POM: The Field Marshall diesel tractor which is fitted with a winch and steel rope. These machines were nick-named 'Pom-poms' from the sound of their single-cylinder engines and they were ideal for driving the threshing mills; powerful, smooth and reliable. (T)

POOCHES: Pockets, as in a garment. 'Rype (search) yer pooches, min. Ye'll maybe fin a sweetie.' (B) A 'hanky pooch', a 'hip pooch', an 'oxter pooch' (inside breast pocket) and even a 'poacher's pooch' in a coat, big enough to conceal a rabbit, a hare, or a brace of pheasants. (T)

POORTITH: Poverty. (T)

POOSHIN: Poison. 'Ae man's mait (food) is anidder man's pooshin.' A difference of opinion; a matter of taste. (T)

POT-BUN: Pot-bound; root-bound. A plant or flower which has out-grown the pot in which it was planted. 'My fuschia's pot-bun, Liza. I'll hae tae gie't a bigger pottie.' (T)

POTESTATER, or in slang POTTYSTARTER: At the height of one's career; in full prosperity; on the crest of a wave. 'Ye shid a seen Calum Pittendreich fin he wis in his potestater. He wis nae smaa drink I tell ye, an there wisna mony that could touch him at yon game!' (T)

POVEREESE: To rob, starve or reduce to poverty. 'There's nae girss in at park, min. Ye're povereesin at nowt.' There is no grass in that field, you are starving the cattle. (T)

POW: Head. 'See oor Tam, aye shakkin is pow!' (T)

PRAN: To punish. 'He sellt the place ower ma heid, Jock. I'll pran im for that! As a sittin tenant I shid a been consultit, bit I'll see ma lawyer aboot it yet. It's nae aa bye, jist you wyte an see!' (T)

PREE: To taste. (T)

PREEN: A pin. There are common preens, hat preens, tie preens and hair preens. (B)

PRESS: A cupboard. 'Pit the dishes in the press fin ye hiv them dried.' (B)

PREVOO: To shun, avoid or abstain from. 'Gee whiz, ye've fairly prevooed hiz! We nivver see yer face noo.' 'Johnny's fairly prevooed the drink noo. Signed the pledge, I'm thinkin.' (B)

PRIG: To beg, plead or implore. In the past tense 'priggit'. 'Mullie hid tae prig wi his foreman tae get im tae bide. He socht the biggest fee in the market an Mullie hid tae gie im't, (give him it) and half-a-croon for arles.' Arles was the shilling paid by the farmers to their servants as bargain money, in good faith or to seal the agreement that both would abide by its terms. It was like the King's shilling when you joined the army, but if you asked the farmer for half-a-crown (to buy your dinner) you sometimes got it, as Mullie's foreman did, and he didn't have to prig for it. (T)

PRILE: Three cards of equal value, e.g. A prile of Kings. (B)

PRIMPIT: Affected; suffering from self conceit. 'A silly, gypit, primpit cratur, yon. Spil't aa her days.' (B)

PROOD: Proud; snobbish. 'Prood, bigsy an conceited.' Few will admit to this fault. **PROOD FLESH:** Flesh open to the gaze. (B)

PROP: A land-mark; a memorial; a monolith. Usually on a hilltop like the 'Prop o Ythsie' in Formartine or the 'Prop o Bogengarrie' in Buchan. (T)

PROTICK: A caper or ploy. 'We had some rare proticks fin we were bairns.' (B)

PUCKLE or PUCKLIE: An indeterminate amount or number. 'A wee pucklie o peys wid fairly improve that broth.' 'A gweed puckle', a substantial amount or number. (B)

PUDDEN: A pudding. **PUDDEN DISH:** A pudding basin, but oblong in shape and usually enamelled. Ideal for desert pudding such as stewed rhubarb, new caffie's cheese, yerned milk, tapioca, semolina or rice. (T)

PUDDICK: A frog. Also a heavy sledge pulled by horse or tractor and used to clear stones. **PUDDICK'S EGGS:** Frog's eggs. A nick-name for sago or tapioca pudding. **PUDDICKSTEEL:** A toadstool (T)

PUDDLIN: Drenching; soaking. 'Puddlin his men.' Working his men outside in wet weather. 'Puddlin ootside in wither like iss, it's aneuch tae droon the tattie-boodie (scarecrow) nivver mind the men folk!' (T)

PUGGLED: Exhausted, usually by heat or by over-eating. 'I canna thole this het wither – I'm jist aboot puggled.' (B)

PUTTEN: Sent (on an errand). 'I wis putten ower tae speir gin it wid be aa richt if we dem the ditch atween you an hiz for a day or twaa, mebbee a wik, tae lat wir nowt get a drinkie in the merch (march – boundary field) park?' 'Aye fairly, Wullie, jist ye dem the ditch. We wunna hae beasts in oor side o the merch for a file (while) yet, the girse is gey bare. We're sair needin rain, Wullie!' (T) **PUTTEN:** Past participle of the verb 'to put'. 'I widna hae putten up wi that!' 'He's gone an putten 'putten' where he should o putten 'put'! (B)

PYKIT WEIR: Barbed wire. 'Watch an nae leave yer sark on the pykit weir, my loon.' (B)

PYOCH: To cough. **PYOCHERIN STIRK:** A bullock with the hooze or some other distressing lung affliction that laboured his breathing, especially when prodded forward. The condition was sometimes caricatured on human frailty. (T)

PYOKE: A small sack or bag. Nowadays when I ask for a pyoke o chips I am met with a puzzled stare, yet I can remember when a great many commodities were provided in pyokes, a sheet of paper skilfully twirled into a container like an ice cream cone. The country shoppie wifies were expert at this and had your sweeties in the pyoke and weighed by the time you got your money out. (T) 'Foo mony sexes are there, my loon?' 'Three sir. Saicks, pyokes an bags.' (B)

QUAET: Quiet. Ye're affa quaet the nicht, Geordie. Hiv ye faa'n an trumpit on't or something? Cheer up, min, it mith (may or might) nivver happin!' (T)

QUAIK: A heifer or young cow. Also called a coy. (T)

QUARRY REID: The red mush from the granite quarries, used for surfacing paths and driveways. (B)

QUEEL: To cool. 'The loon took aff his hose an sheen tae queel his feet in the burn.' (T)

QUEENIE ARABS: Peterhead harbour was originally a channel between the island of Keith Inch and the mainland. The channel was called 'the Queenie', a name which was later transposed to mean the island. 'Ower the Queenie' meant 'across the channel'. Nowadays it means 'on Keith Inch'. The folk who lived on Keith Inch (the Queenie) were known as 'Queenie Arabs'. The survivors of that gallant clan are very proud of their title. (B)

QUEER YOUMER'T: Queer humoured; moody; temperamental; changeable. 'Dod wis a bittie like a widder-cock; queer youmer't an nivver lang in the same direction.' (T)

QUEETS: Ankles or lower part of the shin-bone. 'Ower the queets amon dubs (mud)!' 'Forty years stannin aa day ahin the coonter, nae winner oor grocer wis vrang amon the queets.' In the bothy ballad 'Drumdelgie' we hear the grieve say:

> Sax o you'll gyang tae the ploo
> An sax tae caa the neeps
> And the owsen wull be efter ye
> Wi strae-rapes roon their queets.

It is most likely the plough-oxen the grieve is referring to. They had ropes of straw twisted round their lower legs to protect them from the mud and frost of the plough-rigs. 'Better oot at the queets than oot o fashion!' (T)

QUINE: A girl. Probably derived from Queen. 'Oor Tibby's jist a bit slip o a quine yet, nae aal aneuch tae get merrite.' (T)

RAAN: Fish roe. The Japanese now look upon herring roe as a great aphrodisiac, consequently Japanese buyers come to Scotland to buy great quantities of herring, simply for the roe content. The Russian klondykers are quite willing to do a deal with the Japanese for the roe, which fetches fantastic prices. The herring itself is not wasted. A great change from the days when we saw great catches of herring, aphrodisiac and all, being dumped back into the sea. (B)

RAG: Temper. 'Lose yer rag.' Lose your temper. 'Tak the rag o them.' Take the size of them; to humble or belittle them in the presence of others. (T)

RAGGLISH: Wet and misty. 'Nae a great day for the bairns' picnic, Miss Chisolm, gey ragglish.' (T)

RAIKINS: Rakings. Loose stalks of unthreshed straw left on the stubble in harvest time. Once gathered in by hand, but now gleaned by the combine-harvester. 'We jist feenish't the raikins the day afore Hogmanay in nineteen twenty-seivin. That wis the latest corn hairst I ivver saw!' (T)

RAIP: Rope. **SLEET-RAIPS:** Ropes of sleet. (T)

RAISE O THE WIND: An expression used if someone appeared wearing a new garment or astride a new bicycle, or who somehow seemed to be better off than he or she had been before. 'Aye man, Mike's gotten a braw new suit; he's surely had a raise o the wind.' Another one in similar vein could refer to the opposite sex: 'Hey Lizzie, did ye see Rosie wi that new frock? There's surely been a fire somewye.' Meaning Rosie had managed to salvage the frock from the blaze, for everyone was sure she couldn't afford to buy such an expensive garment. (T)

RAITHER: Rather. (T)

RAIVEL'T: Ravelled; in a confused state. 'Yer hair's aa raivel't, quine. Better rin the kaim throwe't.' 'He wis clean raivel't fin he cam oot o the anaesthetic. He didna ken his ain folk.' (B)

RAMMY: An uproar. 'Fit a richt rammy in the toon fin the pubs come oot.' (B)

RAMSHACKLE: Ruin or ruinous. 'The steading at Bogeyseat is jist a ramshackle. It needs a new reef for a start.' (T)

RAN-DAN: Rampage. Often describes a boisterous escapade or night out. 'I heard ye wis on the ran-dan again. Are ye ivver at hame nooadays?' (T)

RANDY: A girl of loose moral behaviour. (T)

RAW: A row. (T)

RAX: To stretch; to overtax. Boy trying to be polite: 'Scuse me raxing over for the tatties.' 'Sandy's nae neen weel. I hear he's raxed his hairt.' (B)

RAX A THOCHTIE: Stretch a little. 'If ye want the motor, Harry, ye'll hae tae rax a thochtie. I'm nae lattin't awaa at that price. The figure ye're offerin wid hardly buy the spare wheel or the jack, nivver mind the kit o tools yer gettin in the deal; na na, ye'll hae tae rax a thochtie, a gey thochtie for that model!' (T)

READIN SWEETIES: Conversation lozenges. A very popular heart-shaped, square or round coloured sweet, pink, yellow or white, with a flat surface bearing intimate, romantic endearments printed on them. These were love tokens or sweet nothings that could be passed around in the company of friends or between couples without embarrassment and with considerable amusement just for the fun of it. 'I think you're swell', or 'I like the colour of your eyes', or 'Can I see you home?' are just a sample from memory of the conversation pieces and others with 'Yes!' or 'No!' etc. were also provided to keep the ball rolling, and at two-pence a quarter or eight-pence a pound you could have quite a bit of fun with the readin sweeties. The sweets were quite easily broken and there was always the crack about the mean shop-keeper who had 'haaver't (halved) a readin sweetie tae gie ye exact wecht!' (T)

REAMIN FOO: Brimming full. 'Ye've gotten an affa jaa (splash) o melk the nicht, fadder. The fluggin's jist reamin foo.' (T)

REDD-UP: To clear or tidy up a mess. 'I'll hae a richt redd-up in that sheddie (hut) someday.' 'Sic a redd-doon, sic a mess, ye wid think aathing hid been coupit oot o a cairt. It'll tak some reddin-up!'
'Redd yer throat!' Clear your throat.
'Redd yer hair!' Comb your hair.
'Redd oot the grate!' Clear out the ashes.
'Redd yer crap!' Get it off your chest.
'Redd a road for the binder!' Scythe a bout (swath) round the field verges. (T)
'Redd the line afore ye bait her.' clean the hooks before you bait them.
'Get redd o yon dog afore it bites somebody.' (B)
'Redder' is not quite the same word and means 'rather' or 'raither'. (T)

REEF: A roof (of a building). May also apply to the ceiling. 'Fiten the reef.' Whitewash the ceiling. 'A thackit reef.' A thatched roof. 'Ging throwe the reef.' Go through the roof; explode with anger. (B) **REEF A DITCH:** Roof a ditch. 'Ye'll hae tae reef a ditch.' You'll have to put a roof on a ditch. This was sometimes said to a cottar (married farm worker living in a tied cottage) if he hadn't found another situation and a house for his family within weeks of the Term Day on 28th May, when he had to quit his present employment whether he had found a new home or not, because a new worker would be moving into his old home on that date. Usually somewhere was found, even a rented house if all else failed, but it was an anxious period for some in those days when labour was cheap and competitive in a populous market. All this was governed by unwritten law and very few cases went to court. Looking back I think it is amazing that everything went so smoothly in the chaos of this nomadic form of livelihood when every cottar who was moving house flitted on the same day, when every occupant had to be out of his house by twelve noon so that another could move in, even though he had to stack his furniture outside or a lorry or carts arrived to move him. This didn't often happen and the best of tempers prevailed over the whole proceedings with the odd rankling of course, but nothing serious, and most of the people involved accepted the situation in good holiday spirit. 'Reef a ditch', indeed, but it never quite came to that. (T)

REEFER JAIKET: A half-length overcoat. Not unlike the modern car coat and popular with ploughmen. (T)

REEK: Smoke. (T)

REEM: Cream. (T)

REEMISH: To rummage. 'Fit are ye reemishin in that drawer for?' (B)

REENGE: To roam or ramble. 'Ach, Dod, that dog o yours, ye shidna lat it reenge aa ower the place, ye shid hae it on a tether (lead)!' (T)

REESE: Praise. 'The dominie didna gie oor Billy muckle reese for his sums or his spellin, bit I ken he's a gweed scholar for aa that.' (T)

REESHLE: To rustle, shake or agitate corn on a riddle so that you hear the 'reeshle' of it; a sharp sound that indicates its firm, hard quality. (T)

REEST: To roost. (T)

REET: A root. 'The reet an the rise o't!' The cause and effect, so to speak. A sort of Agatha Christie 'who done it', with all the stops out. 'The root cause' in English, but the Scots version is scarcely understood nowadays. (T)

REETIT: Fleeced or financially cleaned out. 'Keep oot o the bookie, my loon, or ye'll be reetit aathegither.' (B)

REID: Red. **REID FISH:** Salmon (another taboo word at sea). **REID ROTTEN:** Bone lazy. **REID-MOUSER'T:** Red-moustached. **REID EEN:** A red one; a new net.

> Since ivver they sailed the stormy sea
> Their cod had aye fower heids.
> An the hens o them that wis fairmer folk
> Laid eggs wi twaa big reids.

Thus 'reid' is egg-yolk. (B)

REIST: To rest. 'Mind an reist the fire, Janet, afore ye gyang tae yer bed!' It was the peat fire that had to be reistit or rested overnight to make it easier kindled in the morning. This was done last thing at night by taking the tongs and gathering most of the red hot embers or peat cinders in a heap in the centre of the grate and covering them with a shovelful of ash from under the brander. The embers were still smouldering in the morning, and by adding fresh peat and blowing vigorously with the bellows, the fire was soon alight and the kettle boiling for the men's brose. (T)

REIVER: A thief. (T)

REMEID: A remedy. (B)

RESURRECTION BROTH: Broth of third day's vintage. (T)

RETOUR: An outfit (usually a renewal). 'She nott a hale retour o new dishes aifter the loons cowpit the table.' (B)

RICHT: Right. **RICHT DIVERT:** Real entertainment. **RICHT TEEN ABOOT:** Handled with skill. 'I canna be deein wi mait that's nae richt teen aboot.' (B) 'I canna be deein wi wark that's nae richt teen aboot.' (T)

RICHTAFEE: To rectify, adjust, put right. 'Ye'll hae tae richtafee that accoont Dougie. I'm nae gaan tae pey twice for ma order!' (T)

RICK: Smoke. The new smoke alarm has survived in the Doric as a 'smoke-detector' and so far hasn't been humbled with the 'rick-detector' label. (T)

RICKLE: A heap or cairn. To 'rickle peats' or set them up on end in clusters to dry. First they had to be spread out on the lairs to dry on one side, then set up in rickles to dry all round before carting home. 'We'll hae tae gyang tae the moss, lads, an spread the peats.' A fortnight later, if the weather was dry, the grieve would say, 'Hud back tae the moss then, lads, an rickle the peats.' But rickle can also mean ruin, like the steading on the farm of Skatebrae, 'It wis jist a rickle o steens.' (T)

RIFT: To belch or burp. 'A soor rift.' A sour burp. The sort of burp which brings the taste back up again. 'There's naething like an egg for a soor rift!' (B)

RIG: To dress. 'See the time? It's time ye wis riggit for the kirk.' **RIG:** To put the ropes on a net in proper fashion. 'If Sandy riggit the net, ye needna be neen feart to buy her.' **RIGGIN:** The ropes and masts on a ship; the roof of a house. **RIG OOT:** To prepare a ship for the fishing season. Also an outfit of clothing. 'Ye'll need a hale new rig oot for the mairrage, Beldie.' (B) **RIG or LEA RIG:** A section of a field in ploughing. **RIGGIN:** Ceiling; roof; head. **RIGGIN O THE NICHT:** After midnight; at dead of night. Riggin can also mean roof, the roof of the night. 'Sic a din in the riggin o the nicht. It wis like the haimmers o hell jist ootside yer windae. A gas leak or something and they waar tearin up the tar macadam wi een o yon compressor things, aneuch tae waaken the vera deevil imsel, an I hid tae pit cotton oo in ma lugs or the hinner eyne o't!' (T)

RILE: To anger. 'I wis fair rile't in the store the day fin the wee mannie jumped the queue. (T)

RIME: Frost. (T)

RINGIN STORM: A severe gale. 'It's nae this day we'll lowse the rope! It's jist a ringin storm!' (B)

RINGLE-EED: Wall-eyed; the iris of the eye blotched with white, especially noticeable in horses and supposed to indicate bad temper. 'I dinna like yon mere that Snorlie bocht at Tarset's roup. She his a ringle-ee an could be a thrawn bitch an ull-naiter't forbye.' (T)

RINK: To romp about, as bairns will do when put to bed. 'If ye dinna stop rinkin aboot up there, I'll come up an gie ye Fa broke the hurley?' An unspecified form of chastisement. (B)

RIPPER: A hand-line for catching cod. No bait is required, but the hooks must be bright and clear and lures may be attached. Fishing by this method has several titles: 'The murderer', 'The poor man's friend' and 'A lump o leed at ae end an a feel at the ither.' The last one is the best definition. (B)

RIPPER YOLE or YAWL: A small boat used for ripper fishing. (B)

RIPPIT: A riot; a disturbance. 'There wis a party neist door last nicht. Some rippit, I'll tell ye.' (T)

RISTIN: Resting. (B)

RIVE: To tear or wrench apart. 'I'm nae gaan tae rive ma guts oot tae please naebody.' (T)

RIZZON: Reason; sanity. 'Boris lost his rizzon, the breet, an they took im awaa in the Black Maria.' (T)

ROADIT: On the road; on the way.

ROASSEN: Roasted. 'I'm fair roassen wi that sun!' **ROASSEN FISHIE:** Roasted fish. Here's a treat for you. Get a nice fresh, plump haddock and split it open like a kipper. Do not skin it. Dust it lightly with salt and leave it for an hour or two, preferably in the sunshine (mind the cats). This is called 'lettin the fishie blaa'. When you can wait no longer, roast the fishie on a brander over an open fire, and just listen to the juice sizzling in the red hot coals. I assure you your mouth will water. If you have no open fire, just use the grill, not forgetting a bittie butter on the fishie. She'll sizzle quite nicely there. When she is nicely browned, serve with buttered breid (oatcake). I'm sure this'll fess tee yer hairt (rejoice your heart). (B)

ROBSORBY: A make of scythe blade that was very popular in the old Buchan harvest fields in the days of manual labour. It was made from well-tempered steel that was easily sharpened and kept a cutting edge longer than most other makes of its period. If it was a day for scything out flattened patches in the corn field the grieve would tell his men 'Haud back tae the Robsorby, lads. It's nae a day for the binder – ower weet!' He never had to mention scythe. The maker's name was synonymous with his implement. (T)

ROCH: Rough. **ROCH SHOOERS:** Rough showers of rain. (B)

ROCKY-ON: A childhood game whereby a cairn of stones was built where the incoming tide would surround it. The boy who stayed longest on the cairn won the game. (B)

RODDIN-TREE: A rowan tree. (T)

ROOSED: When herring were being held back for gutting next morning, they were 'roosed', heavily salted. **ROOSIN TUB:** A huge wooden vat into which the herring were salted overnight. (B)

ROOSER: A watering can fitted with a perforated rose for spraying plants. (T)

ROOSTY: Rusty. (T)

ROSET: Resin or rosin. For fiddle-bow or shoemaker's thread. 'I say, jiner, there wiz an affa lot o rosety-knots in yon timmer ye gid me, and fin the knot fell oot it left a hole, bit I suppose it's gweed aneuch tae mak a hen coop, an the chuckens wull see oot at the holes.' (T)

ROTTANS: Rats; vermin. Now greatly decreased on the farms since the introduction of Warfarin poison, which is also used in the treatment of humans with heart complaints, surely the Alpha and the Omega in medical science. (T)

ROU'D or ROW'T: Rolled. Having rolled or trundled something along the ground. Retired blacksmith referring to the joiner who worked next door to the smiddy: 'Oh aye, the vricht (carpenter) made the cairt wheels and rou'd them roon here and we put iron rings on them, het fae the fire we kennl't (lit) roon the wheel-base in the close, an we fittit the mountins (thirled iron) on the naves forbye. But that's aa feenished noo wi the rubber tyres.' Also means to wrap up. 'I row't it intil a parcel for the postie.' (T)

ROUNDERS: Ungutted fish. A crew may, if fishing is good, gut only the bigger fish and land the small fish as 'rounders'. This is simply a time and labour saving expedient. (B)

ROUP: An auction sale. 'Dowpie's surely gaan tae hae a roup: he hiz aathing trail't oot o the big shed an lyin in the close roon the steadin.' 'Weel, Stashie, a body wid easy ken ye wiz a stranger here. Dowpie hiz a roup ony day o the wik that wye o't! He aye hiz aathing lyin aboot, an files oot o sicht amon thistles an dockens in the simmer time. Naethin new in at Stashie.' (T)

132

ROUSE or ROOSE: To anger.

> I'm nae ull tae roose
> So tak care fit ye're at
> And nivver ye mention
> A new lum hat. (T)

ROWE: Roll. **ROWE THE BOWE:** To go right back to where one started to shoot a fleet of lines, and there start to haul. (B)

ROWIE: A flaky bread roll made with plenty of butter and ideal for breakfast after heating in the oven or cooker grill and spreading with more butter, margarine or marmalade, or both. 'Ging doon tae the shop, Betty, for half-a-dizzen rowies; it'll save me bakin afore the folk come for their tay.' (T)

ROWTH: Abundance; profusion. (B)

ROYT: Boisterous. **ROYT GEETS or NACKETS:** Boisterous children. 'Betsy his a curn gey royt geets. I couldna pit up wi yon din in the hoose aa day – ah wid be roon the bend or up the waa. Na na, ye need a firmer (stricter) haan yonder. Betsy's ower saft an easy goin an lats the bairns aff wi onything!' (T)

ROZETTY: Resinous. (T)

RUBBIT: A rabbit. On no account must you use this word on a fishing boat. You must say 'fower fitter' or 'mappie'. Taboos must be observed, you know. (B)

RUCK: Rick; corn or hay-stack. **RUCK-FOON:** Stack foundation, usually a circle of stones and boulders, straw, whin or broom. **RUCK-POST:** A wooden pole or similar strut for supporting a stack which is slightly off plumb. **THACKET RUCK:** A stack which has been thatched for the winter. **WATTER'T RUCK:** A stack which hasn't been properly built and is absorbing rain, causing the grain to sprout, which renders it useless. **HET RUCK:** A ruck or stack steaming from fermentation caused by an accumulation of damp from a crop that hasn't been long enough in the stook to mature or dry out and has been stacked too early. 'Yer rucks are aa stemmin, Forbie. Ye'll hae tae mak twaa oot o een tae cool them doon a bittie. I shoved ma airm intae the ribs o een o them an nearly burnt ma fingers, het aneuch tae bile an egg. Ye've fair connached yer crap, man, an there's aye the maist danger o that in a gweed year atween the cut an the lead, leadin ower seen afore the crap's wun (matured). Folk hinna patience tae wyte an there's mair ull deen in a gweed ear than a coorse een.' In extreme cases the above is not an exaggeration. (T)

RUG AND RIVE: To wrench and pull hard. 'Ruggin the swingletree.' Two men sat on their bottoms facing each other, their boot soles together and legs straight, both holding the same staff and pulling against each other. The one who pulled the other to his feet was the winner. (T)

RUMMEL-GUMPTION: Common sense. (T)

RUMMLE: A rumble; to rumble. 'A rummle o thunner.' A rumble of thunder. Rummle can also refer to speech, 'Ye canna believe aa that Frunkie says, he jist opens his moo an lats his belly rummle!' (T)

RUMP: To romp or jump about noisily. 'Rumpin bairns.' (B)

RUN KNOT: An over-tightened plain or reef knot on a string or bootlaces. 'Ye've a run knot on yer pints (bootlaces) again, loon. Ye'll nivver get at lous't athoot shears. Ye shid tie them wi a doss (loop) ye can get a hud o.' (T)

RUNK: Rank; flush or overgrowth; lengthy. 'The combine leaves a runker stibble than the aal horse binder.' Also means potent, rife or strong. **RUNK POOSHIN:** Rank poison. **RUNK AN FILE:** Rank and file. (T)

RUNT: The smallest pig in a litter. (T)

RUNTIT: Bankrupt; broke; penniless. 'Sodger hisna a maik tull his name – he's fair runtit.' (T)

RYE: Children's rhyme said along a row of children counting one out each time until only one was left then he or she restarted the game. (T)

RYPE: To search. 'Rype yer pooches, min, an see if ye hiv a tabby (cigarette butt). (T)

RYPE UP: To trace someone's ancestry. 'Lookin for yer roots, are ye? Ging an see Isie – she'll seen rype ye up.' (B)

SAACH WAAN: A willow wand. (B)

SAACHLESS: Naive; guileless. 'A saachless breet, Sandy; easy led, I wid think.' (B)

SAAT: Salt. 'If ye skail saat it's unlucky. Ma mither aye said that if ye skail't the saat ye hid tae throw a pinch ower yer left shooder or yer luck wid be oot. And she wid nivver lat ye pit saat back in a packet; if ye poor't oot mair than ye wis needin tae saat yer tatties she gart ye throw awaa the rest o't or ye wid be unlucky. It's a gweed job it wisna expensive stuff or ye couldna cairry on like that for lang. An of coorse, if ye borret saat fae somebody, ye nivver gied it back.' **SAAT-LICK:** Salt brick. These were slipped into brackets in the byre wall in front of stalled cattle, one for each animal to lick at leisure. They probably contained other nutrients but the salt encouraged drinking and good metabolism for putting on weight.

During summer grazing the salt bricks were left at field gates and around drinking troughs for the same purpose and the animals seemed to enjoy them. To be worth your salt-lick was considered a compliment in human terms. (T)

SAB: To sob. (T)

SACKIT WI DEBT or IN A SACK O DEBT: Hopelessly in debt. As far as I am aware, this is the only time the word 'sack' is used. (B)

SAIR: Sore or painful. 'That's a gey sair finger ye hae!' As a measure of degree: 'I dinna think he's sair seekin her. He's nae neen ower keen.' 'This liver's ower sair deen. It's as teuch as an aal beet.' **SAIR FECHT:** A sore fight; a difficult period. 'It's been a sair fecht to get this far, but things should be better noo.' (B) **SAIRLY:** Badly. (T)

SAIR COME AT: Grieving; sorrowful; touched; upset. 'The fairmer's wife wis sair come at fin she read oot Andy's daith in the paper.' (T)

SAIR HANKIT: Constricted. (B)

SAIR HEIDIE: A small sponge or cheese-cake in a paper wrapping like a bandage round a sore head. (T)

SAIR MADE: Hard pressed; under the weather; struggling. 'Murdo's gey sair made in yon craft (croft) at Scrapehard. Needin aa is time tae get ends tae meet. Gey hard caa'd wi ae thing or anither. An yon wife o his – Tibby Bruce! Weel, we aa ken Tibby: siller rins throwe her fingers like watter fae a spoot, an that disna help, ye ken.' (T)

SAIR'T: To have one's fill of. (T)

SANSHICH: Curt. (T)

SAPPY: Heavy in the water, laden with fish. (B)

SAPS: Milk and bread sops. (T)

SARK: A shirt. 'I got a het sark trumpin draff yesterday.' 'If I gid ye a button wid ye shew a sark tee tull't?' **SARKIN:** The wooden boards hammered across the joists to carry the slates on a roof. 'See that ye pit felt on at boords noo, afore ye pit on the slates!' (T)

SATTLE: To settle. 'It's time ye wis merrite min an sattl't doon.' (T)

SCABBIT: Scabbed; inflamed. (T)

SCAFFIE: A street sweeper; a refuse collector. (There is nothing derogatory in the title.) 'The scaffies come roon on Tuesday, so ye'd better hae yer wheelie-bin oot.' (B)

SCALDERS: Stinging jellyfish. Red or blue in colour, with long slivvery stringles, these filthy brutes are the bane of the fisherman's life, especially at the herring fishing. The scalder would keep sliding down the net, covering it with particles of itself, particles which were shaken out along with the herring and affected any human face or fingers with which it might make contact. The result was a stinging sensation around the eyes, ears etc. where the skin is tender. It is enough to drive a man frantic. Towards the latter end of the drift-net fishing, crews had taken to wearing nylon stocking masks to protect their faces. The scalder (well named), is a filthy menace. If you see one on the beach, leave it alone. Note: See slivvery doctors. (B)

SCAMMED: Singed; very nearly burned. 'I threw paraffin on the fire an got my hans scammed for bein sae silly. They're still nippin yet.' (B)

SCAPH: A type of sailing boat (from the Latin *scapha,* a boat). The 'Fifie' boat had a perpendicular stem and stern. The 'Zulu' boat had a perpendicular stem, with a raked stern. The 'Scaph' or 'Scaffie' had a sharply curved stem, with a raked stern. (B)

SCLAVE: A gossip or scandal-monger. 'She his a tongue that wid clip cloots, sclavin aabody, and she wid argie wi her ain shadda if it could spik back!' (T)

SCOB or SCOBBIT: To put in splints. 'Aye, Benny, I see yer doggie's three an cairry wan this mornin. Fit ivver happened tae the craiter?' 'Oh, Donnie man, a steen fell aff the dyke an broke his leg. I hid tae tak him tae the vet and get it scobbit. Ye'll notice it's a hin leg and it's warst fin he's needin a wee-wee, ye wid think he wis on stilperts (stilts).' (T)

SCOMFISHED: Suffocated. Sometimes by a very disagreeable smell. 'I couldna stand the wark in the silage tooer at Nether Bracklin. It wis like bein in the jile, near sixty feet abeen the grun an concrete waas aa roon ye an nae a starn o fresh air, an fut wi the sickenin guff o the silage I wis nearly scomfished. Na na, nae mair o that for me!' (T) 'I'm jist aboot scomfished! Did somebody open their handbag?' (B)

SCORIE-HORN'T: Calloused. (T)

SCOUR or SCOOR: To scour or rub something with fine sand or some abrasive mixture, such as Vim or Brasso. You could also get a 'scoor (slap) in the lug' for some misdeed, or when you grew up you could get the wife and bairns into the family car and 'scoor (tour) the hulls' for a day and enjoy the scenery and freedom of the countryside. Scour or scoor is also a name in English and Scots for an

136

infectious diarrhoea in calves which often proved fatal before the days of modern antibiotics. (T)

SCOUTH or SCOWTH: Elbow room; freedom of movement; open space. 'The bairns hiv plenty o scouth tae play.' (T)

SCRAICH: To screech. (T)

SCRAN: To scrounge. 'He's aye on the scran, yon lad. Jist a proper mooch.' It was common practice for youngsters to scran herring i.e. those which had fallen from overflowing baskets, or had been left in odd corners. Some fish wifie would pay tuppence the dozen, but there had to be fourteen in the dozen and they had to be in first class condition.
It was also common practice for parents to keep their bairns from school, to scran the pieces of coal which might fall from the lorries or carts when a steamer was discharging a cargo. Weird and wonderful the excuses for absence presented next morning. (B)

SCRAT: A scratch. Also a runt. 'A scrat o a cratur.' A poor specimen. 'At scrat o a mannie'll nivver lift at bags o coal.' (T)

SCRATH: The shag or cormorant. 'Yon lang thin deem wi the black goon aye mines me on a scrath.' (B)

SCRAUCH: To screech. (B)

SCREETH: The surface of the water. 'We had jist gotten the bonny fish to the screeth o the watter, fin we lost her.' (B)

SCRIEVE: To write. (B)

SCRIMP: To give short measure; mean. 'Ye're affa scrimp wi the meesher joug this mornin, melkie. Hiz the coo gaen dry or fit?' **SCRIMPIT:** Stinted. (T)

SCROG or SCROGS: A stunted shrub or bush. 'That's nae a shrub, min, it's jist a scrog. Nae mair like a berberis than the tae o ma beet (boot) – throw't oot, ah tell ye. The scaffie'll get it!' (T)

SCRUNT: Someone or something stunted in growth. (T)

SCUDDLIN CLAES: Casuals, somewhat threadbare, patched or darned and well-worn. Not your best attire, almost workday. What used to be known to men as a 'go-ashore suit', reserved for social pleasures. (T)

SCUDDY: Short measure; scarcely enough. 'Ye've been a bit scuddy wi the curtin, Jonin. It hardly meets in the middle o the windae.' (T)

SCULL: A shallow basket where the fisherman kept his smaalins. (B)

SCUM: Perks for the black squad. The hauling of a fleet of herring nets required that the ship be dragged ahead slowly by heaving on the heavy messenger rope. This provided sufficient slack for the crew to haul the nets into the ship. If the herring were 'below the han' (hanging from the underside of the net) many of them dropped into the sea, sinking slowly as the ship moved ahead. Some of these fish could be retrieved with the use of a 'scummer', a sort of giant butterfly net. This was wielded by the chief, who was seldom required until the nets were hauled. The herrings thus retrieved were called 'scum', and were always big and plump. The cash from the sale of 'scum' was divided between the chief and the fireman, although the cook could be included, depending on local custom. The chief and the fireman were always known as 'the black squad'. (B)

SCUNNER: Disgust; loathing; revulsion (see Jandies). 'Fish five times a wik? Aneuch tae scunner a body.' 'I'm fair scunner't wi the repeats on T.V. Time we had something fresh.' 'Come awaa, min! Ye're a proper scunner, trailin ahin like that.' (B) 'He's a scunner o a mannie yon, aye pickin is nose or clawin is doup.' 'I've aetin haggis or its comin oot at ma lugs an am fair scunner't o't. I couldna look at the stuff – the sicht o't wid gar me spew!' (T)

SCUTTER: To dawdle; to waste time. 'Faith, but Lewie's scutterie. He taks as lang tae gyang an eerin ye wid think he wis makkin the thing.' (T) 'Stop scutterin aboot, min. Get on wi the job.' **SCUTTERY WARK:** Intricate sort of tasks. **AA TAE SCUTTER:** All to pieces. 'That caas yer aal fashioned ideas aa tae scutter, surely.' (B)

SCUTTER'T-KIN: Disadvantaged. (T)

SEAM: The hem or pleat in a garment. 'The mair seams the mair lice.' In the old days of the horse plough and broadcast sowing of grain, narrow ploughing was favoured on the assumption that 'wi nerra furrs ye'd mair seed', or 'the mair seams the mair lice', a pun I think the Scottish soldiers of the First World War brought back with them from the trenches, referring to the lice in the plentiful seams or pleats in their kilts. Deeper and wider tractor ploughing with heavy discs and powerful rotovators to make a deeper tilth for drill sowing has changed all that. The horse harrows merely scratched the surface and the broadcast corn or barley trickled into the sharp narrow furrows, to be covered up by repeated harrowing and a flatten out with the stone or metal rollers, whereas the modern combine-drill can complete the whole operation in one go, except perhaps for a final 'straik' with the light harrows to smooth the surface. This procedure with the drill-machine can even include fertiliser distribution, before the final rolling, so that the 'lice' are abundant without the seams. (T)

SEAMAW: An old Buchan name for the seagull. 'Damned fishers' hens,' Hilly called them. 'I wish they'd bide at hame an aet their ain stinkin herrin!' (T)

SEARCH: A milk sieve. (T)

SECK or HARN APRON: A sack-cloth apron worn by the women folk for the more menial or dirty tasks, like cleaning the fireplace or scrubbing a stone floor. 'Pit on yer harn aprin, quine, an blaiken (black-lead) the fireplace.' A 'harden' or harn towel of similar material for drying dirty or greasy hands was always kept handy on a nail at the back of the kitchen door. (T)

SEDARIN: A scolding; a reprimand; a severe admonishment. 'Sic a ragin', 'sic an owergaan', 'sic a kyardin', 'sic a sedarin I got for brakin the wifie's flooer pot. I've a gweed mind tae buy a flooer't chunty tull er tae mak up for't. Yon lully o the Nile that she hiz wid look fine in a funcy dirler!' (T)

SEDDLE: A saddle. 'Pit the seddle on the richt horse.' Blame the proper person or culprit. No false witnesses. (T)

SEEG: To scold. (T)

SEELYHOO: A cowl or skin cap on the head of a new born baby. It is an extremely rare occurrence and is supposed to portend luck or fame or a very special talent for the child. 'Oor Kirbie wis born wi a seelyhoo an see far he is the day, bidin in yon big hoose an plenty o siller.' (T) Also a knitted Balaclava helmet. (B)

SEGS: Rafia work in coloured straw; reeds growing in marshy places. (T)

SETTLE: A sofa. (T)

SEYPIN or SEYPIN WEET: Absolutely soaking. 'Ye'll be seypin in twaa meenits if ye ging oot in that rain!' (B)

SHACKLE BEEN: The wrist joint or bone. 'Aa that forkin shaves, it's sair on yer shackle beens!' (T)

SHAFT-BELT: A leather strap under the horse's belly and fixed to the shafts on a cart. If the load was 'licht on the back' of the horse and too heavy at the rear, the shaft-belt helped to balance the cart and prevent it toppling backwards. (T)

SHAFTER: A slang word for a sleeved waistcoat, which was more or less a light jacket without lapels and a popular garment in the horse era of Scottish farming. 'I swung my shafter ower ma heid tae pit it on an nearly knockit doon the hingin lump.' (T)

SHAKKIN BRUTE: A local misnomer for 'shooting brake'. (B)

SHAKKIN SPOOT: A square wooden chute suspended on lath sticks and driven by belted crank-shaft motion in the threshing mill to shake or convey corn to an elevator taking it to the granary loft. (T)

SHAKKY: Shaky. 'The briggie ower the burn's gey shakky.' (B)

SHAKKY-DOON: A make-shift bed, made up on the floor. A great delight for bairns who have a proper bed (of course). (B)

SHALL SAN: Shell sand. Sand from some stretches of the Buchan seashore, and particularly from the beach at St. Fergus, which farmers carted home as grit for their hens. (T)

SHALLIE O TAY: An old term for a cup of tea, carrying a hint of friendliness and fellowship. (B)

SHAMMEL'T: Uneven; irregular; misplaced. 'Drucilla is a bonnie quine but her teeth are affa shammel't. She could get a brace on them fae the dintist.' (T)

SHANK: A garment in the process of being knitted. 'I aye tak ma shank wi me fin I'm baby-sittin. It gies me something tae dee.' (T)

SHAPIT: Shaped; formed. (T)

SHARGER: An extremely thin or emaciated person or animal (The 'g' is hard, as in 'bag'). 'Ye're gettin to be a proper sharger, min. Ye're surely nae gettin mait.' (B) **SHARGER BAIRN:** An under-sized child but not necessarily under-nourished. If the bairn was the last of a bigger family it was sometimes considered to be the dregs, or 'the shakins o the pyokie (bag)!' but in this case rudely referring to the scrotum. (T)

SHARN: Cattle excrement. Also a growth or substance which affects fishing nets so that they seem to hold a fantastic amount of water, and squelch beneath your feet. (B)

SHAW: The green shoot or leaf from a vegetable. (T)

SHEAVE: A slice. 'A sheave o loaf an treacle.' (B)

SHEE: A shoe. **SHEEN:** Shoes. 'Tak the buckles fae yer sheen, my bonny lassie-o.' **ILKA-DAY SHEEN:** Shoes for everyday wear, as distinct from Sunday sheen. **SHEENIES:** Small shoes. **SHEENICKIES:** Affected, baby-talk for babies' shoes.

> 'Twis Kirsty this, an Kirsty that,
> An Kirsty's needin sheen.
> But Kirsty's darlin sheenickies
> Maun come fae Aiberdeen. (B)

140

SHEELICKS: Small, third rate oats that fall through the riddles at the threshing mills. (T)

SHEELTERS: Shelled mussels. It was the women-folk's job to gather the mussel bait from the family mussel bed on the shore. This mussel bed was called the 'scaap', and was stocked with mussels from the Ythan estuary, although it was not uncommon for mussels to come from as far away as Guardbridge, near St Andrews. It fell to the women to do most of the baiting as well. To tell the truth, the women did most of the work. Before the days of proper sea-boots, it was the wife's duty to hitch up her skirts and carry her man out to the boat, so that he would go to sea dry-shod. Note: A skipper who is enjoying a run of good catches may be said to hae them 'scaapit'. (B)

SHEEP TROCH: A sheep dipping trough. A solution of selected chemicals is prepared and every sheep on the farm is submerged in a dipping trough for at least half-a-minute, twice yearly, as a protection against scab, fly-strike and other scourges. The dipping is supervised by law with heavy penalties for neglecting it. Crofters who haven't a 'sheep troch' are obliged to 'muck in' with the bigger farmers in having their small flocks submerged. (T)

SHEEPIE'S KNEES: A child who is very sensitive to tickling around the knees has 'sheepie's knees'. (B)

SHEET-IRON: Corrugated iron. The Buchan chiels never got their tongues round a word as fancy as corrugated, so it was just simply sheet-iron. (T)

SHELT: A light work horse or larger pony. **SHELTIE:** A small pony. (T)

> I think I'll get a sheltie, a quaet shaggy breet,
> An yoke him 'tween the trams o a cairtie wi a seat,
> Syne tak the road throwe Buchan, fae the toon o Peterheid,
> Wi twaa-three bits o thingies that a fairmer's wife micht need. (B)

SHEUCH: To transplant or set aside. 'That cabbage plants, Doddie, sheuch em intil a corner eyvnoo.' (T)

SHIEL: A galvanised metal scoop for filling herring into baskets. In days of yore such scoops were made of wood. (B) **SHIEL or SHIEL OOT:** To clean up or clean out. 'The foreman left Burnside at the Mey Term an aa the ither lads got a shiel oot. "A clean toon", they caa'd it.' (T)

SHILPIT: Of poor physique. 'A peer shilpit-like cratur, Sandy.' (B)

SHIM: The old single horse shim was a light-weight plough-shaped implement fitted with tines or sharp prongs for tearing or cutting out the weeds between the turnip or potato drills. It was usually a job for the loon or the orra-beaster. (T)

141

SHIPPIE: A term, usually affectionate and usually used by the women folk for the steam drifter. (B)

SHITMIRAC: Hopelessly drunk, stupified and helpless. 'Kylie wis shitmirac last nicht. He fell in tae the strang hole on the wye hame. Sic a sotter!' (T)

SHIV: To shove or push. And also diversely, 'Shiv in time.' Fill in time during an idle period. (T)

SHIVERIN JIMMY: A fancy teacake. (T)

SHOCHLE: To shamble or walk with effort. 'Eppie's like a ship on a stormy sea the wye she shochles doon the road.' (T)

SHOCK: A stroke. 'Sandy took a shock last ear. He cower't that, but he took anither shock this summer, an that feenished im.' (B)

SHOGGLY: Shaky, as a rickety ladder might be. 'Sometimes, on the telly, ye'll see a briggie slung on ropes across a ravine. I couldna taikle yon – it wid be far ower shoggly.' (B) **SHOGGLY-WULLIE:** A table jelly. Probably so named because it wobbled in the dish when mither spooned it out round the table. (T)

SHOODER: Shoulder or to shoulder. 'Dennis shooder't the seck o tatties an cairrit it up the stairs.' (T)

SHORT ON THE TROT: Short tempered. 'Ye're affa short on the trot the day noo, Basil. Wis the wife lyin on the tail o yer sark?' (T)

SHOT or SHOTTIE (depending on amount large or small): A catch of herrings (or fish). 'Nae muckle deein in local waters, but I hear there's some fine shots comin fae Stronsay wye.' Also used to inform someone it is their turn during a game. 'It's your shottie.' (B)

SHOUDIN-BOATS: Carnival swing-boats. A big attraction at Aikey Fair. (T)

SHOUTHER-THE-WIN: Shoulder-the-wind. With one shoulder higher than the other. 'The set o his beens made him shouther-the-win.' (B)

SHOWD: To swing; a child's swing. 'If ye look fair an spik square, maybe fadder'll pit up a showd on yon tree in the gairden.' (B)

SHUE or SHOO: To sew. 'Will ye shoo a button on my sark, Ma?' **SHOO:** Past tense of the verb 'to sow'. 'Hilly shoo his corn gey late.' (B)

SHUITED: Pleased; well satisfied. **FINE SHUITED:** Very well pleased. **NAE NEEN SHUITED:** Not at all pleased. (B)

SHUNNERS: Cinders. May apply to coke. 'A bag o shunners fae the gasworks disna cost muckle, I'm sure.' **SHUNNER ROADIE:** A path laid with cinders. 'Harn bags an shunners.' Sack-cloth and ashes. (B)

SHYVE: To throw out. Applies only to rope or fishing line. 'Gie the rope a gweed shyve, noo! Gie the man on the pier a chance tae catch it.' (B)

SIC: To seek. 'He's siccan a len o my bicycle, mither. Wull I gie im't?' (T)

SIC or SICCAN: Such. (T)

SICCAR: Secure; certain. **MAC SICCAR:** Make sure. (T)

SICHT: Sight. (T)

SICK LAMB: An orphan lamb fed with the bottle, but in Buchan the pronunciation was more like seik or sik rather than purely sick lamb, which it wasn't, but unfortunate enough to lose its mother. Calling the lamb at feeding time was 'sic-sic-sic-sic-sic-sic' which may have resulted in the sick lamb tag, and the animal became a pet around the kitchen door and had no fear of the farm dogs. I have seen a farmer's wife with a really sick lamb in the kitchen oven, or wrapped up in a hot-water bottle to revive it, even treating it to a teaspoon of whisky. It didn't have to be a motherless lamb, but genuinely ill with pneumonia, or at a later stage with wool-ball obstruction, which is quite different from the adopted orphan known as the sic lamb. Disguised with the skin of a dead lamb on his back he was sometimes fortunate in finding a surrogate or foster mother in a bereaved parent, otherwise he romped around the farmhouse and steading in complete freedom and was coddled and petted by everyone, especially the bairns, and sometimes even had a name to go with his sex, Sam or Polly or whatever. When Sam or Polly was weaned he or she was returned to the flock, and just as well, because when market day came round they had to be sold, especially if it was a castrated he, and you can understand the heart-break if he had still been prancing round the kitchen door. (T)

SIDE: Hard or severe punishment; strict admonishment. 'Dinna be ower side on at loons, noo, tho they dintit yer car. Mind ye wis eence young an feel yersel!' (T) **SIDE or SEYDE:** Detrimental; having an adverse or harmful effect. 'It wis fine to hae the big car, but oh, boys, she wis side on the petrol.' (B)

SIDELINS: Side-saddle; sideways. (T)

SILLER: Silver; money. 'Aye, Stobbie's fadder live't afore im an left im weel aff. He wis born wi the siller speen in is moo.' (T)

SILLERTON LOONS: The original students at Robert Gordon's College, Aberdeen, who lodged at Sillerton House dormitory. (T)

SILLY MADE UP: Applies to a youngster who delights in impish behaviour, not taking life too seriously. (B)

SIMMER'S BITS: Light weight attire for summer. 'Isn't this a richt fine day? Time ye had yer simmer's bits on.' Note: There are, of course, also winter's bits. (B)

SIN: Son. 'My sin's ma sin, tull he gets a wife; bit ma dother's aye ma dother aa the day's o her life.' (T)

SIN SYNE: Since then; in the past. (T)

SINKER: A small but heavy wooden ball with a hole in the centre for a rope or chain, binding a horse to a stable manger or forestall. (T)

SIREE: A soirée, usually a social evening in the church hall. The French pronunciation was, and still is, completely disregarded. 'The Mission mannie's fite bonnet aye mines me on a siree table.' (B)

SIT SAFT: To enjoy an easy life. 'Wullie winna sit saft wi yon deem. She's jist a proper tartar.' (B)

SITT: Soot. 'Hiv ye heen yer heid up the lum? Ye're jist yirdit wi sitt.' (B)

SIZE: Chives. A slender plant of the leek family with a slight onion flavour. 'Chappit tatties an size.' A mixture of mashed potatoes and chives was a frequent diet in the Buchan farm kitchens. 'Tatties an girse (grass)', the lads called it jokingly. (T)

SIZZON: Season. **SIZZEN'T:** Seasoned, like seasoned wood. 'The timmer they used tae mak yon shed wisna sizzen't. It'll warp come time an faa tae bits, nae doot.' (T)

SKAAS: The barnacles which will grow on a boat's bottom, if it is not kept properly painted. (B)

SKAIL: To spill or scatter something granular, like sugar, salt, tea or rice. 'Watch an nae skail the saat, quine.' 'Gyad sakes, ye've skail't the pail.' (T) **SKAIL:** To spill. 'Ye've skail't the mulk, ye dosey quine.' 'At half-past-three the skweel skail't.' The school emptied. (B)

SKECHAN: Fastidious about food; jaundiced; a feeling of disgust for anything edible. 'I'm fair skechan, an I couldna look at onything mair than a rich tea.' Referring to McVities' Rich Tea Biscuits. (T)

SKEELY: Skilful. 'Sandy's a richt skeely han wi the fiddle.' (B)

SKELBIN: A very thin slice; a sliver. 'Jist a skelbin o cheese noo, mistress. I dinna want a thick slice – ye ken it gies me hertburn.' (T)

SKELLACH: The charlock weed, with bright yellow flowers like those on the oil-seed rape. Before the days of weed-killer sprays it was rife in the cultivated coastal areas around North-East Scotland. The seeds lay dormant in grass for many years but the plough awakened it and it sprang to life in succeeding crops. It was particularly annoying in turnip fields where the seedling plant resembled the turnip at the same stage and was sometimes left in the drills at hoeing time as a healthy young turnip. (T)

SKELP: A wallop; a thrashing. Also used to describe a substantial area. 'A fair skelp o gairden.' (T)

SKELPIN: Hurrying. 'He wis fairly skelpin doon the street.' (T)

SKELVES (pronouce the K): Shelves. (T)

SKEP: A bee-hive. **SKEPPIT:** Handled bee-hives. (T)

SKICE: To make off quickly; to disappear or escape. 'Alan skiced afore the bobbies cam on the scene. He wis ower the dyke an throwe the park like a hare jist efter the crash. I think he'd been drinkin and wis feart tae be catch't!' (T)

SKICHENT (ch as in loch): Having a superior, condescending manner. 'She's a proper Lady Muck wi her skichent wyes.' (B)

SKIDADIL'T: Ran off; took to their heels. 'The bairns aa skidadil't oot the back door fin they saw the minister comin in the front. Bit the man in black diddil't (confused) the geets the neist time fin he jinkit roon the hoose an cam in at the back.' (T)

SKIMMER: A circular, extremely shallow, tin plate with a handle, used for skimming the cream from the milk in the old-fashioned earthenware basins. Outdated by the introduction of the hand-driven mechanical milk separator in the early nineteen-twenties. While we still refer to 'skimmed milk', technically, it should be separated milk. (T)

SKIRL: A scream; a high-pitched cry which is often associated with the highland bagpipes. (T)

SKIRLIE: Oatmeal and onion fried in a sizzling hot pan. The stuff would actually skirl in the pan. It was strictly a working class meal, whose main virtue was its cheapness. (B)

SKIRPS: Splashes or drip marks. 'Nae table manners, yon chiel. See the great skirps o soup aa ower his weyskit.' (B) **SKIRPIT:** Sprinkled; dribbled; splashed; splattered. Same as spleitered. (T)

SKITE: To squirt, spurt or spout water at someone as from a water-gun or pump. **SKITIN:** Slipping; sliding. **SKITIT:** Rebounded. (T)

SKITTER: Diarrhoea. (B)

SKLATE AND SKAWLIE or SLATE AND SCAALIE: Fine smooth slate framed in wood and slate-pencil were used in the schools before the introduction of jotters and exercise books. Although it was forbidden, some of the bairns spat on their slates and rubbed out a former exercise with their sleeve, a habit that was blamed for spreading disease. The slates were taken home once a fortnight for scrubbing. 'Hiv ye scrubbit yer slate yet, Jockie?' would sometimes be asked at bedtime. 'Fut wull the teacher say if ye hinna scrubbit yer slate?' The slates were mostly provided by the Education Authority and the scaalie or slate-stone pencils could be bought in packets for a few pence at the local shoppie. The pencils were quite easily broken but were still usable and most loons always had a bit scaalie in their pooches. Some scholars carved their names on the frames. (T)

SKLENTIN: Glancing. (T)

SKLITER: To slip awkwardly. (B)

SKLYTER: An expanse. 'A sklyter o dubs.' A quagmire of muddy puddles. 'An affa sklyter o dubs at Breemies fairm close. I wis nearly ower the moos o ma sheen!' (T)

SKOOK: To sulk. 'She skookit aa day.' (T)

SKRAICH: To screech, shreik or scream; to reject or object to something. (T)

SKRUNKLED: Washing which is almost, but not completely dry, is said to be 'weel skrunkled'. (B)

SKUDGE: To drudge. **SKUDG'T:** Drudged. (T)

SKUM: To skim. (T)

SKUSHLE: To shuffle. 'Skushlin aboot in her aal slippers.' (T)

SKWEEL: School. 'I say, wuman, ye'll hae tae gar (insist) at loon gyang tae the skweel the day. He's been playin truant again an if he disna gyang ulkie (every) day, the wheeper-in wull be roon at the door.' (T)

SKWEENGIN: Scrounging. (T)

SKYCE: To skurry. 'Skycin aboot the place like a feel hen.' (T)

SKYOW-FITTIT: Splay-footed, like the hands on the clock at ten minutes to two. (T)

SKYRIE: Dazzling bright in colour. 'That's an affa skyrie colour o a car ye've bocht Lewie. Folk'll think ye're sellin ice-cream or something wi a motor like at. Bit folk'll fairly see ye on the road, Lewie. That's ae thing in yer favour!' (T)

SLACK WATER: The tide, besides rising and falling, flows like a river. On the East Coast of Scotland, the flood tide runs southward for six hours, then there is a pause, before the ebb takes over, to run northwards for six hours. The 'pause' (maximum one hour) is 'slack water' or 'the slack'. (B)

SLAKE: To quench. (T)

SLAMMACH: The silvery strands of gossamer seen clinging to hedgerows and fences. A sure sign of wind and rain. (B)

SLAP or STILE: A gate or opening in a hedge or dyke or a platform where you can step over a fence. 'Tell the grocer's vanman tae leave my eerins (provisions) at the slap an I'll pick them up later.' (T)

SLEEKIT: Sly; stealthy. 'He's a sleekit mannie, yon. He wid steal yer knickers aff the tow if he could hide ahin a sheet. He wid steal the worm fae a blin hen fin she wisna lookin.' (T)

SLICH or SLEEK: A deposit of silt or sludge in the estuaries of tidal rivers, usually rich in reed growth, as on the river Ythan, which divides Buchan from Formartine, at 'The Sleeks o Tarty' approaching Newburgh, known locally as 'the Neebra'. (T)

SLICHT: Slight. **SLICHT O HAN:** Slight of hand. Faster than the eye can follow. 'Faar did that doo come fae?' (T)

SLIDDERY: Slippery. (T)

SLIVVER: Excess saliva. 'Dicht yer mou. Ye're slivverin like a nowt beast.' (B)

SLIVVERY DOCTORS: Harmless jellyfish often found on the beach. These are a pale blue in colour, with four rings on the crown. In consistency they are like firm table jelly. If one doesn't know the difference between a scalder and a slivvery doctor, better play safe. (B)

SLOCH: The Sloch, the village of Portessie near Buckie in Banffshire. (B)

SLOCK or SLOCKIT: To slake or quench a thirst. 'Naething like a cup o gweed het tay tae slock yer thirst. Aa that lang ale an ice-cream jist maks ye thirstier on a warm day. There's nae end til't. An fullin yer belly wi gas – na na. If ye're richt dry, there's naething tae beat a cup o tay tae slock ye.' (T)

SLOPE: A shirk or skiver. 'So an so wis jist a slope, nivver tee wi ither folk.' (T)

SLORACH: To eat or drink messily and noisily. 'A slorach o nowt.' (T)

SLUBBER: To sup noisily as with broth; to slubber like swine at a trough. (T)

SLYPE: A lazy, worthless sort of person. **ORRA SLYPE:** An even worse sort of worthless person. (T)

SMAA-BOOKIT: Small; undersized; slim. 'Aye, oor Jeckie's smaa bookit, nae muckle o im, bit he can cairry a seck o corn up the laft stair wi the neist ane, an nae muckle the waar o't I can tell ye. Aye, he's aa there oor Jeckie, an there's mair in im than the speen pits in.' (T)

SMAA DRINK: Small drink; inconsequential. 'Nae smaa drink.' No small drink. Someone who has climbed the social ladder above his former equals. (T)

SMAA WATTER: Calm water. 'As lang's ye keep the water smaa, I'll be content wi jist a scrape.' (B)

SMAA WEET: A drizzle of soft rain. 'Aye, it's rainin again.' 'Aye, bit it's jist smaa weet.' (T)

SMAAD: A blemish on a garment. 'Nivver smaad nor patch wis seen on Kirsty's bonny frocks.' (B)

SMAALINS: Small lines. Lightweight lines with small hooks baited with lug worms or mussels to fish inshore for haddocks, whiting or codling. (B)

SMACHRIE: Same as grulshicks, the cheaper assortment of sweets favoured by the bairns who have as much pocket-money as their grandads had wages. (T)

SMARRACH: A swarm. (T)

SMATCHET: A youngster whose irritating behaviour really annoys you. 'Fin I get a hud o yon impident smatchet, I'll gie her a sair skin.' (B)

SMEDDUM: Energy, spirit or vitality. Or in Scots, 'gumption, spunk or gurr and a likin for hard wark.' (T)

SMIDDY: A blacksmith's shop. (T)

SMILER: A small rake, with a shaft, pulled by a rope from the shoulder. 'Aye, Skirlie, ye're in the smiler the day. Ye wunna rin aff wi that thing trailin ahin ye.' (T)

SMITH: The blacksmith. 'Ye'll hae tae get the Smith on the job 'cos the binder's throwin dogs' legs!' Undersized sheaves little thicker than a dog's leg. It required the Smith to adjust the threading mechanism on the binder. (T)

SMORE: To smother or choke. **SMORIN:** Congested. 'Smorin wi the caal.' Congested with the cold. Stuffed up or 'stappit'. 'I'm aa egg shallies the day. Jist smorin wi the caal.' (B) **SMORE DRIFT:** Smothering snow. (T)

SMUCHTERIN: Smouldering. (T)

SMUCHTY: Descriptive of the close, oppressive atmosphere on a warm, still, summer evening. 'It's gey smuchty the nicht. I doot we're gaan t' hae thunner!' **SMUCHTIT:** Choked up. (B)

SNAA: Snow. **SNAAVIN:** Snowing. 'It's snaavin again, Brucie. Time ye hid in a store o neeps.' **SNAA-VRAITHES:** Snow-wreathes. **SNAA-BREE:** Slush. (T)

SNAP AN RATTLE: Breid (oatcakes) toasted at the fire, afore bein murlled doon in milk, to be suppit wi a speen. (B)

SNAPPIE: The school attendance officer. 'If ye scoff the school (play truant), the Snappie'll be aifter ye.' (B)

SNECK: An iron door handle with small thumb lever attachment fixed on the outside which can be used from within where it is fitted into a slot in the jamb. 'I jist liftit the sneck an gaed in.' A wooden bar was used to secure the door on the inside and was thrust into the hasp at bedtime. These contraptions have been long out-dated by the key lock and door knob. (T) 'Sneck tee the door, an sit in aboot.' (B)

SNECK-HARLED: Plastered. Covered with cement or mud or clay or similar adhesive. 'Mighty Lenny, faar hiv ye been? Ye're sneck-harled. A body wid think ye hid faan intae the mason's troch. Ye'll hae tae tirr (strip) tae the skin tae get redd o that mess, an ye'll need a dook forbye. Ye look like een o yon gremlin chiels in a horror video!' (T)

SNEED: A snood. (B)

SNEETLE: To dilly dally on the way. 'We sneetled ben the road tae the skweel, then we hid to mak a breenge tae be on time.' (B)

SNEEVIL or SNIVEL: Sniffle. A cold in the nose causing a nasal intonation in

149

the speech. 'Aye, Dondee, ye hiv a drap at yer nose the day. I doot ye've gotten a sneevil o the caal.' (T)

SNIB: A small thumb catch for keeping a press (cupboard) door closed. 'Hiv ye snibbit the press door, Sally?' The word is sometimes used as a rebuke for an unpleasant remark or incident. 'Beenie fairly snibbit (silenced) Andra ower the heids o yon racket aboot the hens.' And of course, 'Snib (extinguish) at fag, min. Ye're nae supposed tae be smokin in here!' (T)

SNIFTER: A nasal irritation. 'A snifter o the caal (common cold).' (T)

SNOCHER: To snifter as with a running nose. (T)

SNOD: Trim and tidy; neat and smart. 'Dyod bit she's a snod deemie yon that delivers the papers. Nae a hair oot o place, a fine laachin facie an a trim rig-oot. I widna mind my sheen aneth her bed!' (T)

SNOD IN ABOOT: A hair cut. 'Aye Kenny, ye've gotten a fine snod in aboot. I hardly kent ye withoot the thack!' It could also have been, 'Aye Kenny, is't a connie ye've gotten? A body wid think ye wis new oot o the jile.' The 'connie crop' refers to the almost 'bare as a neep' haircut of the convicts in Peterhead Prison in the days when the inmates were under armed guard. Another hairstyle for men was the 'bowl crop', as if a bowl had been placed on the head and the barber had used it as a guide, leaving a ridge or undershelf all round the head. The salutation then would have been, 'Aye Kenny, ye've been at the barber, an he's left ye like a thackit ruck (thatched corn stack).' (T)

SNOOT: A snout; a nose. (T)

SNORL: A muddle; a confusion; a tangle. 'Ma claes (washing) are aa in a snorl, wuppit (wound) roon the tow wi the win.' (T)

SNOWK: To sniff about looking for information. (T).

SNYAUVEN: Snowing. 'It's been snyauven again, Erchie. The road'll hae tae be cleared or we get oot aboot.' (T)

SNYTE: To blow the nose, one nostril at a time, using the thumb and the forefinger. This is known as 'the fairmer's hanky'. Fishers do it regularly. (B)

SNYTIT: Stunted. (T)

SOD or DIVOT: A slice or shaped cutting of turf that can be used to patch a lawn. (T)

SODJER'S SUPPER: A soldier's supper. Pee and go to bed. 'It's a sodjer's supper for you, my lad, if ye dinna behave yersel.' (B)

SOFTIES: Bread rolls; baps. (B)

SON AFORE THE FATHER: The flowering currant, so called because the blossom appears before the leaves. (B)

SONSIE: Well built. Only applied to females. 'A sonsie deem, oor Elsie; a richt fine oxterfae.' (B)

SOO MOO'T: Sow-mouthed; chinless. The lower mandible so much in recession to give the physiognomal impression of a sow. 'Elsie's affa soo moo't, the cratur. A peety tee, she's sic a fine sinsible lassie, ken?' (T)

SOOCE: To simmer. 'Jist lat it sooce awaa at the side o the fire for a fylie. At'll dee't fine.' (B)

SOOIE: A little ball of oatmeal mixture, before it was rolled out. Highly prized by the bairns. (B)

SOOPLE: Supple. (T)

SOOR: Sour; distasteful. 'Josie his a face that wid soor yer melk!' An unpleasant facial expression. (T)

SOORICK: A type of common wild sorrel which has a bitter taste but is considered edible. 'Dyod, Tam, ye've a look on yer face like ye'd been aetin sooricks.' This weed was a tit-bit for country bairns on their way home from school. (T)

SORRA: Sorrow. (B)

SORT: To repair. 'It disna look like a lot o damage, but it'll need a lot o siller tae sort it.' (B)

SOTTER or SOSS: A frightful mess. 'I nivver saw sic a sotter in aa my days. Ower the boot-heids, among the sharn an dubs an aa mortal thing!'

SOTTER: To potter about. (B)

SOUGH, SOUCH or SEUCH: A sigh; a murmur. The sound of wind. 'Nivver a soun but the sough o win, an the girn o the wintry sea.' (B) Also used to describe a calm state of mind. 'Keep a calm sough, Geordie. It'll nivver happen.' Don't worry, everything will turn out all right. (T)

SOUTER: A shoemaker. **SOUTER'S DEEVIL:** A shoemaker's last or foot. (T)

SOWDER: To solder. (B)

SOWEL: A soul. 'He's a gweed sowel, Magnus, nivver says a wrang wurd on onybody, an gweed-wully tee (good-hearted too). If onybody wuns tae hivin, I think it shid be Magnus. He shid be at the heid o the queue, wytein for Sint Peter tae open the yett.' There's also the bad sowel who would slander you behind your back and do you a bad turn if he could. 'Oh him! He'll get fire an brimsteen in the deevil's foondry, rowin coal for Aal Nick in a barra wi a square wheel, an nae a yoke nor lowse for im in aa time tae come. That's fut he'll get for his pains!' (T)

SOWFF: A simpleton. 'Peer sowff.' Poor fool. (T)

SOWPIT: Turned into soup. Descriptive of potatoes which have been boiled too long. Also referred to as being 'throwe the bree.' (B)

SPAINGIE: ('ng' as in 'thing') Osiers for basket-making, an art in which some of the old fishermen excelled. (B) **SPAINGIE BONNET:** A cap fitted or stiffened with a piece of fine cane bent into a circle. The spaingie bonnet was quite the fashion from about the turn of the century to the middle of the 'twenties. It was very popular with the farming chiels and most of them had a spaingie hoop in their kists. (T)

SPANG: The length of a stride, step or leap. Also the span from the tip of the thumb to the tip of the little finger when the palm is outstretched, a measure used when playing bools (marbles). 'Faa's nearest the kypie?' A shallow hole in the ground to catch the bools. (T)

SPAVER: Trouser fly. It used to be fastened with buttons but now it's generally the zip-fastener. Two Buchan farms are known as Spaver Neuk but I don't think the postman knows them by that name. (T)

SPEED O FIT: Speed of foot. A stoutish lady told a farm hand she thought rabbit flesh was good for slimming, whereupon he advised her it would be an added bonus if she could catch the rabbit herself by 'speed o fit!' which would do her more good than the eating. (T)

SPEEN: A spoon. **SPEEN ABOOT:** Spoon about. Each of the horsemen, loons and bailies had a spoon but they all supped their soup or broth from the same bowl or basin. (T)

SPEIL: To climb, clinging by the fingertips. 'Ye wid hae tae speil for coconuts in Africa!' (T)

SPEIR: To enquire; to ask. 'Ging ower an speir at Snypie gin he wid gie's a len o his peat spaad?' (T) Note: You do *not* speir somebody. You speir *at* them. (B)

SPELDIN: Fresh haddock, straight from the sea, split, cleaned and salted before being hung up to dry in the summer sun. At any time during the drying process they could be roasted over an open fire and proved so delicious that folk came from Aberdeen to enjoy the delicacy. I have heard a local man say that, as a youngster, he would take a roassen speldin and scoff the lot, leaving 'naething but the lug been'. I'm sure he was telling the truth. Any fish unsold were allowed to dry bone-hard, to be used in the winter months when, reconstituted, they were just as sweet. Note: Whitings could be similarly treated, but first choice was haddock. (B)

SPELLS: Wood shavings. 'A larry load o spells dis fine for deep litter for the hens.' (B)

SPENT: Spawned. 'Aifter this breeze, the herrin'll be proper shargers, clean spent. Also means 'weaned'. 'A hantle o spent calfies at the mart the day.' (B)

SPIEL: To recite. (B)

SPINNLE SHANKS: Spindly legs. (B)

SPITTEN: The junior form of 'tartar'. 'I some think (it is my considered opinion) yon lass'll hae a job gettin a lad; she's jist a proper spitten!' (B)

SPLATTRICK: A youngster who simply cannot remain at peace for five minutes, but contrives to be a likeable creature at the same time. (B)

SPLEET NEW: Split new; brand new. 'Froggie his a spleet new cairt!' (T)

SPLEETER: Splutter. 'A spleeter o win.' A splutter of wind; a pretentious speech, full of sound and fury, signifying nothing. (B)

SPLEETER: A spilling. **SPLEETER O WEET:** A heavy shower of rain. 'That's a spleeter o weet, Archie. It's fair dingin doon.' (T)

SPLEUCHAN: A leather tobacco pouch lined with material to keep the tobacco moist. 'Grandad says he's nae wantin a tibacca pooch for his birthday kis he gets it in a plastic spleuchan ulkie time he buys an unce nooadays.' (T)

SPILE: To spoil or ruin. 'Ye're spilin at loon. He wunna dee a stroke o wark fin he leaves the skweel.' (T)

SPLIT-THE-WIN: A Y-junction. 'A mile or so ben the road ye'll come tae a split-the-win. Tak ee the fork tae the richt.' (B)

SPLORE: An exploit or adventure. 'We got up tae some gey splores on the road hame fae the skweel fin we were bairns.' (T)

SPLYTERS: Splatters. (B)

SPOOT: A spout; a rone pipe. **SPOOTIE:** Mostly refers to an open pipe running drinking water. (T)

SPOOT HOLES: The wide apertures in the granite walls of the herring curing yards, to permit the transfer of kits of herring from the carts to the staging (platform) within the building. From the staging, the kits were teemed (emptied) into the farlin, the long wooden trough from which the quines gutted the herring. Spoot holes (all closely shuttered) can still be seen in the fisher toons. (B)

SPOTTY: Fish in isolated, erratic shoals are 'spotty'. (B)

SPRAG: To put a stop to something; a spanner in the works. 'I'll jam a stick in is spokes, that'll fairly sprag is wheel.' (T)

SPRAGS: The fisher term for medium-sized cod. (B)

SPROD: An implement for dislodging limpets from the rocks. This was usually a table knife, with the handle thickly bound with flannel, to protect the hands. The sprod had to be used with a pushing action. To use it like a dagger was to risk leaving the skin of your knuckles on the barnacles. (B)

SPROOT: To sprout or grow. (T)

SPROTTS: Reeds and bullrushes used as thatch for the cornstacks. (T)

SPUD: A potato. Grieve to school kids at the tattie howkin: 'Stop throwin spuds you bairns. I'm nae carin though ye hit een anidder or no, bit ye're mixin the seed.' Mixing different varieties of potatoes planted in the field. (T)

SPULLINS: Spillings. 'Michty, Geordie, ye hiv spullins aa doon the front o yer jersey; a body wid think ye hid been suppin soup wi a fork. Ye'll hae tae pit on a bib, min, like the bairn, an sook a dumb tit!' (T)

SPUNK: A spirit or energy; a matchstick. 'Crack a spunk.' Strike a match. (T)

SPURTLE: A wooden stick for stirring porridge. (T)

SQUALLACH: To squeal. 'A pucklie squallachin bairns.' A group of howling children. (T)

SQUARIES: Hopscotch. Also known as 'Beddies'. A game of hop, skip and leap over squares drawn on the pavement, kicking a stone from one square to another without dropping the foot. Mostly played by girls. (T)

SQUEEBS or SQUIBS: Fireworks. 'It's surely gey near Guy Fox nicht. I thocht I heard a squeeb gaan aff in the village.' (T)

SQUEEGEE: Squint; off the plomb. 'Yer shed's aa squeegee, Manson. It'll blaa awaa wi the win!' (T)

STAA-COLLAR: A stall-collar. A leather halter where the chain is fixed for binding a horse to a stall in a stable. Horses went to graze in these halters, which were fixed over their heads and made them easier to handle at yoking time. (T)

STAGGERS: A cattle ailment due to a lack of calcium in the blood, probably owing to a deficiency in the diet. This could reach a crisis at calving when a cow couldn't stand up but staggered and fell. (T)

STAIG: A stallion. 'Rick traivl't (walked the roads with) a staig in his younger day. The deemie at Wasties didna like im. She said he wis a fule brute, that he chawed tibacca an spat doon the back o the chaumer bed.' (T)

STAMACK: Stomach. Also means to consume or endure. (T)

STAMYGASTER: A surprise; an unexpected shock; a disappointment. The wifie was visiting her friend at the lodge in the wood when she felt an urgency to go to the outside dry lavvy. Inside the loo, while fastening the door, she saw through the slits that a mannie was approaching and she heard him sneck the door on the outside. The wifie felt a prisoner but she didn't panic. Peering through the slits she saw the mannie making for the lodge, where the woman came to the door. As soon as he saw her, the mannie ran back het fit and took the sneck off the lavvy door, muttering his apologies. He had locked in the wrong woman and got a bit of a stamygaster. It was one of his usual pranks while having fun with the wifie at the lodge. (T)

STANG: A sting. **STANG O THE TRUMP:** The best of all. The best member of the family. (B)

STAPPIT FOU: Packed full. The result of over-eating and drinking. The barn could be stappit fu o strae, like the loon who was forking the straw at the end of the threshing mill. He cried up to the farmer who was feeding the mill on the bench and yelled, 'The barn's stappit fu.' 'Then hud it ootside,' the farmer shouted. 'But it's fu an aa,' the loon replied. (T)

STARNIE: A very small amount. 'Nettie, this breid wid be neen the waar o a starnie o butter.' (T)

STASHIE: A row; an uproar. 'I'm thinkin there micht be a gey stashie if they dinna separate the fans at the match.' (B)

STAUCHER: To struggle. (T)

STECH'T: Overheated. (T)

STEED: Stood. (B)

STEEK: To close. **STEEKIT:** Closed; shut; locked; secured against theft. 'Ye steekit the stable door efter the horse wis stown (stolen).' The story is told of the terrible frost in Buchan when all the tattie-pits were frozen solid and during the night the desperate father of several children chiselled out a sackful of fresh potatoes. Before he steekit the hole again, he took a small sheet of paper and left it inside the pit. On it was scribbled:

> It's nae for greed
> It is for need
> I hope gweed man
> I've left ye seed.

To plant the next year's crop he meant, and he did steek the hole to keep out further frost which may have destroyed the remaining smaller potatoes used for seed. If the theft had been discovered, the starving father could have 'gotten a filie aneth the widder-cock.' A sentence in the local townhouse jail under the spire and the weather vane. (T)

STEEL: A stool. Melkin-steel; washin-steel; piana-steel. **PUDDOCK STEEL:** A toadstool. (T)

STEEN: A stone. **STEENHIVE:** The town of Stonehaven. The Stonehaven tobacco pipes, once very popular, are still available. (T)

STEEPIT LOAF: A bread poultice. 'Gweed for sookin a plook.' Good for drawing a boil. 'Cast thy bread upon the waters and thou shalt get steepit loaf.' (Misquotation.) (B)

STEER: A stirk or yearling bullock. 'Steer the porrage.' Stir the porridge. 'Sic a steer o fowk!' Such a crowd of people. (T)

STEETS: Stout wooden supports, one on each side, to keep a boat upright when she is not afloat. A single steet may be used to keep a boat upright against a pier, to keep her from 'faain aff'. Steets are often used by carpenters in major repairs to wooden vessels. The word is related to 'stilts', but in Buchan stilts are stumperts. (B)

STEM: The very point of the ship's bows. 'Ging forrit intae the stem, an listen for the foghorn.' (B)

STEM-MULL: A steam-mill. The transportable threshing plant hired for threshing on the farm. In oral transmission thresh is always thrash in Buchan. 'I think we'll hae a thrash!' (T)

STEY: Steep. (T)

STEYS: Corsets. (B)

STIBBLE: Stubble **STIBBLE RUCKIES:** Miniature corn stacks, less than knee-high, built from stubble roots by the cottar loons in imitation of their fathers in the stack yard. Farmer: 'Dinna big stibble ruckies in at park, min, ye'll ruin ma new girse!' Where young grass had been sown in with the corn crop. (T)

STICK: Wood; timber. 'Hackin sticks tae kennle the fire.' 'Sticks an steens wull brak ma beens bit bynames wunna hurt me!' **STICK:** A stitch. 'It's time ye pit a stick in at blouse, quine, afore it faas tae bits.' (T)

STICKLY: Peat embedded with resin and rotted wood. (T)

STILPERT: Spindly. (T)

STILPIN: Stalking. (T)

STIME or STYME: The tiniest particle; the slightest gleam; miniscule; infinitesimal. 'My bicycle licht blew oot last nicht and it was that dark I couldna see a stime.' (T)

STINCH: Strict; punctual; adhering to principle and discipline. 'He's a gey stinch mannie, oor Roderick. He likes tae hae his horse (pair) at the troch at the chap o the oor, an his thoom on the sneck o the kitchie door on the stroke o sax (tea-time). Ye could near set yer watch on the meenit Roddie yokes an louses, on the dot. The only time he canna control is fan he gyangs tae the lavvy. That fairly gets his hair-spring in a snorl.' (T)

STIRK: A castrated bullock. Castration is essential in high quality beef production and to protect selective breeding of cattle. The plural 'stirks' could also include heifers (females). (T)

STIRKIE'S STAA: Stirk's stall. When the second baby is born, the older one will get less attention. Figuratively he will be put in the stirkie's staa, like a young bullock, and he won't see so much of his mother. (T)

STITE: Absurd nonsense. 'Ye're spikin stite', or 'Ye're spikin oot o a hole in yer face!' or better still 'I nivver heard sic stite. A man on the meen ye say! There's only ae man on the meen an God pat him there fan the wardle began, though ma mither used tae say he wis putten there for hackin sticks on a Sunday. Fut's that!

It's on television. A moon landin ye say? Weel, I'll believe't fin I see't bit there's nae word o't in the papers yet!' Before the American moon landings any outlandish or unusual suggestion made to your parents was always rebuffed with 'Ye mith as weel flee tae the meen!' But astronaut Alan Shepard put an end to all that with his spectacular moon walk in the 'sixties. And he visited Buchan. In April 1989, he landed from a helicopter at Ardallie School in central Buchan, where my wife attended all her schooldays. Alan Shepard was presenting a first prize to the pupils in a competition on futuristic drawing. (T)

STITER: To stumble. (T)

STOBBIES: Thorns. (T)

STOCK: An unfortunate man. 'He's ull come-at eyvnoo, the stock.' He's having a bad time of it just now, the man. **DECENT STOCK:** A likeable chap. (T)

STOCKET: Stubborn. 'As stocket as a new coggit calf.' It was sometimes extremely difficult to get a newly born calf to drink milk from a pail or a cog, working against nature and the teat, so you had to let the calf suck some milk off your fingers in the bucket until it got the hang of it, and they could be terribly thrawn and stocket, despite thirst or hunger. (T)

STOKER: An odd-job lot of fish, sold by the crew of a ship for cash. The owners of the ship don't claim a share of this income. (B)

STONE GINGER: Ginger beer in a 'stone' bottle whose stopper is removed by hard pressure from both thumbs upon the metal catch. (B)

STOO: To trim or to cut a net closely and neatly. (B)

STOOK: Several sheaves stood in a group to dry in the wind. **STOOK PARADE:** The re-setting of corn or barley stooks that have been blown down by the wind. Usually a job for oil-skin suits when the sheaves are wet. One of the most wearisome and discouraging jobs in binder harvesting, now discontinued with the advent of combine harvesting. (T)

STOORY: Wild and windy. (T)

STOOT: Stout; obese; corpulent. It can also mean sturdy, big and strong. (T)

STOT: To bounce. 'Stot the baa.' Bounce the ball. (T)

STOTS AND BANGS: Intermittent; now and then; not a steady job. A stot is also the Buchan name for a full grown castrated bullock and Stott is a highly respected surname. (T)

158

STOTTER: To stumble. (B)

STOUN or STOON: To stound. A shooting pain or sharp ache. 'I hid an affa stoon o teethache (always the plural in Buchan dentistry). I swalliet a fullin the ither wik an I jist howp it's come throwe me an nae stickin aboot somewye. I hid the sair teeth riven oot the ither day an the hole hisna hale't yet. He shid be a butcher, yon mannie, nae a dintist, I thocht he wid hae ma heid aff or he wis throwe. My hale face is aye stoonin an the swallin's nae doon yet.' (T)

STOVERS or STOVIES: A hash made with potatoes and the remains of Sunday's joint. Very nice with a bittie breid (oatcake), an inchie o beetroot an a gless o milk. (B)

STOWN: Stolen. (T)

STOY: A stoy is the rope which connects lobster pots to their marker floats. Since the floats are almost invariably submerged, except at slack water, the stoys are a menace to passing propellers. (B)

STRABS: Stalks of loose straw lying on the stubble after harvesting. (T)

STRACHT: Straight. 'Stracht as a rash!' **STRACHEN:** To straighten. 'Strachen yersel up a bit, min, an nae ging aboot twa-faal!' **STRACHT-EDGE:** A straight-edge. A slim strip of iron used to align the coulter and sock or feather with the board or body of the horse plough. In his poem *To a Mouse* when Burns wrote: 'I wad be laith to rin an chase thee wi murderin pattle!' he was referring to the stracht-edge, which was carried on the cross-bars connecting the two stilts of the plough, and although it doesn't have a cutting edge, it could be handled almost like a sword. (T)

STRAE HAKES: Slatted wooden frames fixed to the byre walls in front of the cattle for holding hay or straw. They inserted their hard tongues between the slats and pulled out the straw at leisure. (T)

STRAEIN HIS BEETS: Putting straw in his boots. 'Faar's the strapper (groom)?' 'Oh the last time I saw him he wis in the barn straein his beets. He's affa buther't wi caal feet ye ken, an a pucklie fresh, dry strae jist helps tae keep them warm in this frosty widder.' (T)

STRAIK: To stroke. Also referred to a flat stick which was stroked across the rim of a wooden tub containing a bushel of corn thereby skimming off the superfluous grain and giving exact measure. (T)

STRAMASH: An uproar; a squabble; a fiasco. 'There wis a richt stramash efter the dunce. Some o the loons had been ower free wi the naphtie.' (B)

STRANG: Urine. 'Jock fell intae the strang hole. Fit a guff!' (T)

STRAPPER: The groom or horseman who tended and drove the laird's coach and horses. (T)

STRAPPIN: Well-built; handsome. 'A strappin chiel.' (T)

STRAVAIG: To parade to and fro on the street; to wander without apparent purpose. (B)

STREEKIT: Stretched. (T)

STREEN or YESTREEN: Yesterday evening. (T)

STRICK: To strike as in 'hit'. Not industrial action. (B)

STRIVEN: Fallen out; no longer friends. 'Yon twaa's striven noo. Peety that, an them been thegither for years.' (B)

STROOP: A spout or milk stoup. 'A taypot wantin a stroop.' A teapot without a spout. (T)

STRUNGE: Strange. **STRUNGE BREET:** A surly chap. (T)

STRUSHLE: Untidy; slovenly dressed. 'Faith but he wis a strushle breet, Bert Mutch. Nivver even dressed imsel for the marts or a roup, jist oot o the byre in his sharny beets and awaa on his bike wi a piece in his pooch, a fag atween his sulky lips, an maist likely it wid still be hangin there fan he cam back in the efterneen, for he widna licht a fag fin it lestit langer chawin't.' (T)

STUCKEN: Stuck; at a standstill; halted. 'I say, Marcus, yon Englishmin chiel fae Nethermeer, I aye forget his name, he's stucken his combine in yon weet hole on the face o the brae abeen the kirk. Ye'll hae tae rig the pom-pom (diesel tractor) and ging ower an winch im oot.' (T)

STUE, STOOR or STURE: Dust. 'Time this place wis dustit. The stue's lyin thick aawye.' **COAL STUE:** Coal dust. **CANDY STUE:** Tiny fragments of candy from the breaking process, kept by the sweetie shop owner to sell to the bairns. (B)

STUMP: To walk about with an air of importance. **STUMPERTS:** Stilts. 'Ye're a fair chiel, hyterin aboot there on yer stumperts.' (B) 'The loon's growin that fast ye wid think he wis on stumperts.' (T)

STUSHIE: A chaotic situation. 'Sic a stushie at the sale o wark efter aathing wis gyaan at half-price.' (T)

STYTER: To stagger; to walk with an uncertain step. 'Here's him styterin hame again. Fit wye dis she bide wi him?' (B) **STYTERIN FU:** Drunk. (T)

SUB: Subsistence money. A cash advance on earnings. (T)

SUDDREN WID: Southern wood. An old-fashioned garden shrub with a strong minty fragrance when the leaves are pressed between finger and thumb. Produces a scent like bogmyrtle. (T)

SUNG: Singed. A close relative to 'scammed'. 'Hey, quine, this soup's sung! Anither meenit an it wid hae been clean connached.' (B)

SUNK: A sunk is an area of ground usually at the front of a house well below street level which permits some light to enter via the basement windows. (B)

SUNNEL or SILE: Sand eels. A rich source of feeding for the sea-bird colonies and for other fish as well. Now very conspicuous by their absence. (B)

SUP: An indeterminate measure, usually of liquid. 'A gweed sup.' A fair amount. **A SUPPIE:** Not very much. 'A wee suppie.' Jist a drappie. (B)

SUPPER'T: Given supper. (T)

SURTOUT: A long, black coat with tails worn in Victorian times. (T)

SUT: So. **ARE SUT!:** Are so! **AM SUT!:** Am so! (B)

SWAAL: To swell. 'I dinna like this high swaal (of the sea). It's likely the dog afore its maister!' (B)

SWACK: Supple; agile. 'As swack as a saach waan.' As supple as a willow wand. (B)

SWADDISH: Swedish. **SWADDISH NEEP:** A swede turnip. (T)

SWALLI'T: Swallowed. (B)

SWEEL: To swill. 'Gie yer face a sweel, Curly, afore the watter queels (gets cold).' A sweel would be rather better than 'a cat's dicht' and 'gie yer face a dabble' or 'a sloosh' would serve the same purpose. If you dipped your bare feet in a pool of cold water you would be 'queelin yer heels in the peel' so to speak, and to 'jeel yer heels' would be a real frosty dip. (T)

SWEEM: To swim. **SWEEMERS:** Swimmers. 'Twinty meenit sweemers.' Doughballs. (B)

SWEER: To swear. (B)

SWEETY BOOLIE: A round sweet. (B)

SWEIR: Unwilling; reluctant. 'I'm gey sweir tae pairt wi my boatie. She's jist like een o the faimly.' (B)

SWEIRTY: Slothful; lazy; work-shy. 'He wis like the poacher's dog fin a hare rose; aye needin a pish!' (T)

SWEY: A hinged or swivelled gantry for suspending pots over the fireplace. (T)

SWICK: A cheat. 'He's a swick o a mannie yon! He wid sell his grunny's cat tae mak siller an he hiz the gift o the gab tae gyang wi't. "Sales patter" they caa't nooadays. A bittie mair polite mebbee, bit he's still a swick! Ye hiv tae mak yer een yer merchant fin ye're dealin wi lads like him, itherwise it's like buyin the pig in the pyoke, an he hiz plenty o them for sale.' (T)

SWIDDER: To swither. (T)

SWINE'S HOOSE: A pig sty. (T)

SWINGLETREE: A double or two-horse yoke where two horses can be yoked to one implement. (T)

SWIPE: To sweep. 'Swipe the fleer fin ye're feenished.' Also a facial resemblance, not always easily spotted, but quite obvious in fleeting moments. 'Man, ye hiv a strong swipe o yer father! I saw that the meenit ye smiled.' (B)

SWITE: Sweat. (T)

SWULT: To sob deeply, as a bairn may do involuntarily after a bout of crying. (B)

SWUPPERT: Swift and agile. 'Rea wis as swuppert as an eel, as swack as a deer, and as teuch as an aal beet.' (T)

SWYTE: Sweat. **SWYTE DRAPS:** Sweat drops. (T)

SYE: To pour milk through a sieve or gauze filter or percolator. 'Sye the melk, Mima, an dinna spull't on the melk-hoose fleer. It's an affa job tae clean up. Aye, full the brose bowels first an syne (rinse) the basins. See that ye tak richt het bilin watter tae wash the search (sieve) an melk pails. Aye faith, ye're nae a bad lassickie though. Ye'll mak a grand wife tae some lad yet, if I could only get ye up in the mornin!' (T)

SYER: The grill or grating on a drain. 'He's sic a sharger he wid near faa throwe a syer.' (B)

SYNE: Since. **SIN SYNE!:** Since then. **AAL LANG SYNE:** Long ago. (T)

SYPE: To seep. (T)

TAARICK: The arctic tern. This name probably comes from the bird's cry 'Taarick, taarick!' (B)

TABBY: A cigarette stub. 'Hiv ye nae a tabby in neen o yer pooches?' This was the sort of question likely to be asked after the night before by someone runted for fags. 'Na Jock, I've ripeit (searched) aa ma pooches an I hinna a gasper left!' 'Weel Chae, ye'll jist hae tae tak a dish o want, kis I hinna ony left edder (either). We'll jist hae tae wyte or the shoppie opens.' (T)

TACKETTY: Covered with tackets. **TACKETTY BEETS:** Boots studded with tackets. (T)

TACKIE: 'Tackie roon the rucks.' A game of catch as catch can favoured by the bairns in the stackyard, but could also be enjoyed in the school playground. (T)

TAE-PIECE: A toe-piece. The half-circular iron tab nailed on under the toe of a tacketty boot. Boy to shoemaker: Keep the right tae-piece weel back, souter. That's the ane fadder kicks ma erse wi.' (T)

TAGGER: Old rope, no longer of use for anything but scrap. 'Time ye wis gettin a hale retour o gear. Ye'll nivver mak a livin wi that heap o tagger.' (B)

TAIK: Stock. 'He took taik', could also be given as 'he took stock or notice of everything.' This has nothing to do with stock-taking in a shop, but simply that he was making mental notes or 'wyein aathing up', and had all his wits about him. A taik can also be a stroll. (T)

TAIKLE: Horse harness. 'Aye, Freddie, ye're for the plooin-match than. Yer taikle's lookin weel. Ye'll mebbee wun a prize wee't. There's some spit an polish gaen intae that, I'm thinkin. Yer collars are shinin like a lookin gless!' (T)

TAINGS: Tongs. 'Tak the taings, loon, an gie's a quile tae licht ma fag!' (T)

TAIT or TET: 'A tait o strae.' A strabble or a few stalks of straw; a small handful or a tuft. 'Tak a tait o strae oot o the ruck tae tie in yer rape, Wullie!' or 'It's nae yer mither's heid yer ruggin, Wullie, rug a tait o strae oot o the ruck an tie in yer rape, an tie't ticht. A slack rape is nae eese fin the win rises!' (T)

TAK SHEET: To bolt or take flight. 'When the storm cam, it gart the windaes dirl an the cat tak sheet wi fricht.' (T) 'Tak sheet' is a legacy from the days of sail, when the 'sheet' was the rope which controlled the sail. (B)

TAK THROU HAN: To discuss. (T)

TAMMY NORY: The puffin. (B)

TANZIE: Ragwort, a field weed with a poisonous yellow flower. Farm animals instinctively avoid it. (T)

TAPNER: A type of sickle knife, heuk or semi-circular blade with a hook on the end for plucking turnips from the drill. There were also straight-bladed tapners and all were fitted with wooden handles. 'Get yer tapner, Ian, an poo a pucklie yalla neeps, bit dinna heid them yet, the shaws are aye gweed for the nowt.' (T)

TAPPIT: Tufted. **TAPPIT HEIDS:** Tufted heads. (T)

TAPSTER: Head of the heap; the one who makes most noise. (B)

TARANEEZE: To torment, tantalise or agitate some person or animal beyond reason. (T)

TARES: Beans and peas grown with oats and cut before ripening for cattle feed. Also suitable for ensilage which is used for making silage-fermented winter feed for cattle. (T)

TARRY-FINGER'T: Sticky-fingered; a thief; a kleptomaniac. 'That tarry finger't deil wid steal yer front door if he could get it aff the hinges.' (T)

TARTAR: A domineering woman. 'Jake winna sit saft wi yon deem. She's jist a proper tartar.' (B)

TASH'T: Dishevelled. (T)

TATTERWALLIP: A tattered outfit of clothing. The sort of outfit you would use to dress a scarecrow. 'Sic a tatterwallip, he's surely tirr't (stripped) somebody's tattie-boodie; I widna be seen in hell wi a rig-oot like at!' (T)

TATTIE-BOODIE: A scarecrow. Most Buchan farmers had one to frighten the crows from their potato field. (T)

TATTIE-CHAPPER: A potato-masher. It was the day for sums at the small country school and the teacher asked wee Johnnie an arithmetical question. 'Johnnie, if five visitors arrived by surprise at your house for dinner and your mother had only four potatoes, how would she divide them?' Johnnie wasn't the brightest of mathematicians, but he answered almost immediately. 'Please ma'am, she widna divide the tatties, she'd chap them!' (T)

TATTIE CLAMP: An earth pit for storing potatoes. Every cottar received a cart-load of potatoes at the end of harvest and to preserve and protect them from winter frost, they had to cover them with straw and earth and form a tattie clamp. **TATTIE PARINS:** Potato skins or peel. 'Dinna throw oot the tattie parins, quine. Pit them in the hen's pot.' **TATTIE-SHAWS:** Foliage of the potato plant. (T)

TAY: Tea. **TAYSPEEN:** A teaspoon. **TAYSPEENFAE:** A teaspoonful. 'I like three tayspeenfaes o sugar in my tay, but I dinna like sweet biscuits.' 'The blades on yon propeller mind me on three tayspeens, they're that smaa.' **TAY-BREE:** Tea brew; tea liquid. (B)

TEE: Also; as well. 'There's a lot o local boats in the bay, an a puckle strangers tee.' Also used as an indeterminate fixing position. 'Come tee a bittie. Ye're ower far awaa. Keep close tee tae me an I'll guide ye the richt road.' 'Are ye gettin the herrin hine aff?' 'No, they're close tee.' If that puzzles you, try this: 'Watch faa ye're pushin tee to up against.' **WEEL TEE:** Getting on nicely (with the work). **KEEP TEE:** Keep abreast of things. **CRY TEE:** To call in. 'Cry tee an see hoo the aal folk's gettin on.' (B)

TEEM: Empty. 'Ye're nae eese tae me wi a teem belly.' 'Teem yer rake!' Empty your stubble rake. Don't bite off more than you can chew. 'Teem barrels mak maist noise.' Ignorant folk often have most to say. (T) 'A hoast like a teem cask.' A cough like an empty barrel. (B) **TEEM YER CRAP:** Get it off your chest. Refers to gossip-mongers getting rid of their claik. 'Yon twaa limmers wir ower at Skliddery Brae teemin their crap an sklavin aabody roon aboot an hardly leavin the neepers wi a leg tae stan on.' (T)

TEEN: Taken. 'I wis affa teen wi Mitchell's car, jist like new!' **TEEN ABACK:** Taken aback; surprised; amazed; shocked; rendered speechless. (T) **TEEN ON:** Pleased. 'I wisna neen teen on wi yon comedian the streen. He wid be neen the waar o sweelin oot is mou.' (B)

TEER: A trait or characteristic feature of similar nature. 'Tessa hiz a gweed teer o her midder in er!' (T)

TEET: To peep; a peeping-Tom. 'Ah wis jist pittin the last deuk egg in ma basket fin I saw the fairmer's wife teetin at me roon the corner. It wiz jist comin doon dark and she widna a kent me, bit I took tae ma heels aa the same.' **TEETIN FURTH:** Peeping out. (T)

TEETH: 'A teeth.' A tooth. (B)

TELLT: Told. 'Ye're jist like the mither o ye; ye canna be tellt naething.' (B)

TEUCH: Tough. (B)

TEUCHAT: The green plover, lapwing or peewit. 'Lookin for teuchats' eggs.' A cold snap in April with snow showers is usually known as 'The teuchats' storm', when the lapwing is nesting in the open fields, exposing herself to sharp frosts, high winds and late snow showers, and running the risk of having her eggs smashed by the encroaching harrows, for it is also seed time on the farms. (T)

TEUCHTER: Someone from the north of Scotland. Also a rough and ready, 'ull shakkin up' sort of character with a ready tongue and free and easy manner. (T)

THACKET: Thatched. **THACKET BIGGIN:** A thatched building, usually a cottage thatched with either straw or heather. **STOB-THACKET:** Stob-thatched. The thatch is embedded in clay. (T)

THAN-AN-AWAA: Long ago. 'I mind fine fin the bairns wrote their lessons on a slate. Aye, but that wis than-an-awaa.' (B)

THE STREEN: Last night. 'We hid a richt fine concert the streen. Aabody enjoyed themsels.' (B)

THEATS: Traces; reins. (T)

THEGITHER: Together. (T)

THIN SKINN'T: Easily offended. 'Vera's ower thin skinn't for the gairden shop an aa yon folk tae deal wi. Ye need a hide like a nowt beast for a job like yon.' (T)

THIRL: To thrill. (T)

THOCHT: A thought. **THOCHT-BEEN:** A thought-bone. The small arch-shaped wish-bone from a cooked hen which was hung on the swey for a few days until it was brittle, then each end was hooked in the cranny (little finger) of two members of the family, and making a secret wish, they pulled until the bone snapped. The one left with the largest part of the bone had his or her wish granted. (T)

THOCHTIE: A very slight degree of difference. 'I think this year's crap could be jist a thochtie better than last year's.' (B)

THOLE: To endure. 'As het as ye can thole.' As hot as you can endure. 'The fairmer's wife bil't a kettle o watter an gart me sit on a cheir wi ma fit in a basin.' 'As het as ye can thole,' she said, 'tae tak doon the swallin.' (T) 'He maan be a hardy chiel tae thole yon woman's tongue.' (B)

THON or YON: Referring to something or someone in the distance or out of sight. (T)

THOOM: A thumb. **THOOM RAPE:** Thumb rope. A hay or straw rope, twisted into shape with the thumbs and fingers without the aid of a thraw-heuk. (T)

THOOSAN: A thousand. (T)

THOWE: Thaw. (T)

THOWLESS: Listless; inert; without initiative. 'Get aff yer erse, ye thowless deil.' (T)

THRANG: Crowded. (T)

THRAPPLE: Throat. To thrapple: to throttle, strangle or choke. 'If Lizzie disna come hame in time tae ging tae the bingo, I'll thrapple her!' An empty threat of course, but it does impress upon us how the speaker feels about the situation. (T)

THRAW: To twist. **THRAW-HEUK:** A twisting hook or spindle for making rope from straw or hay. 'The wifie thrawed her mou.' The lady grimaced. (T)

THRAW MOOSE: A field or shrew mouse. 'The cat's left a thraw moose on the door-step; she nivver ates them.' And this is correct. (T)

THRAWN: Contrary; dour; obstinate; resistive; twisted. 'He's a thrawn kind o chiel; he'll neither lead nor caa.' 'I've been lyin the wrang road aa nicht; my neck's aa thrawn.' (B)

THREAP or THREEP: To insist vehemently; to argue; to preach. 'Fred threapit doon ma throat that moles wis blin an that they didna cairry dirt, bit I kent fine that wisna the case; the man wis clean gyte!' (T)

THREE-NEUKIT: Three cornered; triangular. (B)

THREE-THREIDS-AN-A-THRUM: A cat's purr. (T)

THREEPLETHRAW-HEUK: A brace or handle fitted with three hooks whereby three strands of rope can be twined into one for making heavy rope and horse reins from binder twine. And a threeplet was one born of three – a triplet. (T)

THRISSLE: A thistle. (T)

THROWDER: Untidy; disorderly; slovenly. 'Ye're a throwder vratch, quine. Ging an kaim yer hair an pit a slide an a ribbon in't. Ye canna gyang tae the skweel wi a heid like a hedder beesom!' (T)

THROWE: Through. 'Throwe the reef.' Through the roof. Also means finished. 'We'll seen be throwe wi the hairst.' We'll soon be finished with the harvest. (B)

167

THROWE-COME: The trials and tribulations of life. 'She's heen a sair throwe-come awyte, wi ae thing aifter anither.' (B)

THROWE-IDDER: Lit. Through other; untidy; without method. 'Did ye ivver see sic a throwe-idder place?' Fishers use 'throwe-idder' to describe a confused sea, with the 'motion' coming from more than one direction after a change of wind. (B)

THROWE THE BOWS: Excessive misbehaviour bordering on vandalism. 'Dicey gaed throwe the bows yestreen brakin the hall windaes. There wis nae need for yon cairry on an the bobbies are bound tae catch him yet!' There is also the story of the loon who went 'throwe the bows' and was being questioned by the local bobbie for throwing a snowball (probably with a stone in it) through the manse window. Worse still, the snowball caught the minister in the mouth. 'An wis't the inside or the ootside o the windae that ye broke?' the bobbie asked. 'Baith sides,' said the loon. 'Baith sides!' said the bobbie, 'Faith, bit that's serious. You jist ging roon an tell the minister tae be carefae or I get back an nae swally the evidence!' (T)

THROWE THE BREE: Potatoes over-boiled and dissolving into water. 'Tak aff the tatties ma quine or they'll be throwe the bree!' 'Bree the tatties!' Strain the potatoes. Sometimes used as an excuse to visit the toilet. 'I'm awaa tae bree the tatties!' (T)

TICHT: Tight. **TICHTEN:** To tighten. 'Tichten at bolt min afore it dirls aff.' (T)

TICKET: In the Buchan dialect 'ticket' is used to describe someone's down-at-heel appearance. 'Sic a ticket she wis, an her thinkin she wis the belle o the ball!' 'Jist the ticket' has the sound of approval and is just right for the occasion. 'Jist the verra ticket.' It will serve the purpose to perfection. (T)

TICKIE or PICKIE: A very small amount; a pinch. 'Pit a tickie o vaseline on yer lip, Roddie. It'll hale the crack.' (T)

TIESDAY: Tuesday in the old Buchan calendar. (T)

TIG: Sullen humour. 'Tak a tig.' Take the huff or sulk. It has been known for someone to 'tak a tig' and go off and do something wonderful, or at least unusual, a 'one off' so to speak that surprised everybody. (T) 'Sandy's gaan tae the bowlin, noo. Jist a tig, I'm sure.' A temporary fad or craze. 'Tattie soup taks queer-like tigs it nivver took ashore.' **TIG-TIRE:** Tenterhooks. 'Keep the loon on tig-tire for a fylie.' Keep the laddie guessing for a while. (B)

TILL: To or towards. 'Faa hiv ye bocht the flooers till?' 'Ye're gaan awaa? Far till?' (B)

168

TIMMER: Timber. **SIZZEN'T or WUN TIMMER:** Timber that has been seasoned or dried out. If it isn't sizzen't or wun it will eventually warp. **TIMMER TONGUE:** Timber tongue, a disease in cattle known as actinomycosis resulting in hardening and swelling of the tongue. Mastication and digestion are soon affected and would prove fatal without veterinary treatment. **TAK A TIMMER:** Take a stroll. **TIMMER ON:** Proceed quickly. (T)

TIN-CAN: Corrugated iron. (T)

TINE: To lose. 'But it's nae tint (lost) that a freen gets.' Which could be the acme in consolation or modesty. **TINES:** Spikes. (T)

TINK: Someone with dubious morals who has no concern for their fellow man as long as they themselves are all right. In fact, they are 'jist a puckle coorse tinks.' (B)

TINKIE: One of the travelling people. This word has no reflection on their character. (B)

TINKIE'S MASKIN: A cup of tea, made by putting a few tea-leaves into a cup and adding boiling water. (B)

TINKIN: A telling off. 'Fit a tinkin the loon got for gaan throu the fairmer's park.' (T)

TINT: A tent. **TINTIE:** A small tent, possibly made by the bairns in the back green from 'twaa cheirs an a bed-sheet.' (B)

TIPPENS: Horse hair snoods, made by the fishermen. About eighteen inches in length, these beautifully twined strings were a work of art. The hooks on a haddock line were always on the horse-hair tippins, which were joined to a short hempen 'sneed', which was in turn attached to the line itself. (B)

TIRL: To titillate. To tickle or motivate an object with gentle pressure. 'There's hardly aneuch win tae tirl the tail o a kite!' 'Please Ma'am, Geordie Pittendreich wis tirlin the backs o ma lugs wi a pincil.' (T)

TIRR: To strip off one's clothing. 'Tirr, this meenit, or I get ye richt washen. Ye're fairly yirdit.' Strip this minute till I get you washed. You're in a filthy state. **TIRR A REEF:** Remove the slates from a roof. (B) 'The wind wis tirrin the reef.' The wind was lifting the roof. (T)

TIRRAN: A tearaway. 'A tirran o a bairn at! She's jist new startet tae traivel (walk) an she's in amon aathing.' (T)

TIT: To jerk or pull sharply. 'The beadle titit the towie (pulled the bell-rope) fin he rang the kirk bell on Sunday an gey nearly shook the stang (tongue) oot o her.' 'Tit a tait.' Pull a portion. 'Tit a tait o hey oot o yer cole an mak a thoom rape, Charlie. Ye ken the wye tae mak a thoom rape, divint ye? Pit yer rape ower the centre o yer cole tae hud the heid doon fin the win rises. Fairly that, Charlie. Ye'll be a man afore yer mither yet, min.' (T)

TITHER: The other. 'Fae een tae the tither.' From one to the other. (T)

TOON-KEEPER: The person in charge of the animals on a farm at weekends. Until 1939, when the weekly half-holiday was introduced, it was only Sundays off. 'I'm toon-keeper this first Sunday' or 'Is this your wik-en o the ladle?' were comments that referred to the responsibility of looking after the cattle and horses over the week-end while the other members of the staff were free. On the bigger farms two men were left in charge by turns in a ratio of perhaps twice a month in winter and once a month in summer when the animals were on pasture and one man could cope. (T)

TOONSERS: Town dwellers who were neither fisher nor country folk. Time was, and not that long ago either, when a fisher loon who married a toonser quine, was deemed to have been 'thrown awaa'. (B)

TOOPICAN: A mound or some other upward projection, not necessarily very high, but clearly visible on the skyline. 'I've seen that toopican for years, fae the sea. Noo that I'm nearer han, I can see it's jist a cyaarn (cairn). (B)

TOOSHT or TOOSHTIE: A very small amount. 'Mebbee ye shid sell yer pucklie corn Erchie, afore hairst. Ye canna be sure that the price'll rise efter at. In fack, it micht faa and ye wid hae tae tak less.' 'Ah weel, Hullies, for aa the toosht that we hiv owerby, it wunna mak muckle odds eether wye.' (T)

TOOTEROO: A wind instrument. The term embraces all different kinds including those used by brass and silver bands. (B)

TOOZY: Tangled; rumpled. 'Ye're a fine loon,' said the aal man, an toozled his hair. (T)

TOPPER: A first class person or object. It is an age-old custom for fishers to put toppers on top of a box of fish to attract customers. **TOPPERS:** Rubber knee boots and wellies. (B)

TORY AETIN: Tory eaten. A corn crop ravaged by the tory worm or leather-jacket, the caterpillar larva of the daddy-long-legs. (T)

TOSHIL: A tassel. 'Seggie got a toshil tae hud fin his granfadder wis beeriet.' (T)

TOTUM: A small spinning top which is spun with the fingers. It has six sides, each marked with a score, e.g. Take one, put two, take all. It is really a form of dice. (B)

TOW: A light rope or line. **CLAES TOW:** A washing line. 'Fin the diver gings doon, he has a towie fastened tae his belt. He can signal tae the man in the boat by tittin the towie.' 'Them that has a tumble-drier nivver need a claes-tow.' (B) **TOW-HEIDIT:** Fair-haired. (T)

TOWBEETHE: Tolbooth or Townhouse. Peterhead's Townhouse has been an important landmark to many generations of fishermen. Its tall spire is very conspicuous. Fishermen of my generation (and older) always call it the Towbeethe, but when I mention this to young men, I get a blank look. Today's fishermen don't use landmarks, preferring Decca Navigators and the like. (B)

TRACK: An outrageous outfit of clothes. 'Oh mercy, Elsie, jist look at Dora. Fit a track!' Also means a trench or cart-road or footpath, and getting accustomed to wearing new shoes. 'I'll hae tae track ma new sheen.' (T)

TRACKIE: A teapot. 'The tay wiz nearly aye rickit an files it wiz bile't, an the trackie got affa brookie sittin sae lang on the bink at Craigieburn.' The tea tasted of smoke and sometimes it was boiled and the tea-pot was black with soot being so long at the fire. A tea-cosy was unheard of in the Buchan farm kitchen so the enamelled tea-pot was never far from the fireplace. (T)

TRAFFIKE: To have dealings with. Means the same as 'trock'. (B)

TRAIVEL: To travel or walk. 'We traivelled aa the road tae Aikey Fair.' (B)

TRAUCHLE: To struggle against the odds. 'It wis a sair trauchle in the aal days raisin a femily on a pound a wik.' The pound note in Buchan used to be known as 'a cat's face' but I have never discovered the reason for it. (T)

TRAVIS POST: A post which divides stalls in a byre or stable. (T)

TREELIP: A tall gangling person or an overlength dress on a wineglass figure that sweeps the floor. 'She's like een o yon strae wifies at deem, a lang treelip in at frock, an she's deein the scaffies oot o a job swipein the streets.' (T)

TREESH: To entice or cajole someone in a soft-soap, flattering sort of way. To run after, almost subservient. 'Susan shidna treesh efter Henry like yon; she's only makin ersel chep. If he's intendin takin Susan for a wife he wid a been makin a move lang or this time.' (T)

TREETLIN: Trickling; purling; trebbling; like slowly running water. In human terms loitering or 'treetlin on ahin.' Can also mean trotting. (T)

TRENCHER or TRENCHIN SPAAD: A cross-handled spade for digging the top or first turf on a peat bank. 'Tak the trenchin spaad, Isaack, an ging ower tae the moss an tirr (uncover) the peat bunk.' (T)

TRIG: Tidy; neat; presentable. 'Tubby's fine an trig the nicht, nae like the same lad fin he's sober.' (T)

TRINK: A natural trench in the sea bed. 'If ye could get yer troonks (lobster pots) doon in yon trink, I'm sure ye'd get a labster.' (B)

TRINKLE: A straggle. 'A trinkle o bubbly-nibbit bairns at her tail.' (B)

TROCH: A cement watering trough for cattle and horses. (T)

TROCK: To barter or swap; goods for exchange; to have dealings with. 'I'll trock wi ye, if ye like. A black dog for a fite monkey.' (B)

TROONK: A lobster pot. A name used in St. Combs, north of Rattray Head. (B)

TRUMP: A Jew's harp or 'jaw harp'. 'Bella is the stang o the trump!' She is the metal prong which is vibrated to produce the music. In other words, Bella is the woman behind the man. Bella keeps the ball rolling. Bella keeps the pottie boiling. 'Her man widna get naewye athoot Bella.' She is the strings and bow of the fiddle. 'There wid be nae music athoot Bella. She's the stang o the trump.' (T)

TRUNCHER: A trencher; a wooden platter for cutting bread; a bread plate for oat-cakes or biscuits. 'Gie's ower a corter o bried aff the truncher.' (T)

TRYST: To entice, tempt, persuade or beckon; an agreed meeting place; a rendezvous. (T)

TULL'S: To us. 'He cam tull's aboot parkin in front o his gate!' (T)

TUMLIN TAM: Tumbling Tom. A horse-drawn hay gatherer that could be handled to make it somersault or tumble-the-cat in the swath and drop the hay where you wanted it for building into small coles to mature prior to stacking. The Tumlin Tam was made redundant by the tractor hay-sweep in the very early days of mechanisation, around 1936-37. (T)

TUMMLE: To tumble. 'Henry took a tummle on the slidder an broke a leg.' (T)

TURKAS: Pliars. 'Gie's ower the turkas, min, or I rug oot iss nail.' And if you think the 'or' is out of place there, read the next one. 'Lat "see" ower the turkas, min, or I rug oot iss nail.' See! But that was how we said it. (T)

TURRA: Turriff, a market town on the western boundary of Buchan and

Banffshire. 'Turra Turra, far sorra idder?' Turriff Turriff, where in sorrow other? A traditional expression referring to the town which may have originated with the notorious Trot o Turra, a skirmish in the Civil War of 1639, when the Royalists surprised and routed the Covenanters.

The Turra Coo has become legend, and since her glimpse of the spotlight in 1913 she has been modelled in porcelain and painted on canvas and even the bairns had a Turra Coo piggy-bank. She was a white dairy cow confiscated from Mr Robert Paterson of Lendrum Farm because he refused to stamp the insurance cards of his workers when David Lloyd George introduced the Health Insurance Act in 1913. An attempt was made to sell the cow in the square at Turriff but there were no bidders. A riot involving a thousand people ensued and the civil personnel involved in the sale were stoned and clodded to dispersion. Eight men were charged with civil disobedience but were acquitted for lack of evidence. Lloyd George was a Welshman, thus the connotation 'From Lendrum to Leeks' the emblem of Wales. Eventually a body of local farmers bought the cow back from the authorities, thus paying for the insurance stamps, and returned the Turra Coo to Lendrum, where it is said she died a natural death. (T)

TWAA-FAAL: Bent double; bent acutely forward. 'Aal Hughie's boo't twaa-faal, peer stock. I kin mind fin he wis as stracht as a rash!' (T)

TWALMONT: A twelvemonth period; a whole year. 'It's surely nae a twalmont, since last we dauchled here?' (B)

TWEETLE: To whistle. (T)

TWIG: A glance; a quick or side-long glimpse of something. 'I jist twiggit Charlie on the soo's back fin we gaed by!' 'I twiggit Meggie wi the tail o ma ee! She wis stride-legs ower the byre reef!' (T)

TWO-EYED STEAK: The humble herring, the only steak that fishers of my generation were likely to see. (B)

TYANGS: Fireside tongs. 'Tak the tyangs tae stoke the fire, an keep yer fingers clean.' (B)

TYAUVE or CHAUVE: To struggle, wrestle or labour hard. 'A gey sair tyauve' or 'Aye tyauvin awaa, a gey sair pech bit we'll warstle throwe. I'm fair forfochen an ma face is like a burssen cock (fighting cockerel) and I'm breathin like a fobbit yowe, bit we'll get the better o't yet.' (T)

TYE or OH TYE or TYE-TYE: Words used in giving your assent to something, or assuring someone of something he or she had their doubts about. 'Oh tye, wumman, I'll be there the morn on the dot!' 'Tye-tye, wumman, there'll be a dance efter the concert aa richt!' (T)

TYKE: A dog. 'Aye, Muggie, I see ye've gotten a tyke!' 'Oh aye, it'll mebbee help tae keep the muggers awaa.' (T)

TYLIE: A tailor.

> Tylie, tylie tartan
> Gid up the lum fartin,
> Twinty needles in his dock
> An couldna shoo a garten. (B)

ULKIE: Each and every. (T)

ULL-FASHANS: Curiosity. 'His ull-fashans wid triste (beckon) im up a gas pipe or even a strang (urine) drain.' (T)

ULL-NAETER'T: Ill-natured; unpleasant. 'If the foreman sleeps in, he's ull-naeter't aa day.' (T)

ULL PEY'D: To be sorry for someone; to be sympathetic. 'I wiz richt ull pey'd for yon peer aal cratur lossin er purse amon the lang girss. She'll nivver see't again, nae likely.' (T)

ULL STOCK: Ill stock. 'Nae an ull stock.' Not a bad chap. 'Na na, I wunna hear o that! Waldie Podd's nae an ull stock fin aa's said an deen. Aye aye, I ken his fadder liv't afore im an left im weel aff, bit if ye wis on yer last saxpence, Waldie widna see ye stuck!' (T)

ULL-TEEN: A discordant tune; a foul mood; a bad humour. 'Dod's in a richt ull teen the day. He's surely heen a row wi the wife.' (B) Ill-temper; anger; not to be approached or meddled with. 'He's been in an ull-teen for days on en an hisna spoken tae naebody.' 'Faith, bit Archie's been in an ull-teen ivver since yon coonter-louper lad took his quine hame fae the dunce.' (T)

ULL TO THOLE: Hard to bear. (T)

ULL WIDDER: Ill weather. Wet, rainy weather that was like to put a stop to all out-door work on the farm. Sweir (lazy) folk aye bode (foretold) ull widder, because there was always the chance of a sitting job under the steading roof, like picking the sprouts off the tatties in the cart shed. (T)

ULL WINTER'T: Ill wintered; cattle, poorly fed and neglected in winter. 'They're an ull winter't lot at, aa hair an horn, gey dry skinn't, dinna bid on them Charlie, keep yer siller man.' (T)

ULL WULL: Ill will. 'I took a richt ull wull at thon dominie efter he gid ma bairn the tag (tawse)!' (T)

174

UMMAN: Woman. (T)

UNCO or UNCA: Changed, strange or peculiar. 'Dick wis affa unca like the last time I seen im. Ah'm thinkin he winna be lang for this warld.' In medical terms, so much worsened and altered in appearance to be almost unrecognizable. **UNCO:** Uncommonly. **UNCO GUID:** Uncommonly good; self-righteous; pretentious. (T)

UNTODDERLEY: Clumsy or slovenly in appearance. 'Sic an untodderley mess, ye wid think at lot hid been coupit oot o a cairt.' (T)

UPCOME: A quick-witted remark. 'He his some richt up-comes oor Waldie, affa ready-wuttet an aye his an unser for aathing and maistly a clivver een, like yon time he wis teen for drunk drivin an blamed somebody for stealin the steerin-wheel. Fin the shirra speir't foo that cam aboot he said, 'Weel, yer magistrate, I didna ken at the time, bit I wis sittin in the back seat!' (T) An expression or a saying which may be witty, outrageous, hilarious or profound. It will certainly be unforgettable. For instance: 'Fit wye dis a fart hae a smell? For the benefit of the deaf.' (B)

UP TAIL: To depart in a hurry. 'Dougal wis up tail an awaa, nivver waitit or the end o the match tae see the last goal scor't!' (T)

VERRA: Very. **VERRA DUNT:** The very thing; exactly what was required. (T)

VERTY: Keen; enthusiastic; eager. 'Lang seen I hid a hunger for buiks an learnin, bit nooadays I'm nae sae verty.' (T)

VRAITHE: A wreath. (T)

VRANG: Wrong. 'I'm aa vrang the day.' I'm not at all well today. In the Buchan tongue, 'W' often becomes 'V' when coupled with 'R'. (B)

VRATCH: A wretch. 'Jist ee wyte till I get ye, ye impident vratch.' (B)

VRICHT: A wheel-wright; a joiner; a carpenter; a first class handy-man. (B) 'Michty me, wife, the vricht chappit es thoom drivin in a timmer wedge an he's like tae loss the nail on't. Aye, his thoom nail, fit idder? Bit I tellt im I hopit it wid be a thoom tull im aa his days. Weel, fut else could I say?' (T)

VRINGIN: Wringing; soaking wet. 'I'm jist vringin wi swyte.' (B)

VROCHT: Worked. 'Her mither wis a guttin quine that vrocht wi Sandy Wid (Wood).' (B) **VROCHT PENT:** Practised your art. (T)

VRUNG: Wrung. 'I'm that tired, I'm like a vrung cloot (cloth).' (B)

WAA-GYAAN: Going away; departure. (B)

WAACHY: Stale. 'Gaad sakes, Dod, that's an affa waachy smell. Pit yer socks in the press!' (T)

WAAKRIFE: Wakeful. (T)

WAAL: A well. (T)

WAAL-TAMS: The Buchan name for Nicky-Tams, the leather straps with buckles worn by farm workers just under the knees. (T)

WAAR or WARE: Seaweed, adrift from its roots and cast on the beach. **WAAR:** Worse. 'It could hae been waar, min. Ye could hae been kill't.' (B) **WAAR O THE WEER:** The worse for wear. Can be applied to human or motor car in the name of corrosion and rust, in length of days, behaviour and usage. 'Aal thingie-ma-jig, I've forgotten his name, onywye, he's the waar o the weer the stock, boo't twaa faal an hirplin on a stick; vrocht himsel oot o the cases, yet they say that hard wark nivver kill't onybody yet and they blame it aa on rheumatism.' (T)

WABBIT: Tired; exhausted. 'Suntie Claas is a bit wabbit-lookin in at Christmas caird. He's wye't doon wi parcels.' (T)

WACHLE: Frail; jaded; fatigued. 'Gracie wis affa wachle on er feet. I hope she got hame aa richt!' (T)

WADDIN: A wedding. (B)

WADGE: To shake. 'Wadgin her nieve.' Shaking her fist. (T)

WADNA: Would not. (B)

WAESOME: Sorrowful. (T)

WAFF: A faint scent. (T)

WAG: To wave. 'Wag ta-ta tae grunny noo, wag e handie, ta-ta.' (T)

WAH, WAH: An expression difficult to convey into English, simply because the inflexion of the voice can alter the meaning entirely. Can be used as an expression of contempt. 'Wah, wah, fit's the warld comin tae?' 'Wah, wah, we're nae gaan tae swally that, ye ken!' 'Wah, wah, wi the wife that gings oot at nicht.' When the wind backs (against the sun), it is said to be 'gaan oot'. This is not a good sign, being an omen of worse weather to come, especially if it happens at night. This is old weather lore, and has nothing to do with the wife at all – or has it? Woe unto you if ye hiv a wife that gings oot at nicht. (B)

WALDIES: Wellington boots. (T)

WALE: Choice; selection. 'Some folk like tae shop in Aiberdeen, they think there's mair wale there.' 'Wale oot the best o them, syne haive the lave in the midden.' Select the best then dispose of the remainder in the rubbish heap. (B)

WALLOCHIN: Wailing. 'Efter the fecht, wee Jimmy cam hame wallochin.' (T)

WALLOPS: Strapping. (T)

WALLY DUGS: Old fashioned porcelain dogs which decorated a farmhouse dresser or mantelpiece, one at each end. Now regarded as valuable antiques. (T)

WALLYDRAIGLE: Draggletail; the smallest or weakest of a species. (T)

WAME: Stomach. 'Big Tam Cardno fairly likes tae stap is wame! Sic a slorach at is grub.' Big Tam eats excessively, noisily and makes a terrible mess of it into the bargain. (T)

WAMLIN: Scrambling. (T)

WANNER'T: Wandered. 'Oh the rubbitie (rabbit) jist wanner't awaa, bit he'll be back fin he's hungry for his tay-leaves an meal (oatmeal). Na, he's safe aneuch, there's nae futrets here. He'll be back, dinna worry. (T)

WAPPIN: Flapping loudly. (T)

WARK: Work. 'Twal oor a day, an the wark's nivver deen!' Twelve hours a day and the work's never done. (T)

WARLD or WARDLE: The world. Buchan mother to her big family: 'I've a lot tae be thankfae for – ye're aa wise an wardle like.' Her children had all their wits about them and were sound of limb and without deformity. (T)

WARRIEDRAG: A proper slowcoach; one who habitually brings up the rear. 'Warriedrags, towrags an swypins o the pier.' Riff-raff. (B)

WARSSLE: To wrestle, struggle or plod on, with a hint of weariness. 'The plooman warssled hame, ready for is bed.' (B)

WARST: Worst. **WARST AVAA:** Worst of all. (T)

WASHEN or WISHEN: Washed. 'Billy wis washen ower the side an lost is life.' 'See yon claes that she's hung oot? They're nae half wishen!' (B)

WATCH-POOCH: A watch-pocket. A small pocket sewn on to the inside of the trousers at the waist for holding a watch. The double-cased lever watch was attached to a braces button with a plaited leather boot-lace because it was the farm worker's most treasured possession. Latterly, the modern cheaper watches didn't have a pocket, but dangled freely from the braces button. (T)

WATERY PINTS: The straggly ends of a girl's hair when it needs trimming. (B)

WATRENCE: An entry cut through a hedge or an earthen bank so that the animals in a field have access to drinking water in a stream or ditch. Fencing must be constructed so that the animals can not stray along the bed of the stream nor gain access to any other field. (T)

WATRY: The water closet; the toilet. Door to door salesman: 'Is yer mither in the Prudential, my loon?' Boy: 'Na, she's in the watry.' (B)

WATTER-GAW: A broken rainbow or pillar in the sky. 'A teeth in the sky', the Buchan folk used to say, and mostly it was followed by rain. (T)

WATTER-GLESS: Water-glass, a soluble mixture of soda and potash used for preserving eggs. After use, the liquid was ideal for cleaning the old flagstone floors in the farm kitchens. (T)

WATTERY NIBBIT: A drop at the end of the nose or threatening rain. 'Ye're wattery nibbit the day, Tam. It's surely gyaan tae rain!' (T)

WAUCHT: A long draught; a good long swig of ale, swallowed with relish. 'Tak a gweed waucht o that stuff, Spunkie. It'll gar ye cock yer lugs!' (T)

WAUKIT: Shrunk. 'Yer socks are affa waukit, ma loon. I'll hae tae wyve a new pair tee ye.' (T)

WAUP or WAP: A violent or forceful blow; to slam or clash with vigour. 'Open the car door wide, mistress. That wye the win disna get sic wap at it tae brak the hinges.' (T)

WECHT: A weight. 'That's a gey wecht o a chiel at the en o the Wartle tug-o-war team. It'll tak a gey rug tae haal him aff is feet.' (T)

WED: The past tense of weed as a verb. 'I wed aa the gairden the day!' (T)

WEED: A work-horse with one leg noticably thicker than the other three, is said to have a 'weed'. I believe this fault is incurable. (B)

WEEDA: A widow. **WEEDA UMMAN:** A widow woman. (T)

WEEL: Well. **WEEL ACQUANT:** Familiar. **WEEL-FAURED:** Handsome;

beautiful. 'Aal Jean hid seen better days, but she wis still a weel-faured woman.'
WEEL KENT: Well known. (T) **WEEL TEE:** Well forward. (B)

WEELIM: William. (B)

WEER: Wire. **PYKIT WEER:** Barbed wire. 'On the weers o climbin Bennachie.'
Having every intention of climbing Bennachie but never actually doing it. (B)

WEER: To wear. 'Rags, laddie, did ye say? Ye're lookin for rags? The only rags
I hiv I'm weerin im. Fut mair wid ye hae – the sark aff my back?' (T)

WEESH: Washed. 'This is nae yer washin day, Jessie?' 'No, ah ken, bit am
hingin oot a toolie naethin mair, I weesh on Tuesday an got a fine dryin day.' (T)

WEESHT: Be quiet; listen; pay attention. A word formed by a breath on the
tongue with rounded lips. 'Hud yer weesht min, be quaet!' (T)

WEIRD TO DREE: Destiny to fulfil. (T)

WELKIN: The sky. (T)

WERNA: Were not. (B)

WERSH or WARSH: 'My hairt's wersh for a saat herrin.' My heart longs for a
salt herring. (B) **WERSH-SWEET:** Sour-sweet; unpalateable. **WERSH-SWEET GUFF:** A slightly unpleasant smell. (T)

WHAUP: An empty pea-pod. Also refers to the curlew or snipe and human
comparison is relevant with 'So-an-so wis jist a lang teem whaup wi ferntickles
(freckles) an a reid heid.' (T)

WHAZZLIN: Wheezing; chesty; short of breath. 'Aal Punchie hiz an affa whazzle
at his breist an a bit hoast wee't an aa, he surely hiz brunkitis or somethin. Mebbee
it's aa yon fags that he smokes, he's nivver stoppit whazzlin.' (T)

WHEEBLE: The piping call of the curlew and the teuchat (lapwing). Also a
treble sound on a tin whistle. (T)

WHEEK: To whisk, snatch or dash. 'Jeensie wheekit roon the corner.' 'The loon
wheekit the aipple aff the coonter afore the grocer could see.' (T)

WHEELIE-BIRR: A child's imaginary toy motor car. (T)

WHEELING DRAWERS: Long-legged underpants (long Johns) hand-knitted
from thick worsted yarn known as wheeling wool. (T)

WHEEPER-IN: The school attendance officer. 'If ye play truant ower often, he's the mannie that comes roon tae see fit wye ye hinna been at the skweel.' (T)

WHEEPLIN: Whistling. (T)

WHIGMALEERIE: An article of fanciful design, including dress, sculpture or architectural stone carving or some of the more flambuoyant toys children love to play with. (T)

WHIRLIGIG: A merry-go-round; chair-o-planes; a windmill; a helicopter; a revolving chimney cowl. The perfect name for the 'whirlies' that have replaced the clothes lines on the drying green. (T)

WHITE-IRON: Tin-plate. (T)

WHUNDYKE: A whindyke. (T)

WHUP: To whip. (T)

WICKS: Corners. 'Wicks o yer moo.' The corners of your mouth. 'Ye've been suppin the jam, min, ye're up tae the lugs amon't. It's aa roon the wicks o yer mou. If we hung ye up by the heels, ye'd mak a fine flee-catcher.' (T)

WID: Would. **WIDDIN'T:** Wouldn't; would it not? 'Widdin't it be richt fine if we hid watter in the hoose and didna hae tae cairry't fae the waal?' (T)

WIDDER: Weather. **WIDDER GAA:** A weather gaw. It usually appears as a bright, balmy day in winter when it is least expected. Sometimes caused by changes in the phases of the moon. 'Jist a widder gaa, Geordie. It wunna lest, it'll be rain the morn! Yon skirlin eyster-catchers is a sure sign o rain!' A widder gaa was considered as something of a ferlie, 'like a rummle o thunner in the deid o winter', the calm before the storm, even a snow storm. Another ferlie that sometimes foretold bad weather was restless cattle in the byres. 'Ower muckle dancin aboot amon the nowt in the byre, we'll get snaa yet!' And again 'The hennies took shelter in the cairt-shed fae a shooer the day, and that's a gweed sign.' But if the hens stayed outside in the rain it was a sign that they were expecting much more and that getting wet didn't matter. Another bad omen was the cat washing herself behind the ears. 'Ahin the lugs, oh aye, a sure sign o weet!' Rheumatism and stinging corns were further warnings to expect an on-ding, especially if these were accompanied by low-flying swallows and gossamer floating about. 'Aa that slammachs on the girse, an aa they spider wobs on the whuns, and aa that bluidy midgicks aboot, it's bound tae rain!' Before the days of radio and television, farming folk, like the fishermen, took more interest in the weather patterns, and could foretell it at least a day in advance. The sky was a map they studied daily, even at night, when a halo round the moon fore-warned them of a change in the weather. If the halo was distant from the moon, the weather would change soon.

If the halo was close to the moon, about a week later. The new moon on her back or 'the aal meen wi the new meen in her oxter' were also harbingers of weather mood and change and all were carefully noted. Even the stars had something to tell them and the behaviour of the birds, the rumble of the sea on our coasts, broken rainbows, condensation moisture on the walls, the reek fae the lums, sunrise and sunset, nothing much escaped the weather lore of these old sea salts and sons of the soil, but modern technology has robbed us of the skill of these weather-glass men of the past.

> The evenin reid an the mornin grey
> Is aye the sign o a bonnie day. (T)

WIDDIE: A small plantation of trees mostly planted by the old lairds for cattle shelter or ornamentation, sometimes in the middle of a field and sometimes around the farm cottages, a great place for the bairns to play. (T)

WILE: To select; to choose; to pick your way. 'Wile the road, quine, an nae mak sic a mess o yer sheen.' Avoid the puddles on the road and get less mud on your shoes. **WILE WARST:** The worst of the selection; the poorest sample in the heap. The last wile was after everybody had made their choice – a poor or shabby bargain. **WYLINS:** The left-overs. (T)

WIME: Womb; belly; stomach. (T)

WIMPLIN: Rippling; gently flowing . 'The wimplin burnie streamin by.' (T)

WIN AN WATTERTICHT: Wind and watertight; weatherproof. 'Yer hoosie's win an watterticht, Andy. At's the main thing.' (T)

WIN AWAA: Escape; get away. (T)

WIN EGG: An egg laid without a shell. Maybe for the want of grit. (T)

WIN-CAIRDIT: Wind-driven. (T)

WINCEY: A wool and cotton fabric, widely used in the making of sarks (working men's shirts). (B)

WINDLASS: A home-made device for the winding of wool or twine into balls, from the hanks in which such materials were sold. The windlass was simply two flat pieces of wood in the shape of a cross, with a hole in the centre so that the cross could revolve on an upright piece of wood, normally lashed to the back of a chair. Holes in the arms of the cross took pegs for keeping the hank tight. Note: A 'cut' of twine or worsit was always two hanks. (B)

WING: The old penny, when you could get twenty caramels for a wing. The word can also mean a gift, 'a something to yersel', often more than a penny, a gratuity; a tip. Since the usual tip for a message boy was a wing (a penny) the word has two distinct meanings. (B)

WINKERS: Eyelashes. (B)

WINKIN: Brimming. (T)

WINLIN: A bundle of hay or straw twisted into shape in front of the body under the oxters and tied with a wisp to hold it together, much the same as tying up a fleece at shearing time. Winlin making was practised on some farms where straw had to be carried over the close from barn to byre, preventing it from blowing away on windy nights. 'A hale efterneen makin winlins, it's aneuch tae gar baith yer een look oot at ae hole.' The modern mechanical bunchers and baling machines have made the old winlin makers redundant. (T)

WINMULL: A windmill. 'The widder mannie on the wireless says there's gyaan tae be a gale, Wullie, so ye'd better pit the brake on the winmull.' (T)

WINNA: Will not. (T)

WINNER: Wonder. **WINNER'T:** Wondered. 'Fin the slater tell't me fut it wid cost tae sort the reef o the cairtshed I winner't if I wiz hearin richt!' (T)

WINRAW: A swath of hay or straw gathered by a rake. 'Keep yer winraws stracht, min, for balin. Ye're leavin im twistet aa ower the place, like a stot pishin amon snaa!' (T)

WINTER-STED: Beset by winter. (T)

WINTIN AWAA: Wanting away; fading away. (T)

WITHER: Weather. (B)

WITLESS: Irresponsible. A close relative of 'saachless'. (B)

WIVEIN SHEATH: A knitting sheath. A perforated leather sheath or cushion on a belt worn by knitters for lodging a spare knitting needle. Some were made of straw and worn at the side gave some support for the knitter's arms. (T)

WIVVEN DRAAVERS: Woven drawers; men's knitted long underpants. (T)

WIZZEN'T: Wizened; shrivelled; shrunken; wrinkled; dried out. 'The aal tatties wis gey wizzen't or the new eens wis ready.' (T)

WOBBY: Covered with cobwebs. (T)

WORM-AETIN: Worm-eaten; eaten by wood-worm. (T)

WORN AWAA: Worn away; deceased. 'Alfie Paterson's worn awaa. But he wis nae smaa drink an I'm sure he wull be miss't.' (T)

WORRITE: Savaged; mauled. 'The fairmer shot Hebbie's dog kiz it worrite a sheep. An mebbee jist as weel, it could hae been a bairn neist time.' (T)

WORSIT: Knitting wool. 'A worsit ganjie.' A home-knitted jersey. (B)

WORTH I THE QUEETS: Crippled round the ankles. (T)

WRANG SPY: A wrong spy; mistaken identity; to greet or address the wrong person, like someone's double or twin. In another sense it could mean a false alarm or a hoax, or you could accuse or blame the wrong person for some misdeed with an error of judgement. (T)

WRIGG LAMB: A male lamb with only one testicle in the pouch at castration time, known in Buchan as 'Dockin time'. All the castrated lambs had half their tails slashed off as a precaution against fly-strike (maggots), but the rig was left with a full-length tail to distinguish him in the flock as requiring castration at a later date when the second testicle had descended. (T)

WUD: Mad. 'Peer Sandy, he's gaen clean wud!' **WUD:** Wood. 'Gyang tae the wud an gaither sticks!' (T)

WULKS: Winkles. 'I like a fish supper, but I dinna think I could stammick yon wulks that the English seem tae like.' (B)

WULL: Will. **WULLN'T:** Will you not? 'Ye'll surely buy twaa tickets for the raffle, wulln't ye?' **GYANG WULL:** Get lost. 'Mind an meet us at the bus for fear we gyang wull amon aa that new hooses.' (T)

WUMPLE: Entanglement. 'Muggie's washin wis in a fair wumple fin she took them oot o the washin machine for the spinner. It took a bit o sortin oot or she got er claes aa oot o idder (out of each other) for ye ken yersel ye canna pit them in the spinner like at.' (T)

WUN: To win to; to be permitted to attend. 'Will ye wun tae the dunce, think ye?' 'Nae fears, my mither winna hear o't.' 'I couldna wun throwe the door, the place wis fair stappit.' 'I didna wun tae the kirk, we nivver made the lan till supper time.' (B) **WUN:** Dried out, matured as hay, ready for storage. 'The rape seed's nae ready for threshin yet, Wullsin. It's nae wun, the wither's been ower dump is filie. Ye'll need tae leave't lyin anither wik onywye.' (T)

WUN UP: Wound up; excited. 'The bairn wis affa wun up aboot Christmas, an fin she saw Suntie Claas, her een wir shinin like gless bools.' (T)

WUP: To wrap; to bandage. (T)

WUSP: A wisp; a handful. 'A wusp o strae tae strae his beets.' (T)

WUSS: To wish. (T)

WUTTER: The barb on a fish hook. 'Ye'll hae a job gettin that heuk oot o yer finger. It's in ower the wutter.' (B) **WUTTER:** Disagreeable. 'He's a wutter o a mannie, yon: he aye hiz his horn in somebody's ribs.' (T)

WUTTIT: Exasperated. 'I'm fair wuttit at this blastit engine. It keeps stoppin at the maist awkward times.' (B)

WYE: Way. 'Is this the wye tae Aiberdeen?' **FIT WYE?:** What way?; Why? 'Fit wye? I'll seen tell ye fit wye!' **WYE:** To weigh. 'Wye oot a steen o tatties for me.' 'That thing must wye a ton, at least.' **WYE O'T:** Way of it. 'It's nae easy diggin yer gairden, but if ye want fresh vegetables, that's the wye o't.' (B) **AA THE WYE:** All the way. **FIT IDDER WYE?:** Which other way? **FIT WYE'S AT?** Why is that? (T)

WYELED or WEYLEAD: Misled. 'Yon lad wi the holes in his briks wyeled oor Dorothy for a file, bit she hiz mair sense nooadays an bides at hame.' (T)

WYENIN: A rig or section of a field which has been ploughed at a different angle from the rest of it. This was done to suit the flow of surface water at different levels and the angle of ploughing could sometimes be as much as ninety degrees. 'There's twaa wyenins in at park tae suit the hing o the grun.' (T)

WYTE: Fault, guilt or blame, as in the Charles Murray poem 'It wasna his wyte he was late.' Prefixed with 'weel' the word is also used in an expression like 'Weel-a-wyte!' meaning that the person is in agreement with what has been said, or that he is surprised at the announcement, and it might also be translated as 'Is that so!' and amended with 'weel, if I hadna heard it fae yer ain mou I widna hae believ't it,' or 'Weel-a-wyte, fut's the warld comin tull?' Wyte can also mean to 'wait' for someone or something. 'Fit's aa yer hurry? Ye hid tae wyte or ye wis born an ye'll hae tae wyte or ye dee.' (T)

WYVE or WIVE: To knit with wool. 'I'll need tae get a fyow hunks o worsit fae the shop tae wyve a new jumper for the quine.' (T)

WYVER: A spider. (T)

YAAR: Surface corn weed; spurry. 'An affa yaar amon yer neeps, Donal. It's time ye wis startit the secont hyowe.' (T)

YAAVINS: Awns. The beard of barley or oats. (T)

YABBLE: A blether with too much to say. 'Sic a yabble o a cratur yon!' (T)

YAKKIE: The Peterhead name for the Eskimo which is derived from 'Yaqui'. 'Fin I wis a loon, a Yakkie cam tae bide in Jamaica Street, jist across the road fae hiz. Jingers, boys, he took the caal, he took the mirrles, he took the jandies, he took the kink-hoast an aa mortal thing there wis to tak. So they pit him hame tae dee, but it seems the frost kill't aa the germs, cos he lived till he wis ninety-two.' **YAKKIE DALL:** Eskimo doll. (B)

YALLA FISH: Yellow fish; smoked fish, usually haddock. There was a time when only smoke was used to colour and flavour fish, but for many years most processors have used a dye. Same with kippers. 'See if ye can get a bittie hame-smokit, yalla fish, Agnes. I'd fairly enjoy it wi a poached egg for ma tay.' (B)

YAMMER: To cry out in distress; to wail or whine. (T)

YARK: An expression of action which requires no finesse. 'Yark on the paint, afore the rain comes.' 'Yark the door open.' 'A gweed yark on the backside widna dee him ony hairm.' **YARKIT AN BREENG'T:** Slammed things about. (B)

YARP: To carp; to complain. (B)

YARR: Corn spurrey. (T)

YAVAL BROTH: Broth of second day's vintage. A hungry tink was knocking on doors begging a piece. He claimed he hadn't eaten for two days, but nobody responded. At last a friendly looking woman answered a door. He explained his dilemma and offered her his blessing if she would provide him with food. 'Div ye like yaval broth?' the woman asked. 'Oh aye, I like yaval broth,' he said, 'I'm that hungry.' 'Ah weel,' the woman replied, 'come back the morn!' and slammed the door in his face. Third day's vintage is known as Resurrection broth. (T)

YAVAL CORN: Corn grown for the second year in succession in the same field ploughed from lea. This was abandoned in the tractor age when the heavy disc-harrows replaced the horse grubber for the cultivation of root crops, when it became possible to grow turnips directly after lea ploughing. (T)

YAVINS: The beard or bristle on barley oats which comes off in the threshing. When it gets inside the shirt, it causes great irritation and itching on the skin. 'I hid tae change my sark an semmit after a day at the mull threshin barley. I wis jist crawlin wi yavins!' (T)

YAWL or YOLE: A small fishing boat. (B)

YAX: An axe. 'There's naethin like a sharp yaxie for cuttin a ticht rope. (B)

YERNED MELK: Milk warm from the cow, treated with rennet and allowed to set overnight. (T)

YESTREEN: Yesterday evening. (B)

YETT: Gate. 'Dinna forget tae shut the yett ahint ye, min.' (T)

YIM: The thin film which can be seen on an unpolished mirror or on the inside of a car windscreen. A yim is that which makes you feel yer face needs a dicht. 'The bairn's been playin oot there in the sun aa day. Time she wis tirred an intae the bath tae tak the yim aff.' (B)

YIRD: The earth. 'Hud on the yird, min, tae widen yer furr.' Adjusting the bridle in front of a plough to widen the furrow. (T) **YIRDIT:** Absolutely filthy. 'Far on earth hiv ye been? Ye're jist fair yirdit!' (B)

YIRN: To curdle **YIRN'T MILK:** Curds and whey. (T)

YOAM: Aroma or smell. 'Sic a yoam o bil't neeps comin up the stair!' 'Grandad wis smokin es pipe an the hoose wis yoamin foo o rick!' (T)

YOKE: A wooden spar for pulling a plough. Two yokes and a swingletree (double yoke) for two plough horses. Also a shoulder spar for carrying water pails. **YOKIN:** A period of work. **YOKIN TIME:** Time to start work. (T)

YOKIE: Itchy. 'If I come ower, my loon, I'll gar ye claa far it's nae yokie!' If I come over, my boy, I'll make you scratch where it isn't itchy! (B)

YOWE: A Ewe. 'A Broken-moo't yow' An old ewe with some of her teeth missing, considered worthless for further breeding, except by careful crofters prepared to hash her turnips and risk single lambs. Her only value was as butchers' meat in a glutted market, but she was so cheap at the marts the crofters could afford to buy perhaps a dozen from the hundreds on offer, and if they had grass for a winter's keep they could at least sell the lambs at a profit. As one old worthy has it, 'I can mind the days it didna pey tae ploo the grun; the corn wis ower chep, so a lot o folk laid doon their parks in girse an the place wis swarmin wi sheep. Ye could buy a broken-moo't yow at the marts for a shullin, an efter even a year's keep ye could hardly loose on a deal like that.' A shilling, five decimal pence for a healthy ewe – no wonder they were called the 'hungry 'thirties', at least they were for the farmers. (T)

YOWL: To shout; to cry out loud. 'Dinna yowl at me like at, min. I'm nae deef!' (T)

Sayings

How do sayings originate? Let me give you an example. One day, a few years ago, I met a kenspeckle lass, hurlin hame her eerins in an aal coach. The coach wis really ancient, wi smaa wheels, an its belly close tae the ground. 'Aha!' says I, 'That's a richt handy thing ye've gotten the day, Baabie!'

'Jist the bloody dunt, Peter. Jist the bloody dunt!' she replied.

So now, as a family, instead of using the actual apt phrase, we say, 'That's jist the wifie's coachie!' (B)

A belly like a bloated yowe.
Flatulent; blown up; full of wind. (T)

A bigger loss fan a gweed hen dee't!
It was nothing compared to the loss of a good laying hen! (T)

A bite fae the dog.
A remark often used during or just after a hangover and sometimes suggested as a respite from the discomfort and sickness of having consumed too much alcohol the night before. 'A bite fae the dog that bit ye last nicht.' Another dram, but lacking experience, I would suggest strong hot tea to muzzle the dog. (T)

A blink afore a drink.
Bright sun between showers. (T)

A change o a Deil, but aye the same hell.
A change of a Devil, but always the same hell. Moving to another farm. (T)

A doo's claikin.
A dove's hatching from two eggs. In the days of bigger families, when a married couple had only two children, they were considered to have only 'a doo's claikin', assuming the pigeon hatched only two chicks. (T)

A dowpie like an uncie o tay.
A bottom like an ounce of tea. Refers to a baby's bottom. (B)

A face aa roon like a toon clock.
A town clock usually has a face on four sides and this expression describes someone who prefers to agree with everybody. (T)

A face like a broonie.
A scowling, discontented face. Broonie: a corruption of 'bruin', a bear. (B)

A face like a fairmer's erse on a frosty mornin.
Not very prepossessing. I have never seen the object of the saying, but I have

187

seen the fisher equivalent hundreds of times. Gyaad sake, it's nae bonny! (B)

A face that wid spen a foal.
A face that would put a foal off its mother's milk. (B)

A gey tak on.
A challenge; a formidable undertaking. 'For charity ye say! Me loup ower the dryin line on a claes prop? That's a gey tak on!' (T)

A herber for stue.
A harbour for dust. (T)

A hoose like a byre.
An extremely untidy house. 'Nora's hoose is jist like a byre, and the nowt could bide in't. In fack I've seen a byre wi a cleaner greep mony a day, for wi the bairns rinnin oot an in she his a bakit roadie fae the door tae the fireside, an aathing lyin aawye. Sic a redd up is ivver ye saw!' (T)

A lang road tae wun seen hame.
A long road to reach home. The opposite of a short-cut, like 'gaan roon bi the road like a cairt (horse cart) rather than crossing the fields.' To go out of your way for some reason or other on the way home. (T)

A may-be is nae a gweed honey bee.
If you are only maybe going to do something, it can hardly be taken as a promise. But nothing is certain nowadays, except death. In more practical terms, in May the fields of rape-seed blossom provide an ambrosial feast for the bee. (T)

A mou like a torn pooch.
An uncomplimentary description of someone's mouth. (B)

A neck for onything bit soap.
Referring to someone who is bold and rash, but at the same time enterprising, with the will to succeed. (T)

A niz like the jib o a cran.
A nose like the jib of a crane. (T)

A roon O.
A nothing; something of no consequence. (T)

A sodjer's supper – Pee and go to bed.
'It's a sodjer's supper for you, my lad, if ye dinna behave yersel.' (B)

A staanin seck aye fulls best.
A standing sack always fills best. Referring to someone who hasn't a chair and

has to stand at the dinner table. (T)

A stem-stack an a styag aboot er.
A steam-stack and a stallion about the farm. Back in the early days of steam, some farms had a threshing mill of their own, driven by a steam-engine in a shed outside the barn and the tall brick smoke-stack could be seen for miles around. These were mostly hill farms, where it was impossible to collect water in a dam to drive the threshing mill. The smoke-stacks gave these farms a distinction above their neighbours, a sort of dignity not to be trifled with, a 'wha daar meddle wi me?' aspect which commanded respect and envy, and if the farmer owned a pedigree stallion that could be hired in the district, his standing was further enhanced in the public mind. 'On aye,' some outsider would tell a stranger, 'Hullies is a gey toon wi a stem-stack an a styag aboot er!' Some of these smoke-stacks can still be seen on the farms, and still command respect in the sense that they are now regarded as class-B protected buildings. Reminiscent of their day and age is the following rhyme:

> Aal Fernie stood ahin the door,
> And aa that he'd a fancy for
> He pinted tae gyang ben,
> But horsemen, loons and orramen
> Sat roon aboot a muckle dish
> And suppit speen aboot.

This goes back to Victorian times and is the exact opposite of our mill hostess with the mostest on threshing days. It gives a picture of the farmer standing behind the kitchen door selecting his guests for 'ben the hoose' lunch, presumably of better quality and wholesomeness than the blibber of soup in the kitchen where the horsemen, loons and bailies (cattlemen) 'suppit speen aboot' from a big basin or earthenware bowl on the table. Ben the hoose they probably had something that required a fork and knife for consumption, and maybe a dram forbye. (T)

A sweet singin bird the craw.
If you heard someone singing a song grossly out of tune you would remark 'He's a sweet singin bird the craw!' (T)

A willan hert lichtens wark.
A willing heart lightens work. (T)

Aa erse an pooches.
Commonly referring to a man of small stature who had an unwarranted high opinion of himself. (T)

Aa his back teeth are up.
His wisdom teeth are in position. He has all his wits about him. (T)

189

Aa mou's maun hae mait, an them that canna chaw maun tak the pap.
All mouths must have food, but the baby with no teeth must take the teat, bottle or breast. (T)

Aa ower the tyauve.
Making heavy weather of something. 'The wife's up tae her oxters wi spring cleanin the day, aa ower the tyauve.' (B)

Aa tarr't wi the same stick.
All recognised as being similar. (T)

Aabody canny get.
Not everyone merits an invitation. (T)

Aal meen mist, new meen's drift.
Mist at the latter stage of the old moon foretells snow with the new moon. It does sometimes happen. (B)

Ae man's mait is anidder man's pooshin.
One man's food is another man's poison. What suits one may not suit another. (T)

Afore the win.
Before the wind; having a fair wind; having no further worries. 'Bill wis gey sair made for a gey lang time, but he's made a heap o siller this last puckle ear. Aye, he's afore the win noo.' (B)

Ah div sut ken!
I do know! This was sometimes the retort if someone had been accused of ignorance or lack of intelligence on a certain subject. Mostly used by children to protect or uphold their standard of education. 'It is sut!' It is so! is used to confirm a statement or contradiction in which the child is determined to have the last word. (T)

Ah'll see ye past the hen's dish.
The dish containing food scraps for the hens was usually kept near the gate of the farm house, so the saying implied a visitor might steal something on their way to the gate. (T)

An affa big dookit for jist twaa doos.
A very large house for just two people. (T)

An affa skirlin for aa the oo!
Such great effort for small reward. A great noise to little effect. 'A fite elephant for aa the bother it wis.' (T)

An unco come doon.
A step down on the social ladder. (T)

Aneuch's as gweed as a feast.
Enough is as good as a feast. (B)

Are ye ill wi rottans?
Are you troubled with rats? (T)

As broad's ye are lang.
As broad as you are long; having tried a fresh solution to a problem, only to find that it has made not the slightest difference. (B)

As hard as Hinnersin's erse.
Henderson is supposed to be an old Scots nom-de-plume for the devil, and his backside was said to be ten times harder than flint. (T)

As muckle eese as an ae-leggit loon at an erse kickin contest.
Not much use at all. (T)

As peer as the links o the crook.
As lean as the links on the swey chain. Refers to someone who is incredibly thin; skin and bones in fact. (T)

As ye mak yer bed.
As you make your bed, so must you lie in it. If it is the life you choose, you should make some attempt to put up with it, whatever the circumstances. (T)

At's nae wa'cast.
That's not to be thrown away; it has some value, a bargain almost. (T)

Aye aye, ye're aye tae the fore!
You're still alive and kicking, or at least surviving. (T)

Aye hingin thegither.
Managing to survive. (T)

Back tae aal claes an porritch.
This was the resolve after a night on the tiles or painting the town, where a lot of expense had been incurred. Put away the finery. (T)

Bairns get leave to growe as they hing, nooadays.
There is no discipline amongst youngsters, nowadays. (B)

Beery Napoleon.
An expression used by the cottar when he dug a hole in the ground to bury the contents of his dry lavvy pail. The saying probably originated during the Napoleonic Wars when everybody feared and hated Napoleon. It was still done in Hitler's day but the cottars persisted with Napoleon, and even the Kaiser was

omitted in his time. Nowadays most cottars have bathrooms and Napoleon is flushed into the septic tank. (T)

Better than a steen ahin the lug.
In a physical sense almost anything was better than a blow behind the ear from a stone. (T)

Blaa blaa yer kilt's awaa.
An impromptu remark in response to someone who has been boasting. (T)

Buy chep, buy dear!
In other words you get what you paid for with inferior goods. (T)

Caa'd aff yer stotter.
Caught off your balance. To be upset by a change in routine or circumstances. (T)

Chaa-the-poker day.
Chew-the-poker day. The day before pay-day or pension day, when resources may be running low. (B)

Claa oot yer egg an tak up a scone!
A polite way of telling a guest that they are welcome. (T)

Claa yer pooch.
Cost you a fortune. (T)

Cock fire snap!
You placed a piece of bread or a pancake on the dog's snout and dared him to eat it until you had commanded him to do so. Some farmers' collies were adept at the trick, having been trained by the workmen in the kitchen at meal times. It was amusing to watch a fairly big dog sitting patiently on his haunches and his tail brushing the stone floor, the fragment of precious bread balanced on his snout, and his eager eyes watching your face. Then you issued the command, wagging your forefinger in the dog's face thus:

> This is a bit o King Geordie's breid,
> An dinna ye aet it or he be deid.
> (A slight pause and then)
> He's deid lang syne so
> Cock fire snap!

Whereupon the dog tossed the bread into the air from his snout and caught it in his mouth on the way down, chewed and swallowed it, then stood on all fours waiting for the next tribute to King Geordie. One wonders if the trick had a Jacobite origin, taking the raise out of the House of Hanover. (T)

192

Come nicht, come ninepence.

A shore-worker's expression, on looking forward to the end of the day. Not of this generation, of course. (B)

Come throwe the hard.

Come through the hard. To meet with prolonged adversity. This is the fisher equivalent of the country term 'Get the win in yer face.' (B)

Could I borrow a starnie tay, gweedwife?

This was the sort of request made to the cottar wife by the tinker woman when she came to the door with her pack; or it may have been a starnie sugar she was after, or merely a suppie bilin watter tae mak tay, but always the minutest quantity, and starnie suited her purpose not to offend the 'gweedwife' but rather to stimulate her charitable generosity in a more liberal quantity than was asked for, sometimes rewarded with a trinket from the tinker's pack or even a cup and a saucer if the 'gweedwife' had been doubly generous. 'An noo, if ah could jist hae a bittie tibacca for ma pipe ...' (T)

Cut yer feet.

If some sod steals your lass, he is said to have 'cut yer feet'. (B)

Deil the bit!

The response to some sensational piece of information. (T)

Did ye come speed?

Did you succeed in your quest? Did fortune smile upon you? (B)

Dingin doon hale waater.

An absolute downpour. (T)

Dinna tak the doo or ye hae the doocot.

Don't take the dove until you have a dovecot. Don't get married until you have somewhere to stay. (T)

Dog afore its maister.

A high swell which is very often the forerunner of an approaching storm. (B)

Dry breid's gweed ower the watter.

Dry bread's welcome in a land of famine. (B)

Ee'll sup sorra wi the speen o grief.

If you don't mend your ways, a sticky end awaits you. (B)

Ee're nae ilkie body nor yet some folk.

You are someone special being treated like that. (T)

Faan's she gaan to be better?
When is her baby due? (B)

Fae the hey tae the heather.
From the hay to the heather. This meant that the cottar had made a bad flit and would be worse off at his new place of employment. (T)

Fess tee yer hairt.
To revive your heart; restore your appetite; revive your drooping spirits. 'Here's a bonny fresh haddockie, noo. That'll fess tee yer hairt!' (B)

Fint a fears!
Not likely!

Fit sorra idder?
What else could you expect? (B)

Fite the idle pin.
To skive or loiter around when you should be working. The idea of whittling a piece of wood with a pen-knife when you should be better employed. (T)

Flog the clock.
When herring drifters were lying at their nets, one man would be on watch. He would waken his relief at the end of one hour, then turn in. The relief could wait a few minutes before 'flogging the clock', advancing the clock one hour and calling his relief, thus stealing an hour of sleep. (B)

Foo's yer doos?
How are your doves? A friendly greeting similar to the present day 'Fit like?' or 'Foo's yersel?' used either in passing or as a prelude to further conversation. (T)

Frae the stibble tae the clover.
From the stubble to the clover. When a cottar made a move to a better job. (T)

Gang the richt gate.
Do the proper thing; no half measures. 'Ye'll marry that quine an gang the richt gate seein she's wi a bairn tae ye. Nae neen o yer bidie-in affairs!' (T)

Gang yer ain gate.
Go your own way. (T)

Ging inta ma buckie.
Like a molusc retreating into its shell; shying away. (T)

Good al Meggins!
An exclamation of surprise. Same as Govey Dicks! (B)

Guess gin I be barfit!
A challenge issued to all and sundry by an excited bairn. This was to draw attention to the fact that the bairn had new shoes, something of a rarity in those days. Adults would utter the required gasps of amazement, while less fortunate bairns would touch the new shoes with a moistened finger, crying 'First luck!' (B)

Guide fin ye hae, for want'll guide itsel.
Be thrifty in prosperity, that you may have something in reserve for the lean times. (B)

G'waa an flech yer dickey!
Go and pick fleas out of your shirt! Go and jump in the dock! (B)

G'waa an flee up!
Go fly a kite! Get lost! (B)

Hame sweet hame an the fire black oot.
Perhaps the second part of this one has been added as a joke, but with so many divorces nowadays, it may have become a reality. (T)

He couldna tell dirt fae chappit dates.
He was extremely stupid. (B)

He didna get muckle cuttins.
He was not made welcome. He didn't get much thanks for his pains. (T)

He disna ken a bee fae a bull's fit!
He is entirely ignorant. (B)

He hisna a reef in his mou.
He hasn't a roof in his mouth. Descriptive of someone with a cleft palate. (B)

He nivver gee't his ginger.
He never concerned himself whatever was amiss. 'Geordie widna rin tho the place wis on fire!' (T)

He wid skin a louse for its talla (fat).
He is extremely mean. (B)

He wis the favourite for a fylie, but he's aa dirt noo.
He was the favourite for a while, but he's out of favour now. (B)

He'll get faa broke the hurley for that.
He'll be punished for whatever harm he has done, but crime is a noun too strong in this case if all he did was break the hand-cart. Most likely it was something else but he'll get what he deserves. (T)

He's his ain warst freen.
He is largely responsible for his own misfortune. Drunken habits or outspoken attitude the usual faults. (B)

He's makkin siller like sklate steens!
He's making money like slate stones! With an exclamation like that he would seem to be doing alright in any language. Near Huntly, on the Hills of Culsalmond and Foudland, slate stones are overwhelmingly abundant, and if money was as plentiful, there would be silver and gold in them thar hills, and we would all be millionaires. So the chappie concerned seems tae be linin his pooches. He's on tull a gweed thing an deein aaricht! (T)

Heist ye in or I come back.
Haste you in or I come back. Perhaps a token of encouragement but never heard at partings nowadays. (T)

Hey min, ye're sellin spunks!
Being alerted that your trouser fly was open. 'Spaver' was then the operative word, 'Fasten yer spaver, min!' (T)

Hey min, yer wheels are rinnin roon.
Cycling through a Buchan village on a Sunday evening forty years ago, this is what you were liable to hear. Mostly it came from one of the youths gathered at the local fish and chip shop, or in the main square near the war memorial or the Mercat Cross. It was always best to ignore the jibe and cycle on, but at least you could have the last word and cry back at the mild offender 'G'waa an tak a lang rinnin jump at yersel!' But after all it may have been intended as a welcome greeting for a stranger, voiced out of boredom in a community where there was nothing by way of entertainment to keep the young lads off the streets. (T)

Hingin doon aa roon.
Thick clouds threatening rain. (T)

Hingin thegither till coffins is chaiper.
A rather lugubrious reply to an inquiry as to the state of one's health. (B)

His baabees wunna burn a hole in his pooch!
His money won't burn a hole in his pocket! He's a spendthrift! 'Siller rins throwe his fingers like watter; he thinks it growes on trees!' (T)

Hiz twaa an the baith o's.
Both of us or the two of us. (T)

Hud the cat an play wi the kittlin.
Hold the cat and play with the kitten. Sit on the fence; refuse to take sides. (B)

Hud the haanle tae the lum.
In the old days of the traction-engine and the puffin-billy (steam-wagon) this could have meant 'full steam ahead', or in modern times with the motor car, 'hud the fit doon, Stevie!' (T)

Hud yer watter, min.
Hold your horses. What's your hurry? (T)

I didna come up wi the last load o hey.
I'm not so daft as you think. (T)

I say, loon, ye're knockin oot mair than ye're leavin.
The inevitable salutation from an old hand for a young loon learning how to hoe turnips on the farm. It was also inevitable that the loon would knock out more turnip plants than he was leaving, otherwise he wouldn't have been doing his job properly. Before the days of precision sowing of turnip seed it was the only way you could leave one single turnip plant at each end of your hoe-blade, about seven or eight inches apart to allow the bulbs to swell, and besides the surplus turnip plants the loon had to get rid of the weeds, slicing them out with his seven inch blade. The most troublesome of these being the charlock or 'skellach' weed because its leaves resembled those on the early, yellow turnip at this stage in their growth. It was a case of identifying one from the other at a glance and knocking out the right one on the instant or fall behind the others in the squad, so the somewhat harrassed loon had enough on his plate without being reminded he was 'knockin oot mair plants than he was leavin', even though it was true. (T)

I'll hae tae pey the factor! or I'll hae tae pey the rent!
This was the excuse offered on the braid Buchan parks when nature called and you had to go to the toilet, though midden or dung coort or under the watter-wheel would be nearer the truth, for there were no lavatories or even a dry-closet for the menfolk. One farm I worked on had a toilet over the millrace or lade from the water-wheel, and that was the best I ever saw. There was sometimes a flush toilet in the fairmhoose for the weemin folk, but ye couldna gyang in there, so ye jist hid tae bare yer bum tae the elements ahin a steen dyke, mebbee in a shooer o stingin hailsteens, wi naething tae dicht yer doup but a hanfae a frostit girse. So there wis neathing romantic aboot being a fairm Jock I can tell ye! In the cottar hoose at nicht it wis 'Tak in the orra-pail, wumman, fin ye pit oot the cat!' And of course there wis aye the chanty or 'the dirler' as they caa'd it for ony genteel body that micht be bidin the nicht wi ye! There was a flush toilet on the last farm I worked on because it was a dairy farm and under compulsion, but even so, if you were nearly half-a-mile from the steading when nature called you couldn't drop tools and go home. It was a case of on-the-spot relief, or the nearest port in a storm, for on the subject of defecation we were on the level of the animals we worked with, except that we tried to screen ourselves. On one occasion we had a Glaswegian on the job, and when the grieve spotted him strolling home for the toilet one afternoon he threatened him with the sack, or 'doon the road', as they

say in Formartine, if he saw him at it again. 'If we were aa gaan hame for that,' said the grieve, 'the wark wid seen faa ahin!' (T)

I'm jist comin eyvnoo. Can ye nae wyte or I change my sark?
I'm coming immediately, can't you wait till I change my shirt? Must you be so impatient? (T)

I'm nae feel tho I fart in the kirk.
I'm not so green, you know. (B)

I'm nae sae green's I'm cabbage lookin! Toorle oorle aye-doh!
I'm not as daft as I might seem! (T)

I've seen the day but noo it's nicht.
I have lost the image and vigour of youth. I have seen better days and night is falling on my life. 'Ilka doggie has his day!' as they say, and there is nothing we can do to change it. (T)

If at's wir denner wiv gotten, it's ower late, an if it's wir supper, it's ower seen!
A behind the hand remark which might refer to a somewhat frugal meal and uttered by one of the guests out of hearing of the hostess or landlady. (T)

If he hidna been wi the craas, he widna been shot!
A definite if somewhat biased verdict of 'Guilty!' (B)

If it's nae ae thing it's anither.
If it isn't one thing it's another – 'an files twaa things thegither!' (T)

If it's nae ower het, it's nae ower heavy!
A sly observation on the dubious honesty of 'some folk' and their acquisition of certain goods. (B)

In spite o ma neck.
In spite of personal effort. (T)

It aa comes oot o the howel.
It all comes out of the fish-hold. The fisher's observation on seeing signs of prosperity in the shore side of the industry; e.g. posh houses and flashy cars etc. It applies just as readily to the fishers themselves now, but one mustn't say so. (B)

It wunna ging farrer than the skin!
A witty observation when someone is soaked by the rain. (T)

It's a bear.
Prospects are rather bleak. 'Nae word o yon boat yet? I doot it's a bear!' Note:

198

This term is closely related to 'It's a danny' and 'It's a blue doo!' (B)

It's a peer hen that canna scrape for ae chucken.

It's a poor hen that cannot forage for one chicken. Before the days of scientific incubation, and in the most unfortunate instances, there was the occasional broody hen that emerged from the coop with one chicken, the other twelve eggs being either infertile or rotten, and it was amusing to watch the energetic mother fussing about over her solitary off-spring, which had every chance of survival, but for the fact that she sometimes threw it half-a-yard behind her with a mighty scrape of her foot. In the old days of larger families the one-child parentage was considered a luxury, and there was little sympathy for any of them if they got into financial difficulties. (T)

It's a sair fecht for a half-loaf.

It's a sore fight for a loaf of bread. A struggle to make ends meet. Living with empty cupboards from one day to the next on the breadline. The cupboard was the 'press' and a teem press was common place in the old days when there were larger families to feed. The poorest families sometimes made a press of the nearest shoppie, running back and forth for pennyworths of something because they couldn't afford to stock their presses, and where a vanman called it was often the only day there was anything worthwhile on the shelves of the kitchen press. A sair fecht indeed, but I have heard of the bread-winner being treated by his wife to tea in bed on a Sunday morning with 'fine things oot o the press', which could have meant a jeely piece or a sheave (slice) of loaf and strawberry jam she had saved for him. Surely a rarity, and a sharing in poverty, one of the few good things about 'the good old days'. (T)

It's nae a broken ship, ye ken!

An admonition from the mother to her family, not to be greedy. (Broken ships were there for the plundering.) (B)

It's the aal that wins the new.

If something has given good service, you don't grudge a replacement. (T)

It's the first shooer that's nivver gaen aff.

It's the first shower that hasn't gone off. (T)

Keep a thing seiven ear an ye'll get an eese for't.

Hang on to some article or trinket for seven years and you'll find some use for it. This must surely be one for the hoarder and 'the orra drawer full o aathing fae safety-preens an sark buttons, tae nails, bolts an screws an ony ither nick-nack tull the damned thing wull hardly shut.' (T)

Keep him in his neuk.

Keep him in his corner. Keep the upper hand in the matter. (T)

Kick ower the theats.
To lose control of one's temper.

Kirsty's eggs are aye double-yolkit.
Whatever Kirsty had to offer it was always boosted up to be better than anything anybody else possessed. Kirsty's eggs always had double yolks! To deflate Kirsty you would have to say that Kirsty's eggs were all 'win eggs', eggs without a shell for lack of grit in the hen's diet. (T)

Laachin like a tippeny bookie.
Laughing in a silly, affected manner. (B)

Laachin like the claws o a hemmer!
Laughing fit to burst. (T)

Lang may yer lum reek wi ither folks coal.
'Lang may yer lum reek' may have been the original well-wishing epigram, with the second part added mischievously at a later stage in development. (T)

Lat that flee stick tae the waa.
Let that fly stick to the wall. Say no more about it. (B)

Lat the tow gyang wi the pail.
Let the rope go with the bucket in the draw-well. It could mean different things to different people, depending on circumstances, and could refer to partial loss becoming total loss or the failure of a project. The best example I know is the story of the old Scottish farmer who lost a valuable, much treasured mare. She died in harness and the old man knew it would 'claw his pooch' to replace her. While the neighbours searched around for a suitable burial place one of them suggested they take off her shoes for further use. But the old man was touched humanely and wouldn't hear of it. 'Na na,' he said, 'I'm nae for ae thing touched aboot her. I'll jist hae tae lat the tow gyang wi the pail!' And so he did. (T)

Leears wid need tae hae gweed memories.
Liars would need to have good memories. In ither words, the truth aye tells twice. (T)

Like a bress tack in a bleckie's erse.
Like a brass tack in a blackbird's bottom. Referring to a torch with a rundown battery. (T)

Like a circus horse.
Dressed up to the nines. (B)

Like a clew o raivel't worsit.
Like a hank of tangled knitting wool. In a sorry mess. (B)

Like a droon't kittlin.
Someone caught unprepared in heavy rain. (B)

Like a frozen sark.
Stiff with cold. (B)

Like a hawker's rebellion.
A rather noisy gathering, not necessarily violent. (B)

Like a hen amon dirt.
Someone who approaches a task with their nose curled up, merely 'picking' at it instead of getting stuck in. (B)

Like a horse's guts.
All tangled up, as fishing nets may be. (B)

Like a prize doo.
Dressed up in your best outfit. (B)

Like a rippit saithe.
A fish that has managed to break free from a hook. Used to portray the rapid movement of someone in a fearsome hurry. (B)

Like a scart.
An extremely thin person. Probably from the Gaelic *sgalvh,* a shag or cormorant. Could also be from the Buchan 'scart' a scratch. 'Like a scart on the back o the watry door.' (B)

Like a skinned rubbit.
An extremely thin person. (B)

Like a slung steen.
Someone who is heading somewhere at great speed. (B)

Like a spewed whitin.
Pale and sickly in appearance, like a whiting spewed from a cod's belly. (B)

Like Abraham's bosom.
A really safe anchorage. (B)

Like amber.
Pure and spotless. May be used to describe the interior of a dwelling house. (B)

Like deuk's dirt.
Something which slides out smoothly. 'Boys, we didna hae muckle bother gettin that propeller shaft oot. It cam slidin oot like deuk's dirt.' (B)

Like hairy Mary.
A female with unkempt hair or an off-beat hair-do. (B)

Like saiffron.
Precious; dear to one's heart; of great sentimental value. (B)

Like snaa aff a dyke.
Liable to disappear quickly, as food will vanish from the table in a house where there are hungry bairns. (B)

Like suppin saps wi a stob.
Saps or sops is diced bread boiled in milk with sugar added and it goes well with oatcakes. A stob is a small gimlet for piercing holes in wood where screws are to be inserted. Trying to sup or eat saps with a stob would be like using chop-sticks in broth, and the simile refers to work that isn't making much progress, in fact it is a fiasco of endless effort that comes to nothing, like shovelling sand on a beach with a pronged fork. Saps was also known as flannen broth. (T)

Like the angel o Mons.
A tall cadaverous woman, clad in black. (B)

Like the bells that nivver rung.
In a neglected and dilapitated state. (B)

Like the butcher's dog.
Ram-stam full of impudence. (B)

Like the Dutchman's anchor.
Something which has been left at home. (B)

Like the jaws o the sea.
A sudden, angry, verbal onslaught. 'Ron got up on me like the jaws o the sea, an I dinna ken fit I did wrang.' (T)

Like the side o a hoose.
Someone of considerable size or someone who has recently put on weight. (B)

Mackerel's backs an meer's tails.
High cirrus clouds resembling mackerel's backs and mare's tails. A sure sign of strong winds to come.

> Mackerel's backs an meer's tails
> Gar high ships cairry low sails. (B)

Mak yersel at hame, it's far ye shid be!
Make yourself at home, it's where you should be! Not exactly a welcome. (T)

Maselly first, maselly last, an maselly aa the time.
Myself first, myself last, and myself all the time. The epitome of greed and selfishness. (T)

Mirra-hine tae ye.
I'm not interested in what you are saying. 'Ach! Dinna scunner me. Ye mak me sick. Mirra-hine tae ye.' (B) In the country we say 'Merry hind tae ye!' (T)

Monkeys like tae be heich.
Monkeys like to be high. Probably a taunt at someone who has his name on the sign-board above the shop but is incapable or unqualified as a shop-keeper. (T)

Mottie saat's gweed aneuch for hairy butter.
Smutty salt is good enough for butter with hairs in it. Two of a kind. 'We aa ken that Ricky hiz his faats, he's nae jist fit ye wid caa a gentleman, bit Isabella's nae an angel hersel, an mottie saat's gweed aneuch for hairy butter.' (T)

Muckle sic sey.
Little difference, if any. Six of one and half a dozen of the other. 'Fit like's Jean, the day?' 'The doctor's nae come yet, but I wid say she's muckle sic sey.' (B)

My caup's nae aneth their ladle.
I'm not as fortunate as they are. I don't reap the benefits they do. (T)

Nae a drap's bleed.
Not in any way a blood relation. 'Ye dinna need to ging to yon funeral on a day like this. He's nae a drap's bleed to you!' (B)

Nae muckle winner.
Not much wonder. Not surprising. 'Nae muckle winner ye're ravell't in the heid efter aa yon merriges.' (T)

Nae seener said than deen.
No sooner said than done. 'The wirds wir hardly oot o ma mou or he hid the thing birrin!' (Probably an engine set in motion.) (T)

Nae worth a docken.
Not worth a dock leaf. 'That proposal is nae worth a puff o reek, Donal. Nae worth the paper it's written on; nae worth a docken. Dinna sign yer name on't. Pit it up the lum or licht yer pipe wee't!' (T)

Naebody kens fin ye're ower far aff; the hale toon kens fin ye're ower far in.
Advice to a young skipper to keep well clear of rocks. (B)

Naethin in his heid bit beasts.
He thinks of nothing but cattle. Lice is not implied here. 'Young Scroggie yonder,

there's naethin in his heid bit beasts. Nae wunner the lassie Trail jilted im – he canna spik aboot onything else bit nowt beasts!' (T)

Nivver say soo's egg!

This was sometimes used as a sort of epilogue after a disclosure in confidence, and another was 'nivver lat dab' if you didn't want the story repeated. But how 'soo's egg' got into the language is anybody's guess, for we all know that piglets are not hatched from eggs, and that ye canna mak a silk purse oot o a soo's lug, and something almost as ridiculous is the pun 'Wash yer face an gie the soo a drink.' Indeed I can remember my maternal grandmother giving the sow a shovelful of coals in her trough, probably to sharpen her teeth, and she gobbled them up with a grumph or two. (T)

On afore seiven aff afore alieven, on afore alieven, on aa day!

On before seven off before eleven, on before eleven, on all day. Referring to the rain of course. (T)

Ony mair o yer lip.

Any more of your impudence or cheek. 'Ony mair o yer lip an I'll boot yer erse an gar ye claa faar it's nae yokie', or 'Ony mair o yer lip an I'll kick ye on the back o the heid wi baith ma feet at eence', which would have been quite a feat by the performer. Even worse would be 'a sarkfae o sair beens', a proper thrashing, or 'a moothfae o lous teeth', or 'yer nose knockit up in amon yer hair!' Other threats included 'a clout on the lug', or 'a clap on the lug', 'a scoor on the lug', 'a skelpit erse', or 'yer feet knockit fae ye', which would have meant a tumble, and there was always 'dog's brose', or in a gentler mood 'doggie's brose', the same thing but quite painful and eyewatering when someone seized you from behind and held you by the shoulders and butted your buttocks with his knee. And you certainly held your lip when some big brosie loon speired 'foo wid ye like tae be scrapit aff the waa?' (T)

Onything suits a weel-faured face, even a dish-cloot.

Anything suits a beautiful face, even the dish-cloth, but on the other hand you will hear the expression that so-and-so had a face 'as fite as a dish-cloot!' most of which is contained in the traditionally succinct English pun that 'beauty is in the eye of the beholder.' (T)

Oot o reel.

Out of order; not in working condition. 'Dinna pit yer baabees in at parkin meter min, it's oot o reel!' (T)

Oot o yer box.

Showing off; painting the town; making a night of it. 'Ye're oot o yer box the nicht, Erchie, cairryin on like that. Ye better simmer doon a bittie afore ye come tae the bile.' (T)

Or ye ken o yersel.
Before you know. 'Ye're feart tae get oot a teeth laddie? Weel I dinna blame ye. I dinna like the dintist mannie masel, bit eence yer seatit in the cheir it'll be aa by or ye ken o yersel!' 'Or ye ken faar ye are' is another of the same. (T)

Pit a stoot hert tull a stae brae.
Put a stout heart to a steep brae. A sort of forewarned recommendation in the event of a difficult situation that will tax all your strength and perseverance. (T)

Pit in a step.
Walk faster. 'Pit in a step, Bess. Fit are ye scutterin aboot at? If ye dinna hurry up we'll miss the train.' Scutterin and lyterin both have the same meaning, to loiter or lag behind, so the speaker could say 'Pit in a step, Bess. Fit are ye lyterin aboot at?' with the same effect, or 'Hing in, Bess. Mak yer feet yer freen!' (T)

Poultice for a timmer leg.
A poultice for a wooden leg. A fortunate and obvious solution to a problem from an unexpected source. 'Jist fit the doctor order't.' (T)

Richt aff the stotter.
Right off the scent. (T)

Richt intae my barra.
Right into my barrow. This is something that was said if you had been offered an assignment or a job of some sort you were keenly interested in. 'Oh jist richt intae my barra', but on the other hand if someone made a proposition or suggested a plan of action you just couldn't accept, you might have said 'Na na, nae for me, that wid be like rouin a barra wi a square wheel.' (T)

Sair wark's nae easy an workin sair is little better.
Hard work's not easy and working hard is little better. But there is a consolation in the rejoinder that 'Hard wark nivver kill't naebody', which in academic English would read that 'hard work had killed somebody' or as many as you care to read into it. But we'll leave it at that. (T)

Saxteen tae the dizzen.
Sixteen to the dozen. An exaggeration; an overstatement. 'Doss wis hannin oot the fite baps saxteen tae the dizzen.' (T)

Sic mannie sic horsie.
Or 'Sax an half-a-dizzen' were expressions voiced when making a comparison, when there wasn't much difference between the one or the other, a sort of English 'sauce for the goose, sauce for the gander' simile in judging fair play. 'Sic seed sic lead' was another that surfaced in North-East Scotland if good favourable weather had prevailed in the springtime, trusting Providence that harvest time would be similarly blessed, and the 'sic lead' referred to the leading in or carting

home of the crop. Experience has taught us it was the wisdom of false prophets and not to be relied upon. (T)

Side-on, like the Broch holiday.
A remark sometimes made when somebody does something in an awkward fashion. Originally generated by the rivalry between the Broch and the Blue Toon (Fraserburgh and Peterhead). (B)

Sleep till yer ain fart wakens ye.
There are no 'hours' on fishing boats. You work as the skipper and the weather dictate. The grub is good, and the reward at the end of the trip may be excellent, but there is no guarantee of sleep. Six hours of sleep a week is quite common. But oh, the joy of getting into bed at home, for there you can sleep for as long as you like. (B)

Sleep yer heid intae train ile.
Sleep until you are dead to the world. Train oil was the very heavy grease used to lubricate the axles of rail wagons. (B)

Slow at yer mait, slow at yer wark.
Slow at your food, slow at your work. I have proved this saying to be utterly without foundation. (B)

Stan yer han.
Stand your hand. Pay for the drinks. 'Stan ma han! Man, I can hardly stan on ma feet nivver mind ma hans.' (T)

Stee the dirl.
Cope with your responsibilities. (T)

Sunday's bargains dinna stan.
Business shouldn't be conducted on a Sunday. (B)

Suppin the kail afore the grace.
Having pre-marital sex. (B)

Tak a dish o want.
Clearly indicating that if you hadn't a relish for the food on the table there was nothing else for you; a sort of take it or leave it and go hungry. (T)

Tee wi aa the claik.
Up to date with all the local gossip. 'Teenie wull be tee wi aa the claik o the Perrish.' 'Clipe' has a similar meaning but implies the repetition or spread of gossip, like 'Leeby wis the clipe o the Perrish' in that she was wickedly forthright and repeated every tittle-tattle and couldn't be trusted in confidence. 'I widna trust Leeby oot o hearin', for most likely she would repeat what you had just told

her, and telling her not to mention it was like tempting her the more. A scandalmonger. (T)

Teem briks an gaupin leather.
Empty trousers and open boots when you haven't got up in the morning. After a late night of music and song and a bottle of beer with the chiels from the neighbouring farms in the bothy or chaumer the foreman would remark, 'Weel billies, we'll hae tae gyang tae wir beds or we'll sleep-in in the mornin, an the fairmer'll say, "Aye aye, fit hiv we here. Naething bit teem briks an gaupin leather!" An we canna hae that, can we lads?' (T)

Tell a lee tae shun the Deevil.
Tell a lie to shun the Devil, or even justice if it means punishment. 'The maist o fouk wid tell a lee tae keep them oot o the jile, an files they get awaa wee't. That's fit justice is aa aboot I suppose, tae prove em wrang if need be.' (T)

That'll fairly tak the win oot o Phemie's sails.
Common remark in Buchan, even in the country districts if someone in the know had suffered a sudden set-back, either in business or in some domestic affair, and more so if Phemie was a go-ahead person with her fingers in all the local pies, like the Women's Rural Institute or the Women's Guild, when they would certainly rub her nose in it and take her down to their own level. 'That'll fairly tak the win oot o Phemie's sails,' some busybody would remark at the hair-dressers, 'and haein tae close the shop an aa! Faa wid a thocht it? I thocht she wis deein weel aneuch yonder in the middle o the village, but a body nivver kens fits afore them. She wis a bit o a flee-up onywye, but this'll tak er doon tae size!' (T)

That's the price o ye.
You have got exactly what you deserve; you should have known better. (B)

The aal folk hained the siller, but the quines'll gie't the dicht.
The old folk saved the money but their daughters will soon spend it. (B)

The back o his heid's a treat!
It's good to see him go. Good riddance, for he had already caused enough trouble and over-stayed his welcome. (T)

The back o Sunday.
The first hour or so after Sunday has passed. The traditional time for the fishing fleet to leave port. Until recent times, any skipper sailing before midnight on a Sunday would be the 'spik o the toon'. Today, it no longer applies. (B)

The better the day the better the deed.
As the wifie said fin she hung oot her washing on a Sunday. (T)

The Deil's aye gweed tae his ain.

The Devil is always good to his own. Crime so often goes unpunished it would seem there is some truth in this saying. (T)

The fat soo's erse is aye weel creash't.
The fat sow's hips are always well fleshed and rounded. The moral reflects a social injustice inculcated by the scriptural 'He who hath shall receive more.' (T)

The Jews is nae aa in Jerusalem!
Said on encountering a miserly deed. (B)

The mair hurry the less speed, like the tailor wi his great lang threid.
An apt remark when someone was in a terrible hurry to do something but not making very fast progress. (T)

The richt gate.
The real thing. 'Snaa did ye say? It's dingin on the richt gate!' (T)

The richt side o a shullin.
The right side of a shilling. 'Docherty kens the richt side o a shullin, an he's fairly gettin up in the wardle. Siller wis made tae gyang roon an Docherty's jist speedin't up a bittie.' (T)

The road's up.
The road is under repair. 'They're forever howkin holes.' (B)

The same age as ma tongue and a bittie aaler than ma teeth!
This was sometimes the sort of answer you got for your curiosity in questioning someone's age, especially if the person was somewhat guarded on the subject and didn't want to reveal it. (T)

The tae half an the tither.
The one half and the other. 'The tae half wis dry, but the tither half wis jist fair seypin.' (B)

The wardle's ull-pairtit.
The world's resources are not equally shared. But in a mocking sense it could refer to someone being better off than he or she deserves to be. (T)

The win smokes yer fags.
A cigarette burns faster in the wind. (T)

Them that lives langest sees the maist ferlies.
Those who live longest see the most wonders. (T)

There's a first time for aathing.
There's always a first time for everything that never happened before. Like the

mannie's horsie that drappit doon deid. 'That's queer,' says he to an aal freen that wiz standin by, 'That's queer, it nivver happin't afore!' 'Oh na,' says his freen, 'bit there's a first time for aathing, an in this case it's the first and the last time baith thegither for yer horsie!' (T)

There's a midze in the sea.
But what did the old folk mean by this? Did they mean that there was a midst or middle in the sea, which I think they did, or were they talking about the mids or midze or mid-rig in a ploughed field, where the plough-rigs meet? I think they were referring to the middle of the ocean and they meant moderation in life, in financial investment, in business and ambition; don't go too far for even the sea has a midst, it is not limitless, and wisely they didn't involve space, which has no midst and is boundless. 'There's a midst in the sea' was modest and sound advice so long as we know they meant just that, otherwise it is less significant. (T)

There's aye a somethin.
There's always some little problem. A state of perfection does not exist. (T)

There's naethin comin ower's.
We have nothing to complain about. We could be worse off. (T)

There's naethin in Flora bit jist fit the speen pits in.
Flora had little brain power or intelligence and as little commonsense, or 'nae aa there' or 'nae tae ride the watter on' and not to be depended on for responsible behaviour. (T)

There's naethin like skitter, specially fin it skites!
It is really wonderful to behold some folk who seem to get above themselves! (B)

There's naethin sae queer as folk.
Human nature never ceases to amaze one. It is completely unpredictable. (B)

There's ower muckle o im tae be aa there!
He's too large to be complete. There's bound to be something missing in such a large frame, physically or mentally. (T)

They're affa loons, the mull quines.
They're terrible lads, the mill girls. A jocular expression, used in the Peterhead area, where quite a number of girls find employment in the woollen mill. (B)

This is the day the coo calves.
This is often said on pay day, pension day, etc. (B)

This winna get a frockie tae the bairn.
This idleness will get us nowhere. (B)

Throw the line or Fling the line.
Referring to the Grieve or Gaffer giving the farm workers their orders at yoking time. 'Geordie can fair throw the line. Jist in at ae door an oot at the ither, an nae time tae back-speir im.' (T)

Turn the cat.
To do a somersault. (B)

Twaa at the hip an een at the oxter.
A mother with two children at her side and one under her arm. (T)

Twaa breids and a brose and ben the hoose breid.
These were the titles used to describe the two different recipes employed in baking oat-cakes in the Buchan farmhouse. A coarse, tasteless, longer lasting type for the workers, and a more refined, tastier, crisp and tender variety for the parlour or ben-the-hoose folk, which would include the farmer and his wife and family and the guests who happened to call in by. On some farms the kitchiedeem had strict orders from her mistress that the oat-meal dough for the workers' breid was to be mixed with water only, while that for ben-the-hoose was to be mixed with fat, a refinement which resulted after toasting, in a lighter, tastier, more wholesome cake than the thicker oil-cake variety for the workmen. The assumption was that if the men were treated with the more genteel variety they would eat so much of it that the quine would have to bake at least twice a week to keep them going, whereas the coarser, mixed with water type was longer lasting and saved the kitchiedeem a lot of extra work. The theory was correct in that the kitchie breid sometimes lasted long enough to be stodgy and turning green inside and uneatable before it was given to the pigs. This was the 'twaa breids and a brose' variety, but it is to the credit of quite a lot of Buchan farmers' wives that they didn't indulge in it, and those who did were not always obeyed by their kitchiedeems, especially if there was a lad that she fancied among the menfolk, when she would bake thinner cakes for them. (T)

Up a closie.
Cornered. 'He's up a closie. The bobbies'll catch im. Weel weel, it serves him richt for grabbin the wifie's handbag!' (T)

Up tae high doh.
Tense, excited and over anxious. 'It's a gweed job it's nae me. If I hid tae gie a speech at the soiree, I wid be up tae high doh!' (T)

Up tae the eek wi wark!
Overwhelmed with work! (B)

Up the blin side.
Approaching the blind side of someone. To take unfair advantage of someone's ignorance or experience. 'Lang Dod must a gotten up the blin side o the minister's

widda afore she merrite im.' She couldn't have known him properly. (T)

Us, oorsels an the baith o's.
Just the two of us. (T)

We jist bide mix-max, an pairt the bairns at the New Ear.
We just all live together and share out the children at the New Year. A wry expression from the days of gross over-crowding. (B)

We're aa here thegither like the wifie's ae coo!
We are all gathered here together like the woman's one cow. If the woman had just one cow there could be no mistaking the number present. I suppose it means that everyone was there who should be. It's a bit like the Home Guard farmer recruit who asked his sergeant if he could get home before dark to 'look throwe the kye', which was quite in order, and perhaps because he was expecting a calving. But there was the crofter with only one cow and the same problem, and he asked the sergeant if he could get home early 'tae look throwe the coo!' But being an Englishman and probably a townie the sergeant was probably none the wiser and would have given permission if the crofter had asked home to x-ray the coo. (T)

We're jist aetin oot at the door.
After a week-end of unexpected visitors. There is nothing left in the pantry. (T)

We're jist biggit oot wi tatties.
We have received so many potatoes, we are having difficulty finding storage space. (B)

Weel weel, I'll need tae be takin the road.
The reluctant remark of a departing guest who has obviously enjoyed his stay. Whether the host was relieved to hear him say this is anybody's guess. It reminds me of the couple in the dark who were overheard seeing their visitors off in their car after a somewhat long evening visitation with 'Cheerio noo, heest-ye-back, dinna wyte sae lang or yer neist visit, ta-ta, ta-ta!' and as soon as the visitors had departed the husband was heard to say to his wife 'I thocht the buggers wid nivver leave. They wid deave yer erse that lot and am richt glaed tae see the hinner-en o them – thunk Christ for at!' 'Weesht!' said his wife, 'somebody could hear ye!' And somebody did. (T)

Weel weel, maybee; pigs may flee, bit they're nae a commin bird!
Pigs may fly, but they are not a common bird. Not a popular remark but sometimes said if someone has been kite-flying so to speak and giving a false impression of something far beyond its importance and likely to deceive others with less knowledge of the subject. (T)

Weet the bairn's heid.
To celebrate the birth of a child, the father was expected to 'stand his hand'.

When my elder brother's youngest was born (1939?) we were at the 'winter herr'n' at St Monance in Fife. When the telegram arrived, he was immediately required to weet the bairn's heid, so he gave me a ten shilling note to get the needful. 'Good grief!' says I, 'Ye wid be fond to spen aa that siller!' so I went to the baker's shop and bought six large and six small bottles of lemonade (six of a crew) and a box of lovely cheesecakes. Everyone was delighted and, if I remember rightly, I gave him five bob change. Try that today with half a quid! (B)

Wis ye born in a cairtshed?
When someone leaves a draughty door open they are accused of having been 'born in a cairtshed', because a cartshed doesn't have doors, and therefore the offender would never have learned to close them. (T)

Ye aye get the best fart at yer ain fireside.
Because there is less chance of embarrassment. (T)

Ye can queel in the skin that ye het in.
You'll just have to cool off as you got warmed up, nothing has changed. (T)

Ye couldna be liker a nearer freen.
A strong resemblance to the father, mother, sister or brother. (T)

Ye dinna aye dee the day ye get yer daith.
A neglected ailment may have serious consequences. (T)

Ye miss an aal creel fae the door.
You miss an old friend when they are gone. (B)

Ye nivver miss the watter or the wallie rins dry.
We take so much for granted we never think of loss, of making do without or improvising, and mostly we are caught on the wrong foot or with our trousers down, so to speak. In a practical sense you have to live in the country in a dry spell to fully understand the implications of this saying, and the moral effect can be even more dramatic and sometimes devastating, like the sudden unexpected loss of someone dear to us, wife, husband, child or loved one, and we find no comfort or consolation in the what might have been, and we thirst for relief from the well that's run dry. Living in a city tenement with a mains water supply it would take a power cut to have the impact of a dry well, without heat, light, fridge or telly, but of too short duration to theorise upon, unless it were 'We nivver think o the Hydro Boord or the licht gings oot!' But even then, it doesn't have the impact or the seriousness of the dry well theory. (T)

Ye trail an easy harra.
You drag a short-toothed harrow that doesn't bite deeply into the ploughed field. You don't have to work hard for a living, you always have a soft, uncomplicated job. (T)

Ye widna be sellt for a thoosan powen.

This is the very peak of fisher endearment for the bairns. When this phrase was coined 'a thoosan powen' was an astronomical sum, but the words have not been altered, despite inflation. (B)

Ye wunna grou noo unless it's like the coo's tail – doonhull.

Referring to someone who has reached the limit of growth and is likely to remain the same height until old age. 'Ye're gaan aa tae shaws, min!' or 'Ye're fair raxin oot, min!' was sometimes voiced in your favour as a teenager if you were getting taller all the time, but if you were the short dumpy type, the opinion would be a behind the hand expression like 'He wid as ready rou as rin (roll as run)' or 'He's aboot as braid as he's lang, a butter baa!' or 'He's nae the strappin chiel his fadder wiz! He's mair like his midder's fouk – aa laichy-braid (low and stocky).' (T)

Ye'll be a man afore yer mither.

This was a saying often put by grown men to small boys as a sort of compliment, and the boys in their innocence considered it must be something of great importance coming from somebody like the farm grieve and reflecting on some advantage the boy had over his mother, something perhaps she wasn't supposed to know about. Some of the boys told their mother what the grieve had said, and she agreed, though few tried to explain and the lads were no wiser. It was all one of the great mysteries of growing up and the grieve had only complicated matters by revealing something of great importance and failing to explain it. Cross examined on the subject, all that the grieve would say was, 'Weel laddie, yer mither wull nivver be a man!' and the loon had to content himself with this for the time being, or until puberty, when all would be revealed. (T)

Ye'll jist ging tae the waal or ae day.

You'll go to the well for the last time one day. Your day will come. 'Ulkie doggie hiz his day, as they say, an ye canna get bye't. Daith is the only thing we're sure o an we aa hiv tae gyang.' (T)

Ye're a better door than a windae!

'You'd make a better door than a window!' is the sort of rebuke you would get for standing in someone's light when they were trying to read the newspapers in your shadow. Another one was, 'Fut wye div ye expeck me tae see throwe ye?' or 'Get oot o the licht, min' or 'I'll need a spyin gless tae read ma paper!' (T)

Ye're a dirt'n cat.

Said to a female who looks down on others in a supercilious manner. (B)

Ye're affa trailed oot.

If you are a minor centre of attraction, being invited here and there. (B)

Ye're aye sure o the mither.

An observation when there is some doubt about someone's parentage. (B)

Ye're feart for the death ye'll nivver dee!

Perhaps a hypochondriac. Too much concerned about your health. Over anxious about life in general, an attitude that was sometimes greeted with 'Cheer up, Jock. It mith nivver happen!' And mostly it didn't. (T)

Ye're in a gey picher, sair needin a redd oot.

If your house is like a battle-field and you don't know where to start. (B)

Ye're nae needin twaa kitchies.

A kitchie in the old days meant a treat or flavouring or a sort of jam on both sides, as opposed to the English 'Hunger is the best sauce.' Twaa kitchies meant you were putting both butter and jam on your scone or slice of bread when one of either was considered sufficient, or all you were entitled to in the farm kitchens. In my old age I allow myself a thin spread of margarine on my toast and a smear of marmalade on top, but in the farmhouse kitchens of my youth, and even at my parents' table, this was considered an extravagance and was frowned upon, and even hinted at if you persisted in such a luxury. (T)

Ye've droon't the mullart!

You've drowned the miller! An apt remark when someone puts too much water in your whisky. Personally I prefer it neat! (T)

Yer een's bigger than yer belly!

This isn't quite the same thing as having bit off more than you can chew – or is it? Perhaps the moral is similar, but greed is implied more strongly in the first one and hints at left-overs, the sort of thing you would say to a bairn who couldn't eat the plateful he had asked for. 'Yer een's bigger than yer belly!' would be the typical Buchan scolding, rather than 'Ye've bitten aff mair than ye can chaw!' (T)

Yer heid in yer hans tae play wi.

Your head in your hands to play with. A threat of punishment. 'Come stracht hame fae the skweel or ye'll get yer heid in yer hans tae play wi.' (T)

Yon fairly cowes the cuddy!

That really beats everything! 'We've heard aathing noo. Yon fairly cowes the cuddy!' (T)

Proverbs

A bonny bride's easy buskit.
It's easy to dress a bonny bride. That which is naturally beautiful requires little further adornment. (B)

A green Eel maks a fat kirkyaird.
A mild Yule fills the kirkyard. It was believed that more people died in a mild winter because there was a lack of frost to kill the germs. (T)

A gyaan fitt's aye gettin.
Those who are active are most likely to succeed. (B)

A linen Sunday maks a harn week.
A beautiful Sunday is often the forerunner of a week of poor weather. (T)

Aal age disna come its leen.
Old age brings aches, pains and other problems. (T)

An aal maid's bairns are easy brocht up.
Because she doesn't usually have any. (T)

An oor in the mornin's worth twaa at nicht.
Another way of saying 'It's the early bird that catches the worm.' (T)

Atween Ludquharn an Auchtydore. The Deevil traivels back an fore.
Ye fairly pit in a step in the dark on that bit o road for fear the Deevil wis ahin ye. Not knowing which way to turn. (T)

Better the sheen than the sheets.
Better the shoes than the sheets. Meaning that if someone was hard on their footwear it was better than being ill in bed and wearing out the sheets. (T)

Far it's nae gien, it canna be lookit for.
It is pointless to expect a high degree of intelligence in one who is mentally handicapped. This saying may be an expression of exasperation when someone fails to grasp what you are trying to convey. (B)

Feels an aal folk shouldna see jobs half deen.
A tradesman's reply when someone asks a silly question. (B)

Fin drink's in wit's oot.
When you are drunk you become irresponsible. (T)

Fin the aal cock craws the young een learns.
Children learn from their parents and elders. (T)

Fire is a gweed servant but a bad maister.
Fire is a good servant but a bad master. Fire will serve you well, but don't misuse it or you will be burned. (T)

Fit's in yer belly winna be in yer testament.
Eat, drink and be merry, for tomorrow you might be dead. (B)

Fut canna be cured maun be endured.
When circumstances cannot be changed they have to be tolerated. (T)

Fut's natral's nae nesty.
What is natural is not nasty, but quite acceptable. (T)

God aye helps them that help thersels.
God always helps them that help themselves, but God help them that's catched helpin thersels. The second part is fiction but implies that God turns a blind eye on theft in a good cause. God helps those who make the best of their lives, however difficult, would be perhaps the more ethical way to look at it. (T)

Guide fin ye hae, for want'll guide itsel.
Be thrifty in prosperity, so you have something in reserve for the lean times.

Gweed gear comes in smaa buik.
The best things in life come in small quantities. (B)

If aabody had their ain, some folk widna be sae weel-aff.
If everybody received their due, others would receive less. This is a sly hint at some folk's disregard for business ethics. Although names aren't mentioned, one is never left in any doubt regarding the identity of 'some folk'. (B)

If the bonnet disna fit ye, dinna weer't.
If you are blameless say so and stand up for your right to prove your innocence. If you don't identify with the description deny it. (T)

It taks a lang speen tae sup wi a Fifer.
If you associate with a Fifer, be on your guard, they are a smart bunch. Another version of this is F-L-Y spells Fife. (B)

It's an ull win that blaas naebody gweed.
It's an ill wind that blows nobody any good, which can have a domestic, social or commercial implication. (T)

It's fine tae be hungry an ken o mait.
Hunger is all right as long as you know you will soon be fed. (B)

It's nae loss, fit a freen gets.
A personal loss isn't so bad if a friend is benefitting instead. (B)

It's the aal that wins the new!
By wearing old clothes or using a machine or implement until it is worn out, will give you time to earn and save enough money to buy a new replacement. (T)

It's the belly that keeps up the back.
Napoleon meant the same thing when he said that an army marches on its stomach. 'Ye canna work athoot mait!' (T)

It's the steady drap that weers the steen.
A steady worker is worth more than a fellow of fits and starts. (T)

Nae metter foo ull ye be, jist look aboot ye.
No matter how ill you are, just look around you. There is always someone worse off than yourself. (T)

Nae sae Hielan tae be sae far north.
The situation was better than anticipated considering the circumstances. (T)

Oor ain fish guts tae oor ain sea-maas.
Charity begins at home. (B)

Pick the mote oot o yer ain ee first.
Remedy your own faults before you criticise others. (T)

Pooder an pint hides mony a rint.
Powder and paint hides many a flaw. Never judge by external appearance only. (B)

Spik o the Deil an he'll appear.
Sure enough, if you are talking about someone, especially if you are saying something to that person's disadvantage, the one concerned will put in an appearance. (T)

Tak a cattie o yer kind, an yer kittlins'll be like ye.
Marry into your own social class and your offspring will be like yourself. (B)

The biggest bummer's nae aye the best bee.
The person with most to say is not always the one to rely upon. (B)

The Deil's nae a gweed bed-mate.
It's difficult to get to sleep with a guilty conscience. (T)

The souter's bairns are aye the worst shod.
Things are not always as you might expect them to be. (B)

The thickest skin hauds oot the langest.
The survival of the fittest. An arbitrary almost neutral remark by onlookers when a fist fight is in progress. A sort of 'lat them fry in their ain fat!' attitude by those not wishing to take sides. (T)

The willin horse aye gets the maist tae pull.
If you are eager to work, you are likely to get more than your share of it. (T)

There's a slippery steen at ulkie door an some folk his twaa.
Everyone has their share of misfortune and some have a double share. (T)

There's aye some watter far the stirkie droon't.
There is still an element of guilt or suspicion where the verdict was negative or unproven. (T)

There's nae feel like an aal feel.
There's no fool like an old fool. (T)

There's neen sae blin as them that winna see.
Some folk just won't accept the obvious. (B)

Ye dinna aye dee the day ye get yer daith.
A neglected ailment may have serious consequences. (T)

Ye need a lang speen tae sup wi the Deevil.
The further you stay away from trouble the better. (T)

Ye shape yer sheen wi yer ain baachled feet!
Don't blame others for your troubles, it's likely most of them are caused by your own misdemeanours. (T)

Bairn Rhymes and Riddles

My wife played 'Stot the baa' at Ardallie School in central Buchan to this jingle:

One, two, three a leerie,
I spied Mrs Peerie,
Sittin on a basket cheerie,
Aetin jelly-babies. (T)

The following rhyme was recited when selecting the 'mannie' or searcher from a group of children playing Hide and Seek. If you were pointed 'oot' you were the 'mannie'.

Eetle ottle, black bottle
Eetle ottle oot,
Fite fish, black troot
Eerie orrie ee are OOT. (T)

'Coontin a Pie' was the bairns' way of drawing lots.

Eetle ottle, black bottle, eetle ottle out.
Take a nail and push it out
For the dirty dish clout
And O-U-T spells OUT. (B)

Tinkie, tinkie, tarry hat,
Yer hat's nae yer ain.
Ye stole't fae a fisher wifie
Comin fae the train. (B)

Country Geordie, Brig o Dee,
Sup the brose an leave the bree! (T)

As I gaed ower the Brig o Dee
I met my uncle Simon,
I took aff his heid
An drank his bleed
An left his body stannin.
(The empty bottle of course.) (T)

Cripple Dick upon a stick,
And Suny on a soo,
Ridin aff tae Aiberdeen
Tae buy a pun o oo. (T)

Come up an see my hoosie,
Come up an see it noo,
Come up an see my hoosie
It's aa furnished noo.

A broken cup an saucer,
A cheir withoot a leg,
A humphie-backet dresser
An an aal iron bed. (T)

Sandy Bowfie, twaa muckle taes,
Biggit a hoosie on the Pinkie Braes.
The Pinkie Braes began tae faa,
So Sandy Bowfie ran awaa. (B)

Wee Jockie Birdie, toll-oll-oll.
Laid an egg on the windi-soll.
The windi-soll began tae crack
And wee Jockie Birdie roared an grat. (B)

Chin cherry
Mou merry
Nose nappy
Ee winkie
Broo brinkie
On ower the hill
An doon tae stinkie. (T)

Div ye see the P.D. drifters,
Div ye see them yet avaa?
Div ye see the P.D. drifters
Comin hame fae Stornawaa?
Some hae gotten a hantle o siller,
Some hae gotten neen avaa.
Div ye see the P.D. drifters
Comin hame fae Stornawaa?
(P.D.: The registration letters for Peterhead.) (B)

Peter Patter, ower the watter, in a cockle shaal.
The cockle shaal brook, an Peter got a dook,
An aa the men in Scotlan couldna tak im oot. (B)

Cattie at the fireside
Suppin brose
Oot fell a cinder
An burned Cattie's nose
'Oh,' says the Cattie,
'That wis sair.'
'Weel,' says the cinder,
'Ye shouldna been there.' (T)

Paddy on the railway
Pickin up steens
By cam an engine
An broke Paddy's beens

'Oh,' says Paddy, 'that's nae fair.'
'Oh,' says the engine,
'Ye shouldna been there.' (T)

Ha ha ha, hee hee hee,
An elephant's nest in a rhubarb tree. (B)

Oh, look at Mary, she thinks she's affa neat.
Skinny-malinkie-lang-legs an umberella feet! (B)

Oh, we're aa gaan awaa tae the waar,
Oor pooches full o tar.
We drappit a dyke an fell amon . . .
Oh, we're aa gaan awaa tae the waar. (B)

Twaa fite horses gaan awaa tae Fife
Comin back on Monday wi a deid wife. (T)

Pit yer finger in the corbie hole
The corbie's nae at hame,
He's awaa at the back o the barn
Pluckin a deid hen. (T)

Johnnie Raw shot a craw
An took it hame tae his mamma.
His mamma ate it aa
An left the banes tae Johnny Raw. (T)

Nae last nicht but the nicht afore
Twaa great belly-guts cam tae my door.
I oot wi my gun an shot them in the bum,
An they baith ran awaa cryin 'Yum yum yum'. (B)

Nae last nicht but the nicht afore
Three wee rascals cam tae the door,
Een hid a fiddle, the ither hid a drum
And the third hid a dish-cloot
Hingin at his bum! (T)

Nivver say how much ye gie,
Nivver say if it's big or wee,
Gie yer mite if ye feel that wye,
Gie wi'oot fuss then walk away,
An nivver hae nae mair tae say, nivver. (Anon.) (T)

Peer wee Margit Clark, she's oot amon the snaa,
She disna hae a pixie an her scarfie's blaan awaa.
Her sheen are full o holies, nae sockies has she got,
We'll hae tae mak a jacketie oot o her faither's aal coat. (B)

Broon Paper Pyokie

Fin I wis a little wee pirn-taed loonie
They caaed me silly little Jockie,
I eest tae sit on my grunny's windae-sill
Aetin sweeties oot o a broon paper pyokie.

A lassie cam by an offer't me a kiss
A kiss that I nivver thocht o scornin –
She grabbit ma sweeties
Shoved ma heid throwe the windae
And ma grunny tellt me that next mornin. (T)

Grouin Pains

Fin I wis een I gid ma leen
Fin I wis twaa I shot a craw
Fin I wis three I climmed a tree
Fin I wis fower I hid a glour
Fin I wis five I didna thrive
Fin I wis sax I got my smacks
Fin I wis siven I gaed tae Steenhiven
Fin I wis acht I cairiet a fracht
Fin I wis nine I muckit the swine
Fin I wis ten I plucked a hen
Fin I wis aliven I cam back fae Steenhiven
Fin I wis twaal I fell intae the waal
Thirteen, fourteen I gaed tae Aikey Fair
Fifteen, saxteen fut tae dee there
Siventeen, achteen tae buy a grey meer
Nineteen, twinty, they were aa ower dear. (T)

A Lady – A Laird – A Cooper – A Kyard – A Rich Man – A Hangman
– A Bellman – A Thief.

This was how the country bairns used to foretell their destiny on the way home
from school, ticking off their life partner on the seed pods of a rye-grass stem,
starting at the bottom, hoping that the last one at the top would be of the right sex
and the one of their choice. A Laird or a Rich Man was preferable to a Bellman or
a Thief, and of course, if you weren't satisfied with your mate you could always
pull another rye-grass and start all over again, hoping for better luck next time.
This pastime was much the same as blowing the time of day from the fluffy head
of the dandelion in the carefree hours of childhood. (T)

Rise up gweed wife an shak yer feathers.
Dinna think that we are beggars.
We are bairnies come tae play,
Rise up an gie's oor Hogmanay. (T)

222

Tongue Twister

Mull o Rora's fite futret
Ran roon aboot
Mull o Rora's rollers.
And Mull o Rora's rollers
Ran roon aboot. (T)

This is how the Buchan bairns spelled the initials of PREFACE both ways in their primary readers at school:

Peter Rattray Eatin Fish
Andra Catchin Eels,
Eels Catchin Andra's Fish
Eatin Raw Peels.

And the CONTENTS of the book was given thus:
Cows Ought Not To Eat Neeps Till September.
(Turnips were never ready before September in any case.) (T)

Conundrums

I sat lang, I socht it sair, I couldna get it so I gaed awaa wi't.
(A hairst thistle in yer thoom.)

Roon an roon the raggit rocks
The raggit rascal ran.
Tell me foo mony Rs are in that
An I'll caa ye a clivver man.
(There are no Rs in 'that'.)

A similar version was:

Aiberdeen an Aiberdour
Speel ee that
Wi letters fower. (T)

A Buchan riddle

Come a riddle, come a riddle,
Come a rot-tot-tot,
I met a wee man in a bright reid coat,
Wi a staff in his han
And a steen in his throat,
Come a riddle, come a riddle,
Come a rot-tot-tot.
(The answer is the dog-rose berry or rose hip.) (T)